THE MYTH OF THE MODEL MINORITY

THE MYTH OF THE MODEL MINORITY

ASIAN AMERICANS FACING RACISM

Second Edition

ROSALIND S. CHOU
AND JOE R. FEAGIN

Paradigm Publishers
Boulder • London

Copyright © 2015 Paradigm Publishers

Published in the United States by Paradigm Publishers, 5589 Arapahoe Avenue, Boulder, CO 80303 USA.

Paradigm Publishers is the trade name of Birkenkamp & Company, LLC, Dean Birkenkamp, President and Publisher.

Library of Congress Cataloging-in-Publication Data

Chou, Rosalind.
   Myth of the model minority : Asian Americans facing racism / Rosalind S. Chou & Joe R. Feagin. — Second Edition.
       pages cm
   Includes bibliographical references and index.
   ISBN 978-1-61205-570-1 (hardcover : alk. paper) — ISBN 978-1-61205-478-0 (pbk. : alk. paper) — ISBN 978-1-61205-571-8 (consumer ebook)
   1. Asian Americans—Social conditions. 2. Race discrimination—United States. 3. Racism—United States. I. Feagin, Joe R. II. Title.
   E184.A75C515 2014
   305.895'073—dc23
                                                                                    2014015425

Printed and bound in the United States of America on acid-free paper that meets the standards of the American National Standard for Permanence of Paper for Printed Library Materials.

Designed and Typeset by Straight Creek Bookmakers.

19 18 17 16 15   1 2 3 4 5

CONTENTS

Preface and Acknowledgments

Preface to First Edition

I, Rosalind S. Chou, lost my best friend when I was just ten years old. He was not lost due to a tragic automobile accident or accidental drowning during a hot summer. He and I spent almost every day together when I moved in next door at age seven, but that friendship ended abruptly. I lost him to racism. What likely seemed just a petty childhood fight for him was much bigger for me. Joking banter turned a dangerous corner when his teasing of me became racialized. As soon as I became a "Chink" to him and his other friend, our relationship changed then and forever. I could not calmly manage the insult, and was unable to articulate the hurt, but I knew what they were doing was wrong. I went inside my house, got my BB gun, opened my bedroom window, and pushed out the screen. I could still hear them yelling racist epithets as they jumped up and down in the bed of a pickup truck, taunting me. I could see their heads appear and disappear over the fence separating our property. They could see me with the gun and they yelled, "Go ahead, shoot!" So, I did. I was probably twenty yards away. I was so angry that there was no clarity of thought. I remember pulling the BB gun trigger, and everything seemed like it was in slow motion. The next thing I heard was screams. I had hit the other boy right underneath his eye.

Immediately, I knew that I had done something terrible and began to panic. I was still upset about the racist epithets and felt redeemed for a moment, but knew that my retaliation would not be seen as a legitimate way to deal with what the boys did. My parents were very upset to learn of my action and informed me that I had brought shame on the family. They marched me next door so I could apologize. I explained to my parents that I had been called some terribly racist names, but they completely ignored those details and instructed me not to complain about it at all, and it never came up again. The boy who was hit with the BB had to deal with some discomfort for a few days, but his physical hurt is long gone. Twenty years later, I still vividly remember the painful details of the lengthy racist episode. I can still feel the pain of how hurt and betrayed I felt by my supposed friend. Things were never the same.

I learned important lessons from this experience. First, close relationships would not shield me from the threat of white racism. Second, aggressively defending myself against such racist attacks was frowned upon by those adults I respected most. I could not seek out support from family members to talk about these kinds of incidents, for they did not want to make trouble or shame the family. In addition, I learned the terrible lesson that being a target of racism is often a lonely and isolating experience.

Through the years, I have frequently felt similar stings from white hostility and discrimination. What has changed from my youth is that I am no longer surprised when it happens. The threat always exists. I can say that I have been fortunate, so far, to have received only relatively "mild" racist comments and nonviolent taunts, but each event adds to my collection of painful racialized memories, a bucket that I, like other Americans of color, carry in my psyche, and that gets larger and heavier as I age. I no longer make attempts to run and get the BB gun from my closet, but I still feel rage well up inside me when these incidents occur to me or I see them happen to other people of color.

*   *   *

When we first talked about writing a preface for this unique and important research, we talked about using our artistic license to include accounts of Rosalind's own struggles as an Asian American. She was unexcited about this task and for months avoided putting it to paper. She felt some dread in sharing her own experiences but could not put her finger on what made the task daunting. A tinge of discomfort was triggered whenever she thought of having to talk about the everyday racism she faced in her own life. She found anti-Asian racism isolating and, as many of our respondents indicate, she really did not want to share such bad news. This recognition has led us to realize even more fully how brave our respondents were, and still are. We had asked them to open up to a stranger and reveal things that were often very personal and painful. Our respondents took time out from busy schedules to spend a few hours revealing both hardships and triumphs. Yet, once into the interview, not one indicated that he or she was burdened by the interviewing process. On the contrary, once they began to discuss their experiences of racial hostility and discrimination (many initially denied experiencing such), they seemed relieved to have finally revealed to someone their innermost burdens and pain.

Conducting these interviews and writing about them was a difficult process for us as well. We both empathized greatly with our respondents' struggles against racial burdens and barriers not of their own choosing, and we often had some trouble completing our write-ups of their poignant accounts. However, this task was clearly much more difficult for Rosalind. The further into the research and writing process she got, the more Rosalind became aware of parallels in her own life—and thus recalled and relived feelings of confusion, sadness, desperation, anger, powerlessness, and, at times, redemption. As is true for many of our respondents, she has chosen to push certain memories back in her mind in the hope of forgetting them. But she will never be able to suppress many memories of white discrimination, and every day she knows that there is the possibility of adding yet another discriminatory incident to her memory of racial oppression.

This project has made us realize just how groundbreaking this work is for Asian and non–Asian Americans. While we recognize that we do not offer a final or comprehensive analysis of the issues we research and analyze, so far as we can determine no prior book so thoroughly documents the widespread racial hostility and discrimination Asian Americans have faced in recent years. The Asian American experience with white-imposed racism has been *invisible* in most popular and social science analysis.

Indeed, it is this shared experience with white-imposed racism, now for more than a century and a half, that has created a common "Asian/Pacific Islander American" group experience, for there is no identity of nationality or cultural background among Asian and Pacific Islander Americans that creates such commonality. Today, as in the past, those who make up the umbrella realities called "Asian American" and "Asian/Pacific Islander American" are a diverse group with a significant array of home cultures, national identities, and nuanced views and values. These nationality groups have diverse and rich histories that have too often been overlooked or unacknowledged by U.S. scholars and commentators.

There have been multiple incorporations of different national origin groups and cultures from Asia and the Pacific Islands in this country's long history. Beginning with the Chinese in the 1850s, Asian immigration was reinvigorated a half century later, around 1900, by significant numbers of Japanese and Filipino immigrants. More than a half century after that, since the 1960s, ever larger numbers of Asian and Pacific Islander immigrants have entered and settled in the United States.

In spite of their national and cultural diversity, as we show in our data, these groups share one significant common bond: all Asian American and Pacific Islander groups are racially subordinated by whites in the dominant U.S. racial hierarchy and in its associated racial framing. As each new immigrant group has arrived, they and their descendants have faced various forms of white-imposed economic exploitation and/or other substantial racial discrimination. Whites, especially those in the elite, continue to control the U.S. racial hierarchy, thereby making it nearly impossible for Asian Americans to integrate in untroubled, nondiscriminatory, and egalitarian ways into U.S. society. The constant racial "othering" by whites has led to the emergence of the umbrella terms "Asian Americans" and "Asian/Pacific Islander Americans." The discrimination in or exclusion from important white spaces they face daily has created a sense of shared experience and a racialized commonality. Indeed, during the "Yellow Power" civil rights movement during the 1960s, often led by college students and community members, the term *Asian American* was coined as a symbol of unified resistance to racial discrimination by whites. Thus, many of our first-generation respondents never identified as "Asian" or "Asian American" until they were treated as racialized "others" during their early months in the United States.

For many white and other Americans, *Asian American* has become a term associated with "model minority" success. It serves for many as proof that securing the "American dream" is a real possibility not only for Asian Americans but for all Americans of color. As we show throughout this book, however, the stereotypes and images associated with the model minority notion, though often seemingly positive, are in numerous ways constraining and do create intense pressures on and stress for Asian Americans seeking to live up to such unrealistic and racially stereotyped expectations. As we will see, few of our Asian American respondents have chosen to rebel openly against the model minority stereotyping, often out of fear of being ostracized by whites and other Asian Americans alike, and the majority have dealt with the pressures and strains by conforming as much as they can to at least key elements of the model minority imagery. Living up to this white-constructed image of what one should be as an "Asian American," together with their daily encounters with racial hostility and discrimination, challenges these courageous women and men to create their own resistance strategies and self-identities. At this point in the twenty-first century, it appears that in a majority of Asian American families and communities, a *strong* counterframe to the dominant white racist framing of Americans from Asia has yet to be fully developed and circulated, yet we do see aspects of such important counterframing in the ways in which particular national origin groups now align themselves assertively and positively under the umbrella term "Asian American" (or "Asian/Pacific Islander American" and "Asian/Pacific Islander/ Desi American") as a source of group pride. These relatively new developments in Asian American group unity and coalition building are very important and seem necessary to the long-term survival of these groups as well as to the further growth of a democratic multiracial society in this still-racist nation.

Preface to Second Edition

When I, Rosalind S. Chou, set out to write *Myth of the Model Minority*, I was merely a second-year graduate student, finishing up my master's degree. I had not the foresight to see that what I was putting forth, the stories of forty-three Asian Americans, would set me on a course to reexamine all I thought I had known about the world—in many more ways than in the years I was young. I was shortsighted as a scholar and needed time to mature to see how complex we humans truly are. In some ways I look back on the first edition and think I was much too hard on respondents, critiquing their choices to "whiten" themselves. However, as time has passed, I more fully understand that their assimilation is oftentimes a matter of survival. Race and racism already put tremendous pressure on people of color, so that speaking out, fighting back, and resisting can cost someone their livelihood and perhaps their lives. I also had blinders on in terms of the ways that race intersects other parts of identity. The experiences are complex and can vary by geography, age, ethnicity, sex, gender, educational attainment, class, and the list goes on. These other parts of identity further complicate how racism is operating in the lives of Asian Americans. I know now that white supremacy relies on oppression in these other areas to maintain the racial status quo. Today, I mentor students and see the young-scholar self within them. I am reminded of the anger I felt when I started to fully realize the depth and breadth of racism.

Additionally, I have been lucky to work with graduate students who have opened my eyes to some of the ways systemic racism keeps people of color separated from each other. I was asked point-blank in class by one of my African American female students reading my earlier work, "Who cares? Who cares about Asian Americans and racism? What about Latasha Harlins?" Ashamed, I had to admit I really did not know Latasha's story: how this young African American woman was shot in the back just thirteen days after the Rodney King beating in Los Angeles by a suspicious Korean store owner, an incident that was, perhaps, one of the sparks for the 1992 Los Angeles riots. Black and Korean conflict has been documented several times throughout U.S. history, and I understood my student's inquiry. Racism affects all of us, people of color and whites. We become alienated from each other and ourselves. In the moment, I had to put my pride aside, feeling the pangs of how racism keeps us divided, and admitted to the student that I had fear and guilt when writing the first edition of this book. I was worried that other people of color would reject these stories and that we would be embroiled in an "oppression Olympics" of sorts where critics would insist I was trying to argue that Asian Americans had it worse than African Americans or Latinos.

I was also faced with thoughts of doubt, that maybe Asian Americans in fact do not have it that badly, or wondering if I was "too hard" on respondents just trying to make it through each day. I realized when asked in class about why this mattered, that the truth is that everyone's story deserves to be told. Racial groups remain divided in part because the struggle for resources and power is frequently constructed as a zero-sum game. My goal was not to belittle or diminish the obstacles faced by other racial groups; my true hope was to bring visibility to the ways racism operates similarly in the lives of Asian Americans, and that it matters as much as other forms of oppression.

In this second edition, I hope to connect all of us, so this book is not seen as solely a commentary on Asian Americans facing racism, but the ties that bind all of us to racism. People of color and whites, we all suffer because of racism; it tears communities and individuals apart. Asian Americans reading this book will hear the stories of forty-three Asian Americans with various ethnic origins, but they should also know the story of Latasha Harlins. Non–Asian Americans reading this book will hopefully learn that while there are tragedies such as the Harlins shooting in 1991, Asian Americans do suffer from the pains of racial oppression and that their experiences also matter.

* * *

When Rosalind and I (Joe Feagin) set out to do this book on the everyday experiences with white racism that are faced by Asian Americans, we knew that very few scholars had attempted even part of what we were attempting. As Rosalind has eloquently noted above, we did not know just how much our respondents had suffered from the many aspects of U.S. racism, how courageous they have been over long years of this experience, how much they have to teach all Americans about resisting oppression, and, indeed, how much we ourselves would learn in this process.

Since the first edition of this book, a number of anecdotal and essay-type articles and books by scholars and media commentators have argued that certain Asian American groups are now truly "model minorities" or "superior ethnic groups" who no longer face racialized problems in a supposedly "post-racial America." The detailed, revelatory, and painful accounts of the savvy Asian Americans in this book should, if thoughtfully attended to, put such mistaken notions permanently to rest. In addition, much survey and other research since our interviews likewise reveals that there is no such "post-racial America" for Asian Americans, or any other Americans of color. To take just one example, a Pew Research Center survey found that one in five Asian Americans indicated dealing with racial discrimination over the previous months. Many reported racist name-calling and that being Asian had hurt them in getting jobs, promotions, and admission to colleges.

Bringing this reality home to non–Asian Americans, and especially white Americans, is one major reason we have written this book. Over five decades of teaching thousands of college students at six universities, I have learned that, until whites (and some others) have in-depth and meaningful instruction in the contemporary realities of the everyday discrimination and other racial oppression faced by Asian Americans and other Americans of color, most will resist the significant insights and understandings they need to commit to major changes in this country's systemic racism. Clearly, eradicating the centuries-old white racial framing of Asian Americans and the discriminatory actions generated by that framing will necessitate much effort by an array of Americans, including much-improved education about the historical and contemporary experiences that Asian Americans like our respondents have often had with white racism. This book continues to provide one important window into that painful and revealing experience.

Acknowledgments

We would first like to thank our respondents for their willingness to discuss their lives and views with us. Many indicated their appreciation for such research and were glad that "finally, someone" was working on a project that examined the reality of racial hostility and discrimination for Asian Americans. Some explicitly said that they felt some responsibility, to Asian and non–Asian Americans alike, to speak truthfully in the hope that this world could become a much better place for all people. When we began working on this research project, our intention was much the same. Nearing the end of this writing process, we have discovered that these very insightful and articulate respondents have profoundly changed us as well. These amazing people, who are surviving and resisting racism every day, are a true source of inspiration for us and, we hope, for all our readers.

Rosalind would also like to thank her parents, Li-Hsueh Chou and Chuen Cheng Chou, for long years of love and support. Almost forty years ago, they made the decision to leave behind their families and all their friends to make new lives in the United States. They struggled with language, homesickness, and the challenges of a new and different culture. They are truly amazing. My sisters, Nina and Alice, have always been two women whom I have admired. They are both brilliant in their own unique ways. I thank them for being patient with their tagalong baby sister, and I am so glad that some of their studiousness has finally rubbed off on me. I am eternally indebted to the friends who have provided me with security, comfort, and unconditional love. Special thanks go to Deborah Long, Charlene Whitney, Lynn Player, Kirsen Rostad, Gale Wire,

Josh Adrian, Stephanie Dorsey, Tiffany Hall, Rachel Kraft, Marinda Reynolds, Rachel Suniga Osborn, Kelly Frazer, Patty Jervey, Heather Hale, Emily Smith, and Suzanne Uchneat.

Both authors are grateful to a strong community of social scientists who have been so supportive of our research in many different ways, especially Christopher Chambers, Jennifer Mueller, Glenn Bracey, Lorena Murga, Karen Glover, Kristen Lavelle, Michelle Christian, Daniel Delgado, Elyshia Aseltine, Rachel Feinstein, and Ruth Thompson-Miller. We also appreciate greatly the scholarly assistance of several other colleagues and would especially like to thank the late Stuart Hysom, William McIntosh, Leland Saito, Melissa Fujiwara, Bernice McNair Barnett, Terence Fitzgerald, Jacob Van Den Berg, Suzuki Kazuko, Mamta Accapadi, Wendy Leo Moore, Marian Eide, Charles Zhang, Nestor Rodriguez, Adia Harvey Wingfield, Wendy Susan Simonds, and Edna Chun for their helpful suggestions and critical comments at various stages of the research and writing process.

Rosalind S. Chou and Joe R. Feagin

Chapter 1
The Reality of Asian American Oppression

I had a terrible, uneasy feeling in my stomach and I picked up the phone to hear panic in the voice on the other end of the line. "She jumped out the window. Farrah* jumped out of the window." What I thought were irrational fears from the night before had, in fact, become a reality. In late March of 2013, I could not fall asleep. Something was off, something was sitting in my gut and it felt as if I was living out a sociological statistic in real life. It was just before going to bed and I, Rosalind S. Chou, could not get ahold of my friend Farrah. She was not returning any of my phone calls or text messages. She had always been timely in responding in the past few years that we had been friends, and it seemed a little out of character. I had spoken to her a couple days earlier and she just did not seem like herself. I tried my best not to panic, but to explain my nervousness to my partner with whom I shared numerous studies about Asian American women and their high rates of suicide and depression. For some reason, my inability to get in touch with Farrah triggered all the "what if" scenarios.

I slept terribly, and the next morning, I reached out to other friends to see if they had heard from her. I was nervous and anxious for hours. And then I got the phone call. When I answered, I got the news. Farrah had jumped out of a window that morning and was in a nearby hospital. I was stunned. In academia, we scholars are often taught to distance ourselves from our research, but this hit home. This was not a lecture in class where I discuss health disparities and how there is growing evidence that racism plays a role in disparate outcomes. This was someone close to me, in my inner circle.

---

*Farrah is a pseudonym.

I often encourage my students to *feel* when we learn about inequality, because oppression works in a way so that we no longer feel empathy for target groups. My community of friends faced shock and confusion and in the first edition of the book, Joe and I argue that, while it is very difficult to measure how much racism affects Asian Americans and people of color in general, the mental health statistics show that Asian American women are overrepresented in rates of suicide and depression.

In the first edition, we argued that it is a dangerous assumption that Asian Americans are free from racism. Their relatively high levels of educational attainment and household income, and their overrepresentation in professional occupations, make it seem as if they are doing better than other racial minorities or even some whites. However, the white-constructed label of "model minority" awarded to Asian Americans does *not* protect them from prejudice and racism.

The incident with my friend Farrah was not the first one I had experienced with Asian American women I know. In the fall of 2001, R. W., a young Chinese American, bludgeoned and strangled her mother. While her mother lay dead on the floor, she covered her and called the police, confessing her crime. This school valedictorian was an accomplished musician who had begun her education at a prestigious Ivy League school and graduated with honors from her southern university. Her crime received little local notice. Only one full-length newspaper article was published, and after her indictment she was barely mentioned. This tragic incident hit home for the first author because she is acquainted with the family, which was one of the few Chinese families in her hometown. The incident sent shockwaves through the Asian American community of which they were part. R. W.'s failure to stay at her first college program, an elite institution, may well have contributed to her several suicide attempts and eventually to the homicide. She may now live out her years in a mental institution, and family and friends are left stressed and wondering "why?"[1]

On the outside, R. W. appeared to be a model student at her historically white educational institutions. Her demeanor was quiet, which likely suggested to white outsiders only a stereotyped Asian passivity. Thus, even with numerous warning signs of mental illness, she was never seen as a concern. The white-created "successful model minority" stereotype made it difficult for non-Asians around her to see her illness and encouraged silence among the Asian Americans who knew her.

The 2007 shootings of students and staff at Virginia Tech University by Cho Seung-Hui suggest somewhat similar issues. A Korean American student at a historically white institution, Cho was viewed by outsiders as unusually quiet, and although he demonstrated warning signs of mental illness, he was mostly ignored, especially by those with the most authority to take action. Not much has been revealed about his life growing up in a Virginia suburb except that he was an "easy target" at school and endured substantial teasing from white children. When younger, he struggled to learn English, which made it difficult to adapt in his predominantly white environment. Cho seems to have lived as an outcast and in social isolation. Given his parents' success in business and his sister's success as a Princeton graduate, Cho and his family seem to outsiders like a proverbial model family that "lifted themselves up by their bootstraps" and thus are living the American dream.[2] Yet, these stereotyped images and Cho's own struggle to achieve may have worked against his mental health. As the interviews in this book reveal, this young Asian American's struggle to make it in a predominantly white world was not unique in being both very invisible and excruciatingly tormented.

Our argument here is *not* that Asian Americans are distinctively prone to serious mental illness or violence. Rather, we accent in this book the institutionally racist situations in which Asian Americans find themselves—those highly pressured situations that create much stress and deeply felt pain. One major societal problem is that Asian Americans are typically viewed and labeled as "model minorities" by outsiders, especially by whites with power over them. This highly stereotyped labeling creates great pressure to conform to the white-dominated culture, usually in a one-way direction.

In books titled *YELL-Oh Girls!* and *Asian American X,* several hundred young Asian Americans discuss their often difficult lives. These young people recount recurring experiences with coercive pressures to assimilate into the prestigious white end of the prevailing U.S. racial status continuum—to white ways of dress, speech, goal attainment, thinking, and physical being. Most are torn between the culture of immigrant parents or grandparents, with its substantial respect for Asianness, and the burdensome pressures of a white-controlled society. As one young Korean American who grew up in a white community puts it, the dominance of whites explains the "thoughtless ways white Americans often inhabit a sense of entitlement and egocentric normality."[3] Like other Asian Americans, these young people report racialized mistreatment, ranging from subtle to covert to overt discrimination. The successful minority image does not protect them from the onslaughts of discriminatory whites.

Our research here attempts to give voice to numerous Asian Americans as they describe and assess their discriminatory and other life experiences. Using in-depth interviews, we collected accounts of Asian American experiences in everyday life, including incidents of racial hostility and discrimination, responses of assimilation and conformity, and ways that individuals, families, and communities cope with and resist white-imposed racism. Our interviews indicate that Asian Americans suffer from much discrimination, ranging from subtle to blatant, at the hands of whites. The interviews show that, even after Herculean efforts to conform to the dominant racial hierarchy and to the white framing of them—efforts seeking to achieve the fabled American dream—Asian Americans frequently feel stressed, embattled, isolated, and inadequate. Many passively accept that they must hide or abandon their home culture, values, and identity to prevent future mistreatment. Significant educational and economic achievements do not effectively shield them. Some analysts have argued that Asian Americans are "lucky" that they do not face the negative imagery that African Americans experience.[4] This view of Asian Americans is incorrect. The Asian American experience with racial hostility and discrimination is also very negative and largely untold, and such an untold experience is indeed a very *harmful* invisibility.

The Reality of Systemic Racism

Traditional analytical approaches to immigrants and immigration to the United States mostly emphasize various assimilation orientations and processes. Some assimilation analysts have argued that all incoming immigrant groups will eventually be fully integrated into U.S. society, including the more distinctive ethnic and racial groups. Many social science researchers view the adaptation of Asian immigrants and their children to U.S. society since the 1960s through an assimilation lens, one similar to that used for assessing the adaptations of past and present European immigrants. Numerous assimilation analysts have argued that Asian American groups are on their way to full integration into the "core society," by which they mean white middle-class society. For example, Paul Spickard has argued that by the 1980s whites no longer viewed Japanese Americans "as very different from themselves, and that fact is remarkable."[5] To make this case, these analysts usually focus on Asian American socioeconomic progress in areas such as educational and income achievements. However, this limited definition of success in adaptation in the United States is mostly white-generated and ignores other important areas of Asian American lives.

Indeed, the fact that Asian immigrants and their children are heavily pressured to conform to a white-imposed culture, racial frame, and racial hierarchy—and suffer from much racial hostility and discrimination—is usually left out of most assessments of Asian immigrants and their children and grandchildren. Here we go beyond the typical assimilation approach and accent a systemic racism perspective. Since at least the seventeenth century, European Americans have created a complex North American society with a foundation of racial oppression, one whose nooks and crannies are generally pervaded with racial discrimination and inequality. Near their beginning, the new European colonies in North America institutionalized white-on-Indian oppression (land theft and genocide) and white-on-black oppression (centuries of slavery), and by the mid-nineteenth century the Mexicans and the Chinese were incorporated as dispossessed landholders or exploited workers into the racial hierarchy and political-economic institutions of a relatively new United States. Our systemic approach views racial oppression as a foundational and persisting underpinning of this society. From the beginning, powerful whites have designed and maintained the country's economic, political, and social institutions to benefit, disproportionately and substantially, their racial group. For centuries, *unjust* impoverishment of Americans of color has been linked to *unjust* enrichment of whites, thereby creating a central racial hierarchy and status continuum in which whites are generally the dominant and privileged group.[6]

Since the earliest period of colonization, moreover, European Americans have buttressed this hierarchical and entrenched system of unjust material enrichment and unjust material impoverishment with legal institutions and a strong white racial *framing* of this society. In the past and in the present, whites have combined within this pervasive white frame a good many racist stereotypes (the cognitive aspect), racist concepts (the deeper cognitive aspect), racist images (the visual aspect), racialized emotions (feelings), racist narratives (e.g., "manifest destiny"), and inclinations to take discriminatory action. This white racial frame is old, enduring, and oriented to assessing and relating to Americans of color in everyday situations. Operating with this racial frame firmly in mind, the dominant white group has used its power to place new non-European groups, such as Asian immigrants and their children, somewhere in the racial hierarchy whites firmly control—that is, on a white-to-black continuum of status and privilege with whites at the highly privileged end, blacks at the unprivileged end, and other racial groups typically placed by whites somewhere in between. This white racist framing of society is now a centuries-old rationalizing of the racism systemic in this society.

Our concept of *systemic* racism thus encompasses a broad range of racialized realities in this society: the all-encompassing white racial frame, extensive discriminatory habits and exploitative actions, and numerous racist institutions. This white-generated and white-maintained system entails much more than racial bigotry, for it has been from the beginning a material, structural, and ideological reality.

The Exploitation and Oppression of Asian Immigrants

In the classroom, our non-Asian students, regardless of their backgrounds, are often shocked to hear about Asian American oppression. These students have never been taught Asian American history, or been privy to significant events that have shaped these communities in the United States. Students often ask us why these things have been "left out" of their regular curriculum. Additionally, they start to make the important societal connections that Asian Americans do have with other groups—with African Americans, Native Americans, Latinos, working-class whites, and the list goes on. We encourage our students to relearn an accurate U.S. history—and to recognize that our common bonds may keep us from making the same mistakes of the past. Knowing our racial past is imperative to help us with our racial future.

While some Asian Americans today trace family histories back to nineteenth-century immigrants, most have a more recent immigration background. Older members of the families of R. W. and Cho are relatively recent immigrants, and thus these families are typical. Changes in U.S. immigration laws since 1965 have allowed a substantial increase in immigration from Asian and Pacific countries, and thus Asian/Pacific Islander Americans have become the fastest growing U.S. racial group. In 1940 they made up less than 1 percent of the population, but by 2012 their numbers had grown to more than 17.5 million, about 5.6 percent of the U.S. population. The largest Asian/Pacific Islander group is Chinese American. In numbers, Filipino Americans are not far behind, and Japanese, Korean, Asian Indian, and Vietnamese Americans constitute other large Asian-origin groups.

Much scholarship on Asians in North America has addressed Asian experiences with racial hostility and discrimination over a long history of immigration. Scholars have examined more than 150 years of Asian immigration and shown, to take one example, that Asian workers have regularly been pitted against white workers. The first major immigrant group was Chinese. Between the 1850s and 1880s, Chinese contract laborers migrated in large numbers to the West Coast to do low-wage work in construction and other economic sectors. The preference that white employers had for Chinese workers fueled tensions in the racial hierarchy, often pitting white workers against Asian workers. After whites' racist agitation and exclusionary legislation stopped most Chinese immigration, Japanese immigrants were recruited by employers to fill the labor demand on white-run farms and construction projects. (By the late nineteenth century the Chinese were viewed by whites as the stereotyped "yellow peril.") The racially motivated termination of Japanese immigration in 1907–1908 spurred white employers to recruit other Asians and Pacific Islanders (such as Filipinos) to fill labor needs on the U.S. mainland and in Hawaii. This employers' strategy of using immigrant workers from Asia and the Pacific Islands to replace white and other native-born workers has continued in some U.S. workplaces to the present.[7]

In the nineteenth and early twentieth centuries, Asian and Pacific Islander immigrants and their children—mostly Chinese, Japanese, and Filipino—suffered extremely blatant and institutionalized racism. They were negatively positioned, and imaged, by whites as "black" or "near black" on the dominant socioracial continuum. Powerful whites imposed a strong racial framing on these subor-dinated immigrants, with barbed racist stereotypes and images. Reviewing the history, Robert Lee has commented on white constructions of hated "Orientals": "Six images—the pollutant, the coolie, the deviant, the yellow peril, the model minority, and the gook—portray the Oriental as an alien body and a threat to the American national family."[8] For example, from the 1850s onward the first Asian Americans, the Chinese, were stereotyped by white officials and commen-tators as "alien," "dangerous," "docile," and "dirty." At that time, such negative images were not new to the white racist framing of Americans of color. They had precedents in earlier white views of African Americans and Native Americans.[9]

In 1896, even as he defended some rights for black Americans as the dissenter in the *Plessy v. Ferguson* Supreme Court decision upholding legal segregation, Justice John Marshall Harlan included this racial argument: "There is a race so different from our own that we do not permit those belonging to it to become citizens of the United States. Persons belonging to it are, with few exceptions, absolutely excluded from our country. I allude to the Chinese race."[10] In the first decades of the 1900s, this negative view was applied to other Asian Americans as well. U.S. government agencies have played a central role in defining racial groups. Thus, in the important 1922 *Ozawa* case, the U.S. Supreme Court ruled that Asian immigrants were *not white* and thus could not become citizens. The "not white," "alien race," and related racist notions had been generated by elite whites in earlier centuries to stereotype and name Native Americans and African Americans as an early part of white racist framing for a "civilized" Eurocentric society. These ideas have persisted for four centuries, with at least 160 years now of application to Americans of Asian descent.[11]

Racist Framing and Large-Scale Discrimination

New ways of circulating the racist framing of Americans of color were developed by innovative white entrepreneurs in the early decades of the twentieth century. These included a burgeoning advertising industry making use of many magazines and radio stations, as well as the developing movie industry. White advertisers, cartoonists, and moviemakers commonly portrayed Chinese, Japanese, and other Asian/Pacific Islanders as outsiders or villains, who were often crudely stereo-typed as "inscrutable," poor at English, criminal, and dangerous.

For example, between the early 1900s and the 1940s, hostile visual images and stereotypes of "buck-toothed Japs" were prominent in U.S. media, con-tributing to anti-Japanese and other anti-Asian hostility in the United States. With extensive media support and facilitation, white commentators and politi-cal leaders spoke of an alleged alien character and the immorality of Japanese

Americans, sometimes using vicious apelike images.[12] These very negative images and other white racist framing of the Japanese and Japanese Americans contributed greatly to the international tensions leading to World War II, especially the recurring conflicts between the growing U.S. empire and the expanding Japanese empire, both in and around the rim of the Pacific Ocean.[13] This racist framing of the Japanese also contributed to extreme discriminatory actions undertaken by the U.S. government: the imprisonment of Japanese Americans in U.S. concentration camps during World War II. The government's rationale for the camps was openly racist. In 1943 West Coast military commander General John DeWitt articulated what most whites then believed when he argued that "a Jap's a Jap. The Japanese race is an enemy race, and while many second- and third-generation Japanese born on U.S. soil, possessed of U.S. citizenship, have become 'Americanized,' the *racial strains* are undiluted."[14] With no evidence, mainstream commentators and leading politicians, all white, asserted there were enemy agents in this "alien" Asian population. Significantly, one main reason for the existence of this "alien" population was the discriminatory U.S. law prohibiting Asian immigrants from becoming citizens.

Negative framing of Asian Americans during that era can be observed in a 1940s *Time* magazine article on "How to Tell Your Friends from the Japs." Here the white author offered a biologized and blatantly racist explanation of supposed differences between the Japanese and the Chinese—a task taken on because China and the United States had become allies against Japan in World War II:

> Virtually all Japanese are short. Japanese are likely to be stockier and broader-hipped than short Chinese. Although both have the typical epicanthic fold on the upper eyelid, Japanese eyes are usually set closer together. The Chinese expression is likely to be more placid, kindly, open; the Japanese more positive, dogmatic, arrogant. Japanese are hesitant, nervous in conversation, laugh loudly at the wrong time. Japanese walk stiffly erect, hard heeled. Chinese, more relaxed, have an easy gait, sometimes shuffle.[15]

The *Time* editors who published this wildly stereotyped statement probably thought they were saying something positive about the Chinese. Yet, this is a clear example of the arrogant power of *group definition* that has long been part of the dominant white group's historical framing of Americans of color.

However, the white view of the Chinese and of Koreans became more negative with the new conflicts that developed after World War II. With the rise of state communism in China in the late 1940s, Cold War stereotyping again positioned the Chinese, and by implication Chinese Americans, as "dangerous Orientals" in many white minds. Moreover, the U.S. intervention in Korea in 1950 was accompanied by emergency congressional legislation that gave the U.S. attorney general the authority to set up new concentration camps for Koreans, Chinese, and other Asians who might be perceived to be a domestic threat. The U.S. intervention in Korea, and later in Vietnam, further perpetuated an intensive racist stereotyping and framing of Asians and Asian Americans in the minds of many white and other non–Asian Americans.[16]

Even in this crude stereotyping we see a certain ambiguity in white views. Over the past century whites have sometimes positioned Asian Americans at the bottom end of the dominant racial hierarchy, while at other times they have positioned at least some Asian groups in a more intermediate status. From the late 1940s to the end of legal segregation in the 1960s, whites were sometimes perplexed as to where to place Asian Americans in the racial hierarchy, as we observe in this account from a Japanese American speaking about experiences during the legal segregation era:

> I stopped at a McDonald's in Mississippi and there were two lines, one for whites and the other for blacks, well, "coloreds." I stood there confused about which line to join. I stood there and decided to go in the colored line because there was nobody in it and I could get my food faster. When I got up to the counter the guy told me "hey you can't use this line, get in that other line." The line for whites was long and I had gone about halfway up when this guy says, "Hey, you can't be in this line, get in the other line." I just stood there and thought, "Ah, what am I!?"[17]

This recollection indicates not only the stereotyping and subordination of Asian Americans but also a white confusion about Asian Americans' being closer to whiteness or blackness in the dominant racial hierarchy. This placement has become ever more problematic for white Americans with the dramatic growth in the Asian American population since the 1960s.

White Racial Framing: Anti-Asian Imagery Today

Today whites and others still apply numerous elements of an old anti-Asian framing to Asian Americans. As we will see throughout this book, many whites hold inconsistent views of Asian Americans. They commonly view Asian Americans as high achievers and "model minorities," but will often discount the meaning of those achievements as being done by exotic "foreigners," "nerds," or social misfits. For example, some research studies show that Asian American students are often viewed positively by whites, but mainly in regard to educational or income achievements. A recent summary of research concludes that most stereotypes of

Asian American students "are negative, such as non-Asians' notions that Asians 'don't speak English well,' 'have accents,' and are 'submissive,' 'sneaky,' 'stingy,' 'greedy,' etc."[18] To complicate matters, racial stereotyping is gendered and sexualized. Asian American men feel the brunt of emasculating white stereotypes that place them at the bottom of a U.S. masculinity hierarchy, while many Asian American women are exoticized as sexual objects.[19] Racism is often perpetuated through different systems of oppression in an intersectional way—thus, these differences in white-imposed constructions of Asian American men and women.

Subtle and blatant stereotyping of Asians and Asian Americans still predominates in many areas of U.S. society. Consider just a few recent examples. In November 2013, comedian and talk show host Jimmy Kimmel aired a skit on his late night show in which he led a roundtable discussion with children. The discussion topic in the roundtable was the U.S. debt to China and the punch line was delivered by one of the children suggesting that we "*kill* all the Chinese." The broadcasting of the skit demonstrates how Kimmel, and the writers and producers of the show, consider mass genocide of the Chinese as acceptable comedic content. Moreover, in February 2013, Asian American basketball player Jeremy Lin burst onto the NBA scene with "surprising" athletic prowess for the New York Knicks team. During the months of "Linsanity" where media outlets dedicated extensive coverage to the exceptionalism of Lin's play, he was also met with numerous racial taunts and slurs by fans and other athletes. Two ESPN cable channel writers used a racial slur in their headlines about Lin: a "Chink in the Armor" was used on their journalistic website. Floyd Mayweather insisted Lin was not worthy of this attention and was made a celebrity only because of his Asian heritage, not in spite of it.[20] In fall of 2013, a documentary on Jeremy Lin's journey to the NBA was released, and in an interview in the film he noted that racism has played a part in his entire athletic career.

In spring of 2011, a UCLA student, Alexandra Wallace, created an anti-Asian YouTube video titled "Asians in the Library" that went viral.[21] In it, Wallace complains of "hordes of Asians" at UCLA, of their not having "American" manners, and about their parents for "not teaching their kids to fend for themselves." She also makes a mockery of Asians who speak their native languages and minimizes the Fukushima nuclear tragedy in Japan. The university failed to address the racist rant, although Wallace did apologize and resign from the school for personal reasons.[22] She received some notoriety from the racist incident and was asked to appear on MTV. This is one of very few examples of institutional consequences for whites who engage in anti-Asian racism, and of the apparent acceptance of Wallace as a humorous figure in pop culture.

The Adidas company was challenged by civil rights groups for making shoes that had a negative caricature of a buck-toothed, slant-eyed Asian as a logo. In another case, a large pictorial cartoon concerning fund-raising investigations of Democratic Party leaders appeared on the cover of an issue of the prominent magazine *National Review*. The cover showed caricatures of then president Bill Clinton and his wife, Hillary Clinton, as slant-eyed, buck-toothed Chinese in Mao suits and Chinese hats—images suggesting old stereotyped images of Asian Americans' characteristics. Since the nineteenth century, white cartoonists, political leaders, and media commentators have portrayed Chinese and other Asian Americans in such stereotyped terms, often to express a fear of the "yellow peril." When confronted, the *National Review*'s white editor admitted these were negative Asian caricatures but refused to apologize. Such reactions, and the fact that there was little public protest of the cover other than from Asian American groups, suggest that such crude images and other associated stereotypes remain significant in a dominant racial framing of people of Asian descent.[23]

In addition, a U.S. animation company made a cartoon (*Mr. Wong*) and placed at its center an extreme caricature of a Chinese "hunchbacked, yellow-skinned, squinty-eyed character who spoke with a thick accent and starred in an interactive music video titled *Saturday Night Yellow Fever*."[24] Again Asian American and other civil rights groups protested this anti-Asian mocking, but many whites and a few Asian Americans inside and outside the entertainment industry defended such racist cartoons as "only good humor." Similarly, the makers of a puppet movie, *Team America: World Police,* portrayed a Korean political leader speaking gibberish in a mock Asian accent. One Asian American commentator noted the movie was "an hour and a half of racial mockery with an 'if you are offended, you obviously can't take a joke' tacked on at the end."[25] Moreover, in an episode of the popular television series *Desperate Housewives* a main character, played by actor Teri Hatcher, visits a physician for a medical checkup. Shocked that the doctor suggests she may be going through menopause, she replies, "Okay, before we go any further, can I check these diplomas? Just to make sure they aren't, like, from some med school in the Philippines." This racialized stereotyping was protested by many in the Asian and Pacific Islander communities.

Although sometimes played out in supposedly humorous presentations, continuing media-reproduced stereotypes of Asians and Pacific Islanders include old white-framed notions of them as odd, foreign, un-American, relatively unassimilated, or culturally inferior. Noteworthy in these accounts is the connection of more recent anti-Asian stereotyping, mostly by whites, to the old anti-Asian stereotyping of the nineteenth and early twentieth centuries. For the majority of non–Asian Americans, particularly those who control the media, certain negative images of Asians and of Asian Americans (especially Asian immigrants and their children) blend together in a common anti-Asian racial framing. The strong protests of Asian American civil rights and other organizations to all such racialized stereotyping and mocking underscore this important point.

Anti-Asian stereotypes are still frequently encountered in everyday discourse. Asian Americans, including children, often note that they face mocking language and other racially hostile words, such as these: "Ching chong Chinaman sitting on a rail, along came a white man and snipped off his tail"; "Ah so. No tickee, no washee. So sorry, so sollee"; and "Chinkee, Chink, Jap, Nip, zero, Dothead, Flip, Hindoo."[26] A disc jockey at a Toledo, Ohio, radio station called Asian restaurants and made mock Asian commentaries, such as "ching, chong, chung" and "me speakee no English." Similarly, a CBS talk show host mocked an Asian Excellence Awards ceremony by playing a fake excerpt with "Asian men" saying things like "Ching chong, ching chong, ching chong." Comedian Rosie O'Donnell also used a repeated "ching chong" to mock Chinese speech on her ABC talk show. One striking reaction to the O'Donnell comment was hundreds of blogger entries on Internet websites that defended her comments and (erroneously) asserted the comments were *not* racist.[27]

To modern ears such language mocking and other Asian mocking may seem novel, but it is actually an old part of the white racist framing of Asian Americans. White English speakers on the West Coast developed this mocking in the mid- to late nineteenth century as their way of making fun of the English-Chinese speech of Chinese workers, as well as of racializing them. An early 1900s ragtime song goes, "Ching, Chong, Oh Mister Ching Chong, You are the king of Chinatown. Ching Chong, I love your sing-song."[28]

Anthropologist Jane Hill has shown how in the United States such mocking of language links to systemic racism. In particular Hill has studied the extensive mocking of Spanish, such as the making up of fake Spanish words and phrases. Mock Spanish—common on birthday cards, on items in gift shops, and in commentaries from board rooms to the mass media—is mostly created by college-educated Americans, especially white Americans. Similar language mocking has long been directed at African Americans and Asian Americans. "Through this process, such people are endowed with gross sexual appetites, political corruption, laziness, disorders of language, and mental incapacity."[29] Language mocking is not just lighthearted commentary of no social importance, because such mocking usually is linked to racial framing and societal discrimination against the racialized "others." While native speakers of languages such as French or German do not face serious discrimination because of their accents when they speak English, Asian Americans, Latinos, and other Americans of color do often face such discrimination. As one scholar has underscored, "It is crucial to remember that it is not all foreign accents, but only accent linked to skin that isn't white, or which signals a third-world homeland, evokes such negative reactions."[30]

Model Minority Imagery: An Apparent Contradiction?

Today, frequent anti-Asian mocking and caricaturing signal the continuing presence of a strong racist framing of Asians and Americans of Asian descent. Some people, especially whites, may play down the significance of such racist framing and instead argue that a strong positive image of Asian Americans has often been asserted by whites. They note that whites, especially in the mainstream media and in politics, regularly broadcast positive reports on achievements of Asian Americans in schools and workplaces. From this point of view, one should note, an Asian American group has "succeeded" in U.S. society when its attainments on a limited number of quantitative indicators of occupation, education, and income are at least comparable to those of white Americans. A superficial reading of these indicators leads many to view virtually all Asian Americans as successful and thus as not facing significant racial barriers in this society. Such analyses may be correct in regard to a certain type of success measured by particular socioeconomic indicators for Asian American groups as a whole, but not in regard to the socioeconomic problems faced by large segments within these groups or in regard to the various forms of racial discrimination that most Asian Americans still face in their daily lives.

Take Japanese Americans, for example. Recent data indicate that Japanese Americans are more likely to hold managerial or professional jobs than their white counterparts, and their unemployment rate is less than that for whites. Median income for their families is more than for white families nationally, and a smaller percentage falls below the federal poverty line than for whites. However, Japanese American workers mostly live in the West, where there is a relatively high cost of living. We should note too that in California the difference in median incomes between Japanese American families and white families is reversed. Per capita income for Asian American groups is also generally lower than that for whites, who average smaller families. In addition, many Asian immigrants and their children, especially those from Southeast Asia and rural backgrounds, have experienced much poverty and other serious economic difficulties over the past few decades.[31]

Moreover, although Japanese Americans and certain other Asian American groups have achieved significant socioeconomic success, they still face a substantial array of subtle and overt acts of discrimination, as we demonstrate fully in later chapters. Research studies reveal some of this picture. For example, when researchers have examined Japanese and other Asian American workers in comparison with white workers with similar jobs, educational credentials, and years of job experience, the Asian American workers are found to be paid less on average and are less likely to be promoted to managerial positions.[32] In addition, Asian

American workers often face exclusion from numerous positions in business, entertainment, political, and civil service areas, regardless of their qualifications and abilities. Japanese and other Asian Americans periodically report a "glass ceiling" in corporations or exclusion from business networks. About 5 percent of the population, Asian Americans are far less than 1 percent of the members of the boards of Fortune 500 firms; one tabulation revealed that just *one* Asian American headed up a Fortune 500 firm not founded by an Asian American. White executives periodically assert that in their firms Asian Americans are best as technical workers and not as executives. Given this stereotyped view, Asian Americans are often hired as engineers, computer experts, and technicians, but no matter what their qualifications are they are rarely considered for top management positions. Moreover, given this discrimination, many younger Asian Americans have pursued scientific and technical educations and rejected the fine arts, humanities, and social sciences, areas they might have preferred. Career choices are thus influenced by both past and present discrimination. In addition, many business opportunities in corporate America remain limited by persisting anti-Asian sentiment.[33]

The "great recession" of 2008–2009 disproportionately affected Asian Americans, further challenging the "model minority" myth. According to the National Coalition for Asian-Pacific American Community Development, Asian Americans have seen a 38 percent increase in their poverty population while the general poverty population grew by 27 percent during the same time period, with the African American poverty population growing by 20 percent.[34] This poverty rate is not just affecting the newer immigrant population, for 60 percent of the net increase in Asian American/Pacific Islander poverty was in the native-born segment of that population.[35] In 2010, compared to whites, blacks, and Latinos, Asian American workers had the highest share of unemployed workers who were unemployed long term (more than half a year). Additionally, when compared to their similarly educated white counterparts, highly educated Asian Americans suffer from disproportionately higher unemployment rates. Asian Americans with bachelor's degrees are more likely to be unemployed than whites. This is especially significant because 57 percent of the Asian American labor force is in this category.[36] Oftentimes, education is seen as the "great equalizer," but we see that Asian Americans obtaining advanced degrees still face economic disadvantages. In spite of much data contradicting their commonplace view, numerous social scientists and media commentators have regularly cited the educational and economic "success" of a particular Asian American group, one typically described as the "model minority," as an indication that whites no longer create significant racial barriers for them.[37] For example, a 2012 research report of the prestigious Pew Research Center cites this socioeconomic success and asks unreflectively,

"Are Asian Americans a 'Model Minority'?" The report also compares, again uncritically, the supposedly successful achievements of Asian Americans with the lesser achievements of Hispanic Americans.[38]

This continuing use of a white-named and white-framed perspective on Asian Americans is highly problematical. We can pinpoint when this model myth was likely first constructed. In the mid-1960s, largely in response to African American and Latino (especially Mexican American) protests against discrimination, white scholars, political leaders, and journalists developed the model minority myth in order to allege that all Americans of color could achieve the American dream—and not by protesting discrimination in the stores and streets as African Americans and Mexican Americans were doing, but by working as "hard and quietly" as Japanese and Chinese Americans supposedly did. This model image was created *not* by Asian Americans but by influential whites for their public ideological use.[39] One example is a 1960s *U.S. News & World Report* article entitled "Success Story of One Minority Group in U.S." This major media article praised the hard work and morality of Chinese Americans, and its analysis strongly implied that if black Americans possessed such virtues, it would not be necessary to spend "hundreds of billions to uplift" them.[40]

For decades now, prominent commentators and politicians have cited the educational or economic success of Asian Americans as proof that they are fully melded into the U.S. "melting pot," with many "ascending above exclusion" by "pulling themselves up by their bootstraps."[41] Today, variations of this model stereotype remain pervasive, and leading politicians, judges, journalists, and corporate executives assert them regularly.[42] Even other Americans of color have sometimes been conned by this model minority view and declared it to be so true that governments do not need to be concerned with the discrimination against Asian Americans. For example, black Supreme Court nominee Clarence Thomas, at his Senate confirmation hearings, asserted that Asian Americans have "transcended the ravages caused even by harsh legal and social discrimination" and should not be the beneficiaries of affirmative action because they are "over-represented in key institutions."[43]

One of the contemporary ironies of such uninformed views is that private and government reports in recent years have shown that today educational success varies among the Asian American groups and, indeed, that many Asian Americans in numerous groups still face significant obstacles to academic success, in some cases more than in the past.[44] For example, one savvy higher education journalist noted that numerous articles in college newspapers have used Asian Americans as a point of humor, but their portrayals usually feed the "model minority" myth. Asian American students are still often seen as an "invasion" and their demeanors as "inscrutable." On these college campuses lies a "continued pattern of Asian American students being (a) the butt of such jokes, basically the punch line; (b) that the jokes are heavily laden with racial stereotypes; and (c) that these … essays reveal volumes about racial relationships, tensions, and perceptions of Asian American students as all being, in some way, the same—foreigners, math and science nerds, and all around different from the regular average college student."[45]

Assimilation and the "Model Minority" Imagery

Several researchers—mostly Asian American—have challenged the rosy view of Asian American success in the complex assimilation process forced on them in the United States. These researchers have shown that Asian immigrants and their children have long faced discrimination and other serious difficulties in adapting to U.S. society. Some have also explored how the societal conditions of Asian Americans are racialized.[46]

Several social scientists have focused on Asian American adaptation to the dominant culture and society using traditional assimilation theories. For example, drawing on interviews with young Asian American professionals, Pyong Gap Min and Rose Kim report that these young professionals have highly assimilated socially and culturally, and have significant friendship ties to middle-class whites and significant assimilation to white folkways. They found that these Asian American professionals are bicultural, with strong assimilation to "American culture," but express a strong national-origin or pan-Asian identity as well. An earlier study of Korean immigrants by Won Moo Hurh and Kwang Chung Kim reported similar findings, in that their respondents demonstrated what they term "additive" or "adhesive" adaptation—that is, assimilating substantially to the new economy and society, yet maintaining a strong sense of their ethnic and racial identities. While both research studies discuss difficult identity choices of their respondents, like most contemporary researchers looking at immigrant assimilation, they do not examine in depth the harsh racial realities surrounding these choices. In this still-racist society, personal or group identity "choices" by Asian immigrants and their children are severely limited by the racial identity typically *imposed* on them by white outsiders.[47]

In a study of second-generation Chinese and Korean Americans, social scientist Nazli Kibria has also explored the formation of identities. Assessing the adaptation of Asian immigrants and their children, she distinguishes between an "ethnic American" model and a "racial minority" model of assimilation. The old ethnic assimilation model, asserted by scholars and others, has set the framework for Asian assimilation into the core society, yet creates significant problems because it assumes that an ethnic immigrant group is white. In Kibria's view, as

Asian immigrants and their children accent a new umbrella identity of "Asian American," they are updating the old ethnic assimilation model to include their racial minority experience. While Kibria recognizes that her respondents are set apart, discriminated against, and stereotyped as foreigners or model minorities, she keeps her analysis of the perpetrators of this stereotyping and discrimination rather vague and provides no in-depth analysis of the systemic racism context in which these Asian Americans are forced to adapt. Her Chinese and Korean respondents report on some "lessons about race," "race socialization," and not being accepted "by others," yet in her analysis Kibria does not assess the central role of white discriminators or the white-imposed framing and hierarchy in forcing such hard lessons.[48]

One of the few analysts of Asian Americans to explicitly name white discriminators as central is sociologist Mia Tuan. Interviewing nearly 100 third- and later-generation Chinese and Japanese Americans, she found that although most were well assimilated into the dominant culture, most also had a strong sense of a racialized identity because whites constantly imposed the identity of "Asian foreigner" on them. They reported being caught between feeling perpetually outside, as "forever foreigners," and sometimes being given greater privileges by whites than other people of color. They spoke too of the difficulty they had in viewing themselves in terms of their national origin when they were constantly being defined in "generically racial terms" as "Asian Americans" or as "Orientals." Though offering a probing analysis that assesses well racial-ethnic identity struggles and recognizes whites as having a privileged status, Tuan also does not, in our view, provide enough in-depth analysis of the anti-Asian racism that surrounds, and imposes oppressive predicaments on, Asian Americans.[49]

Several researchers have specifically targeted the model minority stereotype. One early analysis was that of the innovative legal scholar Mari Matsuda, who suggested that Asian Americans might be positioned as a "racial bourgeoisie," a racial middle status between whites and other people of color. This protects the white position at the top by diffusing hostility toward them and sets up Asian Americans to be a "scapegoat during times of crisis."[50] In a more recent analysis, Vijay Prashad has shown how Asian Americans are termed model minorities and thus come "to be the perpetual solution to what is seen as the crisis of black America." Prashad does not specifically identify and assess the white agents who have created this crisis for black America. He does note a certain "Orientalism" among white Americans—the view that many have of Asia as being "static and unfree" in contrast to a "dynamic and free" Western civilization. Holding to this framing, whites frequently stereotype Asian Americans negatively as alien, exotic, barbaric, or primitive. Prashad adds that for Asian Americans "it is easier to be seen as a solution than as a problem. We don't suffer genocidal poverty and incarceration rates in the United States, nor do we walk in fear and a fog of invisibility."[51] Ironically, he here evokes part of the model minority stereotype yet does not note that this hoary stereotype often creates an invisibility cloak hiding severe problems of racism faced regularly by Asian Americans.

The pioneering legal scholar Frank Wu has done much to dispel model minority stereotyping. In his work he has explained the benefits that whites enjoy because of that labeling. Reviewing the long history of anti-Asian discrimination, he notes that "non–Asian Americans can discriminate against Asian Americans by turning us into noncitizens, either officially by prohibiting even legal long-term residents from naturalizing or informally by casting doubt on our status. The alien land laws, passed to drive Japanese immigrants out of farming, are the prime example." While he accents well the many decades of anti-Asian discrimination, Wu regularly uses vague terms such as "non–Asian Americans" and thereby skirts around using the word "whites" for those doing such intense discriminating. While in many of his analyses Wu recognizes how anti-Asian racism is institutionalized, at times he seems to play down certain aspects of white racism: "Other than among a few idealists, as a nation we accept discrimination on the basis of citizenship as necessary. But except among a few extremists, as a society we reject discrimination on the basis of race as immoral."[52] Wu here seems to neglect the societal reality that *many* whites still do find it acceptable to engage in racial discrimination against Americans of color, yet may find it no longer fashionable to discriminate openly or assert racist views publicly.

Clearly, these often-pioneering Asian American scholars have moved social science analysis of the adaptive barriers faced by Asian Americans in very important directions. Still, some of them tend to avoid explicitly naming and analyzing fully the role of whites (especially elite whites) as central protagonists in creating anti-Asian racism today—often preferring instead to name vague social agents such as "non-Asians," "the law," "the government," or "the larger society" as generators of contemporary racism. Such analytical practices can be found as well among many scholars researching the racialized situations of other Americans of color. They too are often reluctant to name whites *specifically* as the key actors in past or present dramas of U.S. racism.[53]

One of the few researchers to examine in critical detail the contemporary impact of *systemic racism* on Asian American communities is sociologist Claire Jean Kim. Examining periodic conflicts between Korean American merchants and African American patrons in a few cities, Kim shows that these conflicts should be understood in the context of whites' long-term discriminatory actions against both groups. She illustrates how Asian immigrants have come to be positioned, mainly by *white* actions, between white urbanites and black urbanites, and how these Asian Americans are given a negative evaluation by whites on both the axis of superior/inferior racial groups and the axis of insiders/foreigners. Such intergroup conflict involves more than just stereotyping by African Americans or Korean Americans of the other group, but instead reflects the white-imposed racial hierarchy and its effects on both racially subordinated groups. Like other Americans of color, Asian Americans serve as pawns in the racially oppressive system maintained at the top by whites.[54] White Americans may prize Asian Americans relative to African Americans in certain limited ways so as to ensure white dominance over both. Whites may sometimes place or consider Asians "nearer to whites," a relative valorization, because of Asian American achievements in certain educational and economic areas. Yet this middling status is possible only because other Americans of color, such as African Americans or Mexican Americans, have been allowed fewer opportunities by whites. Whites' use of Asian Americans as a measuring stick for other Americans of color is highly divisive, for it pits groups of color against each other, as well as isolates Asian Americans from white Americans.

Kim underscores well the price paid for becoming the white-proclaimed model of a successful minority: "By lumping all Asian descent groups together and attributing certain distinctively 'Asian' cultural values to them (including, importantly, political passivity or docility), the model minority myth sets Asian Americans apart as a distinct racial-cultural 'other.' Asian Americans are making it, the myth tells us, but they remain exotically different from Whites. Beneath the veneer of praise, the model minority myth subtly ostracizes Asian Americans."[55] In this process of exoticizing and of civic ostracism, whites treat Asian Americans as foreigners not fully assimilable to white culture and society. Exoticized and celebrated for docility, Asian Americans have relatively little political clout and as yet are less involved in the U.S. political process. As Kim's data demonstrate, this lack of political involvement at the local level is often *not* a voluntary choice but results from active discrimination and exclusion in the political realm by whites.

Discrimination persists in many institutional areas. The astute scholar Gary Okihiro sums up the contemporary Asian American situation this way: Whites have "upheld Asians as 'near-whites' or 'whiter than whites' in the model minority stereotype, and yet Asians have experienced and continue to face white racism 'like blacks' in educational and occupational barriers and ceilings and in anti-Asian abuse and physical violence. This marginalization of Asians, in fact, within a black and white racial formation, 'disciplines' both Africans and Asians and constitutes the essential site of Asian American oppression."[56]

The Many Costs of Anti-Asian Racism

Conforming to the Hierarchy and Racial Frame

The omnipresent racial hierarchy and its rationalizing racial frame directly or indirectly affect most areas of the lives of those who live in U.S. society. Whites are collectively so powerful that they pressure all immigrant groups, including those of color, to collude in the white racist system by adopting not only many white ways of doing and speaking, but also numerous stereotyped views and notions from the old white racial frame. The white frame is all-encompassing and has infiltrated the minds both of native-born Americans and of European and other immigrants. By adopting the perspective of the dominant racial frame, earlier European immigrant groups, such as the Irish and the Italians, eventually secured a high position on the U.S. racial ladder and are now considered "white," but this has not been the case for darker-skinned groups such as those of African, Latin American, and Asian descent. Asian immigrants often have a chance at some socioeconomic mobility, but they, their children, and their grandchildren have not been awarded full acceptance by whites. Most whites expect the intermediate positions offered to many Asian Americans on the old racial status ladder to be valued by them, but, as later chapters will demonstrate, this middling position has typically come at the high price of conformity, stress, and pain—and often of abandoning much of a person's home culture and national-origin identity.

Generally, new immigrants quickly begin to conform to the dominant hierarchy and frame or else face significant emotional or economic punishment. On the one hand, they often try to conform well, which they generally view as a method to prevent discrimination targeting them. On the other, conforming is pressed hard on them as the targets of white-generated racism. The dominant white racial frame ensures that those at the bottom of the racial order are repeatedly denigrated. In this situation fighting for one's dignity will sometimes mean that another individual or group will be pushed down and set up for failure. Vying for position in a preexisting racial order creates volatility and conflict. Groups of color are frequently pitted against each other for the title of "top subordinate," while whites as a group remain at the top.

The dominant white group and its elite stand in a position of such power that they can rate groups of color socially and assign them "grades" on a type of "minority report card." Whites thus give certain Asian American groups a "model minority" rating while other groups of color receive lower marks as "problem minorities." However, the hierarchical positions that whites are willing to give any group of color are always significantly below them on the racial ladder. Today, some media and scholarly discussions suggest that Asian Americans are now viewed as white or "honorary white" by most white Americans, yet this is not likely the case. In one research study, we gave 151 white college students a questionnaire asking them to place numerous racial and ethnic groups into "white" or "not white" categories. An overwhelming majority classified all the listed Asian American groups, including Japanese and Chinese Americans, as clearly *not white*. These well-educated, mostly younger whites still operate with the old racial hierarchy and racial status continuum in mind when they place individuals and groups of color into racialized categories.[57]

Impact on Mental Health

The previously cited incidents involving R. W. and Cho raise the issue of Asian American mental health in a dramatic way. Are these just isolated individuals suffering from mental illness that involves only unique personal conditions? Or does the reality of anti-Asian racism generate much everyday suffering for a large group and thereby contribute significantly to these conditions? Few researchers have probed Asian American mental health data in any depth. One study of Korean, Chinese, and Japanese immigrant youth examined acculturation to the core culture, but only briefly noted that some of these youth experienced substantial "cultural stress, such as being caught between two cultures, feeling alienated from both cultures, and having interpersonal conflicts with whites."[58] Another study examined only Korean male immigrants and found some negative impact on mental health from early years of adjustment and some mental "stagnation" a decade or so after immigration. Yet the researchers offered little explanation for the findings. One early 2000s study of U.S. teenagers found that among various racial groups, Asian American youth had *by far* the highest incidence of teenage depression, yet the report on this research did *not* assess the importance of this striking finding.[59] Recently, the National Alliance on Mental Illness released a report that Asian American girls have the highest rates of depressive symptoms of any racial/ethnic or gender group.[60]

Asian American statistics on suicide and alcoholism stand out. In the modest statistical analysis that exists, elderly Chinese American women have a suicide rate *ten times* that of their elderly white peers. Although Asian American students are only 17 percent of the Cornell University student body, they make up fully *half* of all completed suicides there. A study of Japanese American men who had been interned during World War II found that they suffered high rates of alcoholism and that 40 percent died before reaching the age of fifty-five.[61] Eliza Noh, a researcher who has done much research on suicide and depression issues for Asian American women, has reported that among females aged fifteen to twenty-four, Asian Americans have the highest suicide rate of all racial groups.

Suicide was found to be the second leading cause of death for these females. Noh concludes from the data that Asian American women live under greater pressures to achieve, including in education, than even their male counterparts, pressures that create the great stress underlying much depression and suicide. In a media report Noh has commented that "pressure from within the family doesn't completely explain the shocking suicide statistics for young women" and that "simply being a minority can also lead to depression." Yet she fails to pursue the implications of this last comment—the likely connection between their stress and depression and the racial hostility and discrimination they regularly face because of this white-imposed racial status. She also does not put the necessary white face on the perpetrators of much of their everyday stress.[62] Indeed, in the rare situations where such data on depression or suicide are examined, researchers and other commentators usually cite background ("Asian") cultural factors and culturally related pressures to achieve in education and the workplace as the reasons for Asian American mental health problems—and not their problems with the pressures of everyday white racism.

Generally speaking, medical and social scientists have seriously neglected the costs of everyday racism for all Americans of color. A growing but modest research literature addresses some of its impact for African Americans. In the 1950s Abraham Kardiner and Lionel Ovesey addressed the impact of extensive racial discrimination on African Americans in a book aptly titled *The Mark of Oppression*. They argued from their clinical data that legal segregation significantly affected the mental health of African Americans. Self-esteem was constantly battered by racism's onslaughts. In the 1960s psychiatrists William Grier and Price Cobbs wrote on the impact of recurring discrimination on their African American patients. The discrimination they faced during legal segregation was again linked to their major physical and emotional problems. Research by Joe Feagin and Karyn McKinney involving in-depth and focus group interviews with African Americans found a similar array of physical and mental health problems stemming from everyday discrimination.[63] It seems likely that systemic racism today has a similar impact on Asian Americans. They endure racial hostility and discrimination by whites and must use much psychological maneuvering to function successfully in their lives. In later chapters, our respondents speak of the numerous defensive techniques that they use to deal with discriminatory events. Such psychological gymnastics are always burdensome to those who must engage in them.

In a pathbreaking documentary film, *When You're Smiling*, communications scholar and moviemaker Janice Tanaka provides a rare documentation of the heavy costs of racism for Asian Americans, specifically Japanese Americans. The documentary covers the racialized internment of Japanese Americans in

World War II concentration camps, then focuses on the psychological effects of this internment on those imprisoned and on their children and grandchildren. In the film, third-generation Japanese Americans (the *Sansei*) share personal stories of pervasive white discrimination. Interviews with the Sansei found that most of their parents (the *Nisei*) were interned as youth in the wartime camps. The Nisei faced much overt and extreme racial oppression during and after World War II. They suffered much psychological trauma, and during and after the war they placed great pressure on themselves and their children to conform to white understandings and racial framing, as well as to the dominant racial hierarchy. (Their parents, the *Issei,* had already accented conformity as a strategy for dealing with white racism since the early 1900s.) Fearful of a recurrence of that extreme oppression, the Nisei responded with a conforming and high-pressure achievement orientation that would later get Japanese Americans labeled the first "model minority." In the documentary, one Sansei talks about how obsessed her family and the Japanese American community were with a local newspaper article that was published each spring. The article spotlighted all the academic scholars in local schools and listed where they planned to attend college. One interviewee said, "You always went to the good schools. Either Stanford, UC-Berkeley, or out of state."[64] Here we see the extraordinarily high expectations that the Japanese American community has long had for its children.

Second- and later-generation Japanese Americans have paid a heavy price for their substantial socioeconomic achievements. The effects of aggressive *conformity* have frequently been negative. Tanaka's documentary shows significant drug abuse among them and discusses the relatively high suicide rate for the Nisei and Sansei. Alcohol abuse was more prevalent among the Nisei than other men of the same age group during the postwar period. Many Sansei reported great personal distress, painful self-blame, mental and physical illnesses, and alcoholism or drug abuse. Some friends and relatives have committed suicide because of these intense conformity-to-whiteness pressures. Not surprisingly, the negative reactions of the Sansei have in turn affected their own children. This documentary destroys the Pollyanna image of a "happy minority" no longer facing racism. The costs of racial oppression do indeed persist over the generations.[65]

In later chapters, we show in detail how anti-Asian racism is a likely reason for many Asian American health problems, just as recent research has shown that antiblack racism is a major factor in the mental and physical health problems of African Americans. For example, the model minority imagery creates very unrealistic expectations for many people. This imagery deflects attention from major racial barriers and hardships, including damaged physical and mental health, that Asian Americans face as they try to become socially integrated into a racist society.

In this book we examine how Asian Americans counter and respond to the racial oppression they face. Experiences with racism accumulate over time, and Asian American children start their collection of such experiences early in life. By the time adulthood is reached, the often substantial and accumulating pain can affect their lives in many detrimental ways. Research studies show that different communities react to racism differently. For example, in many black families and communities the accumulating experience with racism is not just individualized and held internally. An individual's experiences with racial discrimination are often shared, and the burden of those experiences is frequently taken on by the larger family network or community.[66] Yet, as our respondents indicate in their interviews, the situation is often different for Asian Americans, especially those in predominantly white areas with no large Asian American community. Claire Jean Kim suggests that in order to develop a strong Asian American identity not sabotaged by excessive conformity to whiteness, one must at least have access to a strong Asian American community. Many upwardly mobile Asian Americans do not have such easy access and often find themselves—like the families mentioned in the opening of this chapter—in more isolated, predominantly white spaces where asserting a strong Asian American identity becomes very difficult. Kim further suggests that understanding the reality of societal racism can awaken Asian Americans and move them out of a stage of identifying so heavily with white ways. While all our respondents are aware of the anti-Asian racism surrounding them, few have moved to a heightened consciousness highly critical of that white racism and to a strong Asian American self-concept unvarnished by substantial conformity to whiteness.

According to our respondents, most lessons from discriminatory incidents do not regularly get passed along to family members and friends, and thus their substantial stress and pain are often just individualized and internalized. As the opening accounts in this chapter suggest, this internalization, frequently undetected until too late, can create serious problems for families, communities, and the larger society. Asian Americans who deal with racist incidents in such a silent and repressing manner not only suffer alone but also do not create the opportunity for their discrimination to be discussed as a part of a larger societal problem that requires collective attention and organized resistance.[67]

In contrast, many African Americans, with nearly four centuries of experience with systemic racism in North America, have developed a stronger collective memory of racism, as well as a stronger resistance culture and counterframing that enables them to better resist the racial hierarchy and its buttressing frame. By *collective memory* we here refer to how people of color experience their present reality in light of their own, their family's, and their ancestors' past racial experiences. Sociologist Maurice Halbwachs has suggested that one should not view one's important understandings about the society as just "preserved in the brain or in some nook of my mind to which I alone have access." Instead, important understandings and interpretations "are recalled to me externally, and the groups of which I am a part at any time give me the means to reconstruct them."[68] For many African Americans, and some other Americans of color, past discrimination perpetrated by white antagonists, as well as tactical responses to that, are often inscribed in a sustained and powerful group memory. Memories of negative experiences with white Americans, accumulated and communicated by individuals, families, and communities, are joined with memories of *contending with* and *resisting* racial discrimination.[69] In contrast, our data suggest a majority of Asian American families and communities have yet to develop a routine, strong, and effective means of passing from one generation to the next the necessary information about accumulating discrimination, the history and array of anti-Asian racism, and successful countering strategies. Remembering the discriminatory past is painful, yet recovering key elements of that past can have major therapeutic value for individuals as well as major resistance value for communities.

Our Asian American Sample

The Asian Americans we interviewed for this book are a diverse group. Using snowball sampling, we conducted in-depth interviews with a well-educated, mostly middle-class group of Asian/Pacific Islander Americans in 2005–2007.[70] Our forty-three respondents self-identified as Chinese (10), Taiwanese (7), Asian Indian (6), Korean (3), Vietnamese (3), Japanese (3), Filipino (2), Hmong (2), Pakistani (2), Thai (1), Bangladeshi (1), and multiracial but substantially Asian (3).[71] Twenty-six are women; seventeen are men. In an attempt to capture variegated Asian American experiences, our respondents were selected from different geographical regions. Eleven reside on the West Coast, sixteen reside in the Southwest, two in the Midwest, six in the Northeast, and eight in the deep South. Half of these respondents live in urban areas with substantial Asian American populations. Ages range from eighteen to sixty-nine. Thirty-four have college degrees, with nineteen holding advanced degrees. Of those without college degrees, five were currently enrolled in college, and one more had some college experience. All but seven saw themselves as middle class or upper class. Almost everyone we contacted was eager to participate, and we were not able to interview all who wished to be interviewed. For this study we used numerous open-ended questions about the respondents' experiences as Asian Americans, including questions about mistreatment, identity, acceptance in society, and model minority imagery and pressures. We also asked about impressions of progress in U.S. racial relations and their perspectives on the current state of Asian and non-Asian relationships.[72]

Conclusion and Overview

A central goal of this exploratory study was to interview a diverse and reasonably representative group of middle-class Asian Americans about their everyday experiences in the United States. In the following chapters we examine significant questions about these experiences, especially with reference to the subtle, covert, and overt racism that they have encountered in an array of important spaces—from neighborhoods to schools, shopping centers, and workplaces. We are especially concerned with the physical, mental, and emotional toll that racial hostility and discrimination have had on them. We examine the costs that conformity to the racial hierarchy and its supportive racial framing has brought to their lives. In addition, we ask throughout in what subtle, covert, and overt ways they counter and resist racism.

In Chapters 2 and 3, white-generated discrimination in its major forms is clearly and painfully revealed. Not only are Asian Americans faced with overt discrimination and hate crimes but they also must confront an array of discriminatory actions, mostly from white Americans, of a more subtle or covert nature. As we observe, they rarely find places where they are safe from discrimination and its effects. In Chapter 2 we observe that discriminatory acts take place virtually everywhere—in neighborhoods, at movie theaters, in retail shops, and on city sidewalks. In Chapter 3 we see discriminatory acts occurring at all levels of educational institutions and in various workplace settings. Even though most of our respondents are well educated and at least middle class, they all describe instances of significant discrimination at the hands of white males and females of various classes, occupations, and conditions. Their often significant educational and economic resources do not protect them from racial attacks of different kinds.

Chapter 4 probes deeply the many costs of systemic racism for Asian Americans. Materially and psychologically, these men and women, and their families, are taxed daily by the omnipresent threat of racial hostility and discrimination, and they work to defend themselves from this oppression, most often in an internalizing fashion. As we show, they rarely seek significant help from family or friends to deal with serious racist incidents. When dealing with racial burdens they tend to turn inward, frequently trying to block the necessary expression of deep emotions and to repress painful memories. Successive generations of Asian Americans find themselves struggling with white-imposed racial identities.

First-generation Asian Americans feel particularly isolated in this white-dominated society. Later-generation respondents often feel part of both the dominant white culture and an Asian culture, yet they are thereby marginalized in society and sometimes feel they fit in neither sociocultural world. In addition, many appear to be in denial about much of the harsh reality of the surrounding system of racism.

Chapter 5 details how an often unquestioning conformity to the dominant hierarchy and racial frame operates in their lives. Most try to conform well, which they view as a proactive method they hope will prevent white and other discriminators from further targeting them. However understandable, conforming to white folkways, to the dominant hierarchy and framing, is a conservative tactic that has serious personal, family, and community consequences. Even when they assert that they have never experienced an act of discrimination, as many do early in their interviews, the reality of white hostility and discrimination can usually be sensed even then in their coded words or their body language. Moreover, later in their interviews, they usually contradict this initial assertion. Many go to significant lengths to succeed in being the "solution minority" and to "strive for whiteness." As a result of this conformity, they also internalize hostile racial stereotypes, not only about their own group but often about other Americans of color.

Chapter 6 assesses more centrally how these Asian Americans try to *resist* the racial hierarchy and its supportive racial framing. They do this too in direct, subtle, and covert ways. Most of those we interviewed rarely directly confront the white perpetrators of discrimination. As they see it, there is too much at stake to openly resist whites. When such resistance is undertaken, our respondents usually attempt to produce tangible social and political changes for themselves or their group. When working more subtly or covertly, which is more common, they are often creative in the measures they take. To appeal to other Asian Americans, they may even play into anti-Asian stereotypes in order to have an opportunity to eventually educate them about the broader issue of racial oppression. In addition, numerous respondents note how they resist racist views in personal ways; they do not resist for a greater good but rather for their own sanity. Much everyday resistance takes the form of rejecting the dominant racist ideology in their own minds, or sometimes in a small group of Asian American friends.

In Chapter 7 we summarize and assess our findings. We briefly compare the life paths of two Asian Americans who have shared similar starting points, whose lives have run parallel to each other in some ways, yet who over time have diverged dramatically in everyday strategies they use in facing white discriminators and a racist society. One chooses to fully conform and continue to "whiten" in hope of eventual acceptance, with a sense of white-imposed racism being unchangeable.

The other decides to fight against racist individuals and structures, hopeful that her efforts will change the world positively for all.

Briefly examining some history of collective Asian American resistance, we conclude this book with an examination of policy suggestions and theoretical implications arising from the many racialized experiences described by these courageous Asian Americans.

CHAPTER 2
EVERYDAY RACISM

ANTI-ASIAN DISCRIMINATION IN PUBLIC PLACES

In October 2011, Private Danny Chen, age nineteen, committed suicide in his Army post in Afghanistan. Born in New York City, Chen was the son of two Chinese immigrants. In a personal journal and letters he had sent to his loved ones, Chen complained of constant racialized taunting and physical abuse by his superiors.[1] Just hours before his suicide, eight fellow soldiers "pulled Private Chen out of bed and dragged him across the floor; they forced him to crawl on the ground while they pelted him with rocks and taunted him with ethnic slurs."[2] The eight soldiers were charged in connection with his death, but sentences were a mere "slap on the wrist," with the longest length of jail time being six months and the shortest, just thirty days.[3] Many of these violent attacks specifically target Asian American men, demonstrating the gendered nature of certain types of racialized violence. Asian American women also face sexualized violence that does, at times, target their perceived racial characteristics.

In the summer of 2006 in Queens, New York, Chinese American teenagers were attacked by whites yelling racist slurs and phrases like "stay out of our neighborhood." This hate crime briefly made local news, but not the national media at the time.[4] In 1999, Benjamin Nathaniel Smith went on a shooting spree "hunting" people of color, and four of his targets were Asian Americans. This event got some national media attention, but most anti-Asian violence receives little media attention. Another violent attack took place in Raleigh, North Carolina, in 1989. This time the Chinese American victim, Ming Hai Loo, was killed by white brothers who thought he was Vietnamese and were angry about the Vietnam War. The brother who struck the fatal blow was sentenced to second-degree murder and assault with the possibility of parole after just four and a half years. This was the *first* successful federal prosecution of a civil rights case involving a racially targeted Asian American.

Most infamously known as a miscarriage of justice that has been extensively written about and the subject of documentaries is the case of Chinese American Vincent Chin. On June 19, 1982, Chin was having his bachelor party in a Detroit bar. Thinking he was Japanese, two white men who had recently been laid off from Chrysler started a fight and beat Chin several times with a bat, leaving him brain dead. He died four days later. The two were fined $3,000 and ordered to pay $780 in court fees but *never* went to jail. Disillusioned with the legal system, Vincent's mother, Lily Chin, moved back to China after attempts to bring her son's murderers to justice failed.[5]

White Americans have directed racial violence and other racial harassment at Asian Americans since the first Asian immigrations of the nineteenth century. Yet, until recently, virtually no government entity collected data on this. Today, numerous anti-Asian crimes are annually reported to police agencies. In just the three months after the September 11 attacks of 2001, nearly 250 hate crimes targeting Asian and Pacific Islander Americans, including two murders, were counted. And in two important counties where many Asian Americans live, Orange County and Los Angeles County, California, local agencies report hundreds of hate crimes each year, with many of them having Asian American targets. These range from painting racist graffiti on homes and businesses, to violent threats via e-mail or phone calls, to violent attacks on individuals and property. Recently, a 2012 FBI report detailed 175 hate-based crimes in which the victims were targeted because of an anti-Asian bias, a statistic much lower than the true number because most law enforcement agencies do not record hate-based crimes.[6]

According to the U.S. Commission on Civil Rights, such racialized crimes are usually underreported. Many Asian Americans are immigrants who distrust the police and have a limited understanding of U.S. laws. The Civil Rights Commission and its advisory boards have found that adequate police protection is frequently not provided for Asian Americans—indeed, even that some police officers and/or their department superiors are hostile to Asian American communities. When residents report a crime, they frequently do not receive an adequate police response.[7]

Societal recognition of the discrimination faced by Americans of color has often been lacking, especially in the white population. For example, in the 1970s, after the 1960s civil rights movements, numerous white scholars and media commentators asserted that there was a major decline in, or even disappearance of, serious discrimination faced by African Americans and other Americans of color. However, numerous research studies from the 1970s to the 2000s have shown that serious discrimination has persisted on a large scale.[8] For reasons of privilege or power, white commentators making assertions about racism's decline, and indeed a substantial majority of all white Americans, seem to be out of touch with societal reality when it comes to the everyday discrimination faced by Americans of color, and most especially that discrimination faced by Asian Americans. Whites are either ignorant of these negative conditions or unwilling to fully acknowledge them.[9] What may add to this problem is how white racism is viewed. For many people, *racism* is individualized and conjures images of extremists associated with the Ku Klux Klan or neo-Nazi skinheads engaging in racial violence. While extreme forms of overt racism have not ceased, they now occur less frequently. Associating these extremely violent images with the idea of racism can mislead a person into thinking that white racism is a thing of the past.

Too often, moreover, when people think of U.S. racism, Asian Americans are absent from this picture. This is true even for some Asian Americans. Asian American invisibility is due in part to the pervasiveness of model minority stereotyping, with its numerous distortions and exaggerated images of economic and academic success. This distinctive, supposedly positive stereotyping distracts people from seeing the discrimination Asian Americans face every day.

Violence and Harassment on Public Streets

Violent Hate Crimes

Seven of our forty-three interview respondents gave accounts of extreme violence directed against them, all of them men. Racism is gendered and sexualized and Asian American men are often faced with physical threats related to white masculine posturing. While there are many forms of violence that both men and women face, it is very important to highlight the way the dominant U.S. masculine hierarchy is a racialized system. A strong characteristic of white dominance has been the attempt to control men of color through physical violence. The men in our sample exclusively experienced these particular masculinity threats, whereas the women faced psychological or sexual threats—which are explicitly or implicitly violent.

Guang, a Chinese American, reported that he grew up in a New England city with a substantial Asian population. He commented, "I didn't have a lot of friends at all. I'm pretty much isolated here. There's a lot of racism. Like people threw rocks at me on the street where I lived … and would try and beat me up, jump me on the street." Violent racism is often associated with the southern states, but in our interviews public attacks took place on the streets and at schools in several U.S. regions. The motivation for these attacks is clearly racial, as can usually be seen in the words or actions of white assailants.

Ethan is a Chinese American who also grew up in a city where Asian Americans were numerous and an important presence in his neighborhood. As a student at a predominantly white university, he recently was the victim of a hate crime. Until the assault, he had not considered himself "a minority." He had apparently accepted a version of the model minority stereotype until this point; indeed, he was a model student who had been well received by whites in earlier schooling. He felt included in the white world until he was walking downtown after a night out. The area is public, and numerous police officers are usually present there at night, yet Ethan still was publicly attacked by a white man:

> Around 2:30 a.m. Friday morning, I was heading back to our car along with three friends…. We stopped outside of a club to say hi to some of our friends…. As I was waiting, a white SUV pulled up to the intersection and stopped near where I was standing. The driver and passenger shouted several racial epithets toward me including "Chink," and I turned around to see where the remarks were coming from. I was worried about a confrontation so I started walking back to my friends. The passenger got out of the car … and runs at me. I turned around to look at what is happening and he sucker-punches me. My front tooth was instantly knocked out, and my mouth began bleeding profusely. The witnesses that were around said that they continued the racial slurs at people in the group. Most of them were Asian, Asian Indian, South Asian…. He continued the slurs and was heard saying, "This might be a hate crime, but I don't care." As I was on the ground, I turned to look towards the car and saw the attacker run back to the car, get in, and speed off. At this point, my mouth was bleeding severely and my lips were swollen and cut from the trauma. Holding the tooth in my hand and unable to get up by myself, my friend helped me up, and someone in the group flagged down a police car that chased down the SUV…. I was angry. It was a serious injury, the tooth was knocked out, they weren't sure they could save it, but they did. My gums were lacerated. [The attacker] was 6'3", 250 pounds…. I kept my tooth, but there is still long-term damage.

As this incident was unlike anything Ethan had ever experienced, he was unprepared for it. A complete stranger randomly selected him. There was no prior history of white racism in Ethan's collective memory, which lent to his shock. Ethan had overheard his attacker saying, "This might be a hate crime, but I don't care." The deep reality of white racism allowed his assailant to be almost carefree. Throughout history, whites have generally been able to avoid consequences for such violence toward people of color.[10] Ethan is now developing a racial memory as he works through healing from the "long-term damage," which is more than physical.

The significant damage Ethan endured was not delivered solely by his attacker, but also by the police who were supposed to protect him. He reports the police officers leaving him helpless:

> Police arrived at the scene about five minutes later, took my information, and called an ambulance. The police pulled them over, talked to the driver, but did not make any arrests. They did note that there was blood on the passenger's fist.... [The police] did get the driver's license, but they were let go and not arrested. The [police department] makes arrests all the time for public intoxication, but no arrest for this. The three witnesses who saw the assault positively identified the attacker, but no arrest was made at the scene.... One reason that I think may be a factor is race. I am not sure. I think it was handled poorly in general. The first step is that it made me lose confidence in the police and D.A. No arrest being made and it was difficult to get the witnesses to I.D. him to issue an arrest warrant. It was extremely difficult to get the witnesses to go to the local police department. They were all South Asian witnesses.... The most important lesson I learned was that when dealing with the justice system they will be very disappointing. I thought this incident would be taken seriously as it was unprovoked and racially motivated.... I talked to the assistant D.A. six months ago to express my disappointment, and nothing has been done.... Anything short of a murder, they aren't gonna act. I had to do this work all on my own. My parents couldn't help; even though they came here for graduate school, their English isn't [good]; they can't communicate as effectively as I could have to the D.A. So, I handled all of this myself, my parents provided financial and emotional support. Others couldn't do it. It's horrible. Nothing's been done. He basically got away with it.

Through some Asian American connections, Ethan was able to reach a key government official. Few hate crime victims have that opportunity, and yet Ethan still struggled with getting any justice. For Ethan's white assailant and accomplice there have been no consequences. Ethan eventually lost faith in the public agency. He struggles to call the poor work of the police racist, but thinks his own racial characteristics "may be" related to it. Numerous research studies show a pattern of police *unresponsiveness* to people of color and frequent racial profiling by government agencies.[11] In contrast, when the street victims are white, especially elite whites, police agencies are typically much more responsive.

Also baffling to Ethan was the fact that other Asian Americans were slow or unwilling to help him. Many respondents also spoke of fear they have of disclosing a racist event because of white retribution. Their hope seems to be that they can disassociate themselves from others who are racially targeted so that they will not face targeting too. Ethan assumed that the racially motivated nature of the crime would serve as motivation for the Asian American witnesses to help out, but this was not the case.

While memories of discrimination shared among one's relatives and friends can increase stress for individuals, this is a critical resource in dealing with the damage of white-imposed racism. Research on African Americans indicates that the shared memory of oppression can play a role in development of group solidarity, yet the majority of Asian Americans seem to lack such a shared and strong collective memory of discrimination.[12] Ethan "expected" the witnesses to understand, but they were not eager to help. He even had to call one witness many times to get him to fill out a statement. Ethan concludes,

> I am reasonably educated, graduated from [names university]. I can't see how someone without resources or education could handle all of this. My parents were there to help. I was able to see a plastic surgeon the next day. I had all these resources and help to navigate through the criminal justice system. The [university's] multicultural center director was a big help. I didn't even know that the center existed, if that tells you how little I knew about the Asian American community at school.... I don't know what someone would do if they didn't know where to look and were unaware of the resources.

After being the victim of this horrific hate crime, Ethan was revictimized by the "justice" system supposedly in place to help. Ethan said that he never believed that racism existed before this event, at least "not against Asian Americans." His statement suggests the common stereotype that Asian Americans are privileged "model minorities." To Ethan, this kind of racist incident would have been unsurprising if it happened to another group of color. This demonstrates how powerfully real the model minority stereotype is even in some Asian American minds. He now questions whether a white person would experience the same cold response from the police and district attorney. Ethan was able to use his middle-class status and educational attainment to help him navigate through the red tape of the health care and legal systems. He also had access to community and university resources that many victims of hate crimes do not. Thanks to this incident, Ethan now realizes that his social class and model minority privilege do *not* protect him from racialized violence.

Bari, a South Asian international student who has been in the United States for some years, reports a similar violent incident. Like Ethan, Bari had a jarring experience while riding his bike one evening on his way home. He was riding along a road on the edge of major university campus when two white men drove by and assaulted him: "I was riding my bike until he came in a big white van and hit me with a baseball bat and took off. And he called me names and stuff. They called me 'fucking foreigner' and laughed at me and called me other things. And, it changed the way I looked at [name of city] drastically."

Bari was knocked off his bike and suffered cuts and bruises. Bari too reports this experience as traumatic and unprovoked. Before he started college, Bari had held a "Hollywood ideal" of the United States, but that changed when he began his undergraduate degree at a college in the Midwest, where he faced some racism. It worsened when he moved to another region for his graduate degree. Already feeling like an outsider, Bari now feels that "I don't really want to stay here.... It gives even more reason to leave. And I cannot [stay] with how people view race and the racism and discrimination."

Some might argue that this discriminatory event involved Bari's citizenship rather than racial characteristics, yet the event was clearly racialized. The surface-level interaction, the brief driving by, would make it impossible for the white attacker to tell whether Bari was a citizen, for the attacker could only see his dark skin color. In addition, this attack took place in an area where other Asian students had recently been victims of verbal harassment or physical threats, yet none of the many white international students in the area had been threatened. Immigrants of South and East Asian heritage, although a diverse group from different countries and different ethnic backgrounds within those countries, seem to be lumped into one "undesirable" category by many whites. This issue of citizenship is racialized, as dark-skinned or otherwise physically distinctive immigrants are usually targeted.

In another interview, a Pakistani American husband and wife, both practicing Muslims, share with us accounts of Pakistanis and Asian Indians in their community who had experienced increased discrimination since the September 11 events. The husband provides this story about a Sikh acquaintance who was killed by whites:

> Indian people ... they look exactly the same [to whites]. You see them, you can't tell the difference, but I will know the difference when you look,

but colorwise you don't see any difference. And that's what happened.... They [Indian Sikhs] wear the turban—as part of the tradition they wear always. Not like Muslims; the Muslims they do not have to wear it. But [the Sikhs] wear it; and he was killed by someone here in the U.S. because he was wearing it, and the person thought he was a Muslim.

In his interview the respondent interprets such acts as the product of white "ignorance" and of people being poorly informed by the U.S. mainstream media. White assailants cannot tell Sikhs, who are South Asians, from the media image of turbaned Middle Eastern terrorists. Indeed, the Sikh Coalition, a civil rights group, reported more than 300 hate incidents and crimes targeting U.S. Sikhs in the month after the 9/11 attacks. The trend continues as the FBI reported a 50 percent increase in hate crimes from 2009 to 2010, and another increase from 2010 to 2011, against those who are Muslim or are perceived as Muslim.[13]

In this interview the Pakistani wife adds, "They [whites] don't see it. They don't think. They see the same color. A lot of people die like this." It is a costly ignorance, where the price of such lack of information is a human life. The "ignorance" they speak of is arguably based on racial stereotyping drawn from the omnipresent white racial framing of individuals who are not European in origin. Indeed, one survey of college students found that a majority of well-educated whites regard numerous Middle Eastern and South Asian groups as "not white."[14]

Note too that whites can afford to be ignorant about other racial groups and unfamiliar religions, but people of color must be very knowledgeable about the white world and its dominant racial framing. People of color have, as the prominent black scholar W. E. B. DuBois once put it, a "double consciousness" and must be well informed about the norms of white spaces or suffer being socially outcast, or worse.[15] Part of white privilege is being able to be ignorant about other racial groups and cultures without suffering socially because of it.

In their interview these Pakistani Americans add that one of their close friends had his store set on fire, but then balance this chilling account by saying they were still grateful to be in the United States. Clearly, they have a complicated relationship to their new country and do not seem to see how commonplace and problematical the white racial frame and its anti-Asian stereotypes are, yet they do note the often racialized hostility they and others face. The wife recalls that "after September 11, somebody left a message on the answering machine, 'You Islamic people go back to Islam.' And that was kind of scary, but at the same time kind of funny. Okay, just where is Islam? There you go. People didn't know that Islam isn't a place."

At this point in the interview the couple is becoming more relaxed in sharing accounts of stereotyping and discrimination from their experience and the media, yet they continue to say they are "so glad to be part of the United States." Asian Americans often feel "caught between" or marginalized. They endure racial hostility and discrimination yet benefit from the opportunities of the U.S. economy and educational system. These immigrant Americans spoke of having been wealthy in Pakistan, but having given that up to be in the United States. The wife is especially appreciative of her freedoms as a woman in the United States.

One Asian Indian respondent, Peter, was born in the U.S. Southwest. At the onset of his interview, and indeed throughout it, he says that he has *never* experienced racial mistreatment. Yet, his interview reveals significant evidence of racial inequality, stereotyping, and discrimination in the entertainment industry, where he works. Thus, he says that he often finds himself the only Asian American in a workplace. He notes how difficult it is for him to get work that does not encourage him to perpetuate Asian stereotypes and demean Asian Americans. Although he recognizes the racial bias of white executives in the mass media, he insists that he himself has never had a discriminatory experience in the industry. Outside the workplace, he shares, he has faced significant discrimination. He recounts certain driving experiences that began to happen to him after the September 11 attacks:

> I had a couple of experiences just outside in general. I was sideswiped once. This was like two months after and it's not ... like somebody accidentally did this. I was driving, and I passed somebody, and they zoomed up next to me. Guys always do that where they mad-dog you, and then you drive forward, and then they drove into me and slammed to the side and drove off, that kind of thing. Then I got [intentionally] boxed in one time by two trucks. How stereotypical is that? ... I like to think good of all people, you know. Maybe just, whatever. But you see these people stopped at a stoplight and start yelling and I'm not even going to respond. [Racial slurs?] Yeah, you can hear it through the window. It's nothing nice, that's for sure. And I didn't do anything. I was just driving.... Just yelling all this stuff. Then you get boxed in, and you can tell you're getting boxed in because people are looking back and pointing and laughing. So I had to do one of these things where I had to go out of my way to veer off into the shoulder to get off the road, so I could go home.

Because of his dark skin, Peter has been in harrowingly dangerous situations. The spontaneity of these incidents is alarming, as his white assailants, likely operating out of the old racist frame, only had his skin color as a cue for such discrimination. The perpetrators saw him only through a car window, and they may have associated him and his skin with terrorist attacks. The interaction between the whites in the trucks is notable, as they too were playing off each other in racist taunting.

While Peter experienced these events relatively close to the 9/11 attacks, people of South Asian ancestry are still facing similar racial harassment more than a decade later. In August 2012, there was a mass shooting at a Sikh temple in Oak Creek, Wisconsin. Six people were fatally wounded, and four others faced injuries due to the shooting. This incident was not isolated. Like the terror that Peter had faced on the road, a Florida Sikh man, Kanwaljit Singh, was followed for several miles before he was shot while driving his son in their car in February 2013. Recently, a Columbia University professor who wrote about anti-Sikh hate crimes, Probhjat Singh, was attacked by a group of men in New York City. The attackers yelled "get Osama" and "terrorist" before they beat him.[16] People of South Asian descent continue to be targets of violence because they have been falsely stereotyped by whites and others as dangerous terrorists.

We might underscore the point that Americans of color periodically face retaliatory targeting or heightened racialized scrutiny after widely reported violent incidents involving people of color, such as those on September 11 or the student killings in 2007 at Virginia Tech. When people of color commit these crimes, then people of color who may "look" similar to the perpetrators are often grouped together in a collective category as a possible threat. In contrast, however, when whites are the perpetrators of similar violent acts, such as Tim McVeigh's terrorist bombing that killed many people in Oklahoma City, no one follows up by randomly targeting "Scotch-Irish-looking" white people on U.S. streets. Similarly, after the killings by white males at Columbine High School in Littleton, Colorado, or at Northern Illinois University (NIU) in DeKalb, Illinois, white males did not become the targets of a backlash of violent attacks and racialized surveillance on the streets. Moreover, we can note that the difference in media coverage of these last two tragic events demonstrates how violent whites are more likely to be treated as individuals. In both of these incidents, the mainstream media coverage focused on the shooters as individuals. The media coverage for the shooter at NIU, Steven Kazmierczak, served to humanize him by highlighting his educational and other accomplishments and by focusing heavily on "what went wrong" personally and health-wise with him.[17] Yet, when tragedies such as the Virginia Tech shootings are committed by people of color, the mainstream media portrayals are less likely to highlight an individual's humanity and instead to report in a way that plays into a racialized collective group stigma.

Another respondent, Eve, reports that in her college town assaults against Asian Americans have more than doubled in just the past two years. She lives in a neighborhood where numerous assaults against Asian international students have taken place. Still, she backs away from asserting that racial characteristics are relevant to her concerns about personal safety:

> This is a backwards town, everything is reinforced. I was concerned ... not necessarily because I look like a minority, but because I just look different in general, and someone would be like, "What the fuck is that girl?" So, I wasn't necessarily concerned, because I live right where it happened, and all my neighbors are actually Asian international students.... At night I am kind of cautious, but it's really not because I'm Asian or any minority, because I feel like people look at me different anyways. Because I'm just different, because people stare. Yeah, people stare all the time. They don't say anything to me, because I look like I will kick their ass. Most people tell me, "No one wants to talk to you because you look like you're gonna hit them in the face." People stare, people look.

For Eve, it isn't just her racial characteristics that make her stick out, for she does have visible piercings and tattoos. Yet these latter characteristics are not what have gotten other Asian students assaulted. Potential white attackers would not be able to differentiate her from her Asian neighbors. Local and campus police refused to record any of the assaults as hate crimes even though racist epithets were thrown at the victims along with fists. All the assaults were unprovoked (the victims were walking near the university), were only against Asians, and were committed by whites.

Asked about her thoughts on how Asian Americans are generally treated in the United States, Eve adds this interesting commentary: "I think they are the most accepted minority, because of their stereotypical work ethics and what they've achieved, and blah, blah, blah. As far as being equals, no! Because I don't think anyone thinks they're as equal in this country, except for people that are completely white.... I guess there's no true, completely white, but if they look white, I guess."

Eve is able to identify racial inequality and the preferential treatment received by whites, but labels acts against her as more likely the result of her uniqueness in appearance. In her equivocating view, Asian Americans can only be the best of what whites consider "second class" citizens. Her view demonstrates the complex situation of each respondent. There are moments of racial awareness and admission of the existence of white racism. In another instant, however, they will reveal equivocation, self-blame, denial, and, thus, a repression of naming the oppression. Quite clearly, the Asian American experience cannot be explained by an identity model that accents only self-identity, or that sorts that Asian American experience into one or two neat categories.[18]

Violent attacks on individuals whom whites view as "foreign" (specifically, foreigners who are not white) create pressures for some Asian Americans who are second or later generations to distance themselves from immigrants. For the latter, some Asian Americans and non-Asians use the derogatory term "FOBs," which means "fresh off the boat." This desire by later-generation Asian Americans to disassociate themselves from new Asian immigrants seems to be associated with a desire to "Americanize" themselves in hope of preventing racial discrimination, yet white assailants of course do not stop to question where they were born before committing their acts. As we explain further in Chapter 4, some later-generation Asian Americans also work hard to change their physical appearance and emotional makeup so as to appear "less Asian" to whites.

From a young age, Guang felt the sting of racism by being incessantly taunted and harassed, but our other respondents had faith that they would be protected by the American ideals of freedom, equality, and liberty. Yet Ethan came to realize that even as a native-born American, his racial characteristics have trumped his citizenship. Bari's American dream ended up as a nightmare. Eve seems to equivocate in assessing anti-Asian discrimination in society, while the Pakistani American couple lives in fear and now tries to hide their religious affiliation. This couple and Eve may not be as far along as other Asian Americans in terms of the strong racial awareness and identity that critical analysts like Claire Jean Kim say are important for changing anti-Asian racism, but Bari, Guang, and Ethan are moving in that direction. After suffering a serious hate crime, Ethan said, sadly and poignantly, "I learned about how things truly are in the real world."

More Harassment: "Traveling while Asian"

As we have seen, racial hostility and discrimination can suddenly confront a target, and in almost any public setting. We now consider several other accounts from those who experienced racial discrimination while traveling in public places. Guang notes how he and other Asian Americans deal with discrimination while riding public transportation in his northern city: "I know a lot of people will make fun of us—a single Asian on a train. A lot of the Asian people I know get groped on the train ... because people assume that they will not do anything about it. They will not speak out because they were raised with that Asians don't say anything, it's too shameful. Just be private about it. And that's true because none of my friends that got groped and stuff, none of them spoke out."

These assaults are recent, commonplace, and clearly painful, yet these Asian Americans continue to sit in silence. In her research on third-generation Asian Americans in California, Mia Tuan found a similar tendency in their dealing with racial discrimination: "Stay quiet, behave, and hope that nobody bothers you."[19] By remaining quiet, many Asian Americans show a passive acceptance of incessant harassment. Like many other people of color, they are hesitant to speak up against racist acts in any manner, especially not directly, often out of fear of retaliation. Such fear, in turn, feeds the common white racial framing of Asian passivity.

Another respondent, Ann, relates that she did not respond to a white boyfriend when he made racially insensitive comments:

> We were on the [names city] subway, and he would see another interracial couple and he would go, "Hey Ann, look at them, they are another Asian girl, white guy. It's the Asian invasion!" And I cringed.... It's absolutely ridiculous and I realize that now, but at the time I was just still so young and I hadn't learned about everything yet. So, I knew it didn't sit right, but I didn't understand why.... We had a really bad racial incident where again it was on the [city subway]. This crazy older white man, probably in his 50s ... I don't think he was mentally stable, but the boyfriend and I, at the time, were laughing and joking around on the [subway] and all of the sudden, he jumped up out of his chair, and the [subway] is moving. He gets right up in my face and yells, "*What are you laughing at?*" I froze. This was the first time I have ever been any kind of publicly attacked and I froze, and I just said "nothing" to the man in reply. He just walks away and stares me down until he gets off the [subway]. I am on the verge of tears. My boyfriend at the time, just, he didn't say a damn word. He just sat there and even afterwards he didn't say anything. I'm just like, "These are the things that I have to deal with and you can't just in general, you just couldn't say anything." And when I tried to talk with him about it, I'm like, "I really think it's because you're white and I'm Asian, and he probably didn't like that we're dating." He was like, "That can't be it. He's just crazy." He kept saying things like that, like he wouldn't even be open to the idea of that.

Racial events crash into Ann's life periodically. In the first instance, the metaphor her boyfriend used to describe relationships between Asian females and white males—an "Asian invasion"—implies waves of Asian immigrants coming to "harm" the United States. As cognitive scientists have demonstrated, such metaphors are powerful and dangerous because of the negative images they surreptitiously invoke.[20] In the second example, Ann was harassed by a white stranger on the subway, quite possibly for racial reasons, and her discussion about the incident with her boyfriend only worsened the situation. In an instant Ann was filled with fear and had no idea what this white man might do to her, yet this time her usually articulate boyfriend sat in silence. Later in her interview Ann makes it clear that she no longer trusts white men to understand the personal toll that anti-Asian racism takes on her and indicates that as a result she is wary of dating white men in the future.

In his interview with us, Josh, a Chinese American, initially states that he has never experienced "negative stigma" because of his racial identity, yet later reports a negative experience with white strangers:

> I remember one time I was driving back from an Easter dinner a couple of years ago. I remember my dad was driving. My mom was in the car. My sister was in the car. So, someone started calling us like, started yelling at us.... I remember looking out the window and my sister saying, "Don't look. Don't look at them." And I don't remember even what they were saying.... A traffic light, and they just started taunting us. A car. I don't remember what they said. But she told me not to look at them. [Afterward] we didn't really talk about it at all. I mean, I assume my parents have encountered some kind of mistreatment or some kind of discrimination, they must have, but they never talk about it because my parents kind of move forward with things. So they don't talk about their mistreatment ever, actually.

Even though Josh does not remember the specific taunts, he notes in his interview that they included racist epithets. Josh's family was minding their own business and endured racist taunting that was unprovoked. The manner in which Josh's parents chose to deal with it was by remaining silent, avoiding eye contact, and never speaking of it again. Josh's family did not utilize each other for support to discuss a hostile racial experience they shared.

Uncertainty about Discrimination: High Energy Costs

Not only are Asian Americans being taunted and harassed by white civilians along city streets, but also the people who are hired to serve and protect the community sometimes join in. Charlene recounts this encounter with a white police officer:

> I remember crossing the street. I was in this big group of other Asian Americans and people always cross that street when the walk sign isn't necessarily on, but there are obviously no cars passing because they are beside you in the direction of traffic. This police officer stopped us to tell us that you shouldn't cross this line unless the walk sign is showing. It's so ridiculous because people do this all the time! I don't know, that's an irritating thing about being a person of color because you never know whether or not

someone else's actions occur because of your race or whether or not it's really because that person is a strict cross-light-walker-enforcer.

In previous studies numerous people of color have discussed this issue of trying to decide whether a specific negative experience with a white person is motivated by racist thought or emotions.[21] This is yet another cost of systemic racism for Americans of color. Whites do not have to waste time and energy dealing with recurring discriminatory incidents, including the emotional energy needed to figure out what happened in a particular setting and whether to respond to an apparently discriminatory incident. When one is the target of many acts of overt, subtle, and covert discrimination over the years, as most people of color are, such conceptual and emotional labor becomes necessary, substantial, and enervating. In some cases, as here, the target of the negative action cannot be sure it is discrimination. It is possible that the white officer here was the rare officer who is adamant about laws and safety, but Charlene and the other Asians that were stopped will never know if this was the case or if, as seems more likely given previously cited research showing that whites often view Asian Americans negatively, it was an instance of discrimination.

Interestingly, about three-quarters of our respondents began their interviews by stating that they have never experienced racial mistreatment from whites. This fairly common reaction to questions about racial discrimination has been reported in previous research on African and Latino Americans and seems to be a type of defense against the pain of discrimination. However, as the interview continued, all but one of the respondents contradicted their opening statements, and usually numerous times. They gradually shared instances where they were called racist epithets, racially excluded in various settings, denied jobs or proper service, threatened, or physically harassed or attacked. As with any group of individuals, there are personal and situational factors at play, and some have reportedly had better experiences with whites than others. During our forty-three interviews, however, only one respondent consistently maintained that she had never experienced any racial discrimination. She acknowledged, however, that other Asian Americans did face racial hostility and discrimination. Sadly too, some months after her interview, she called to inform us that she too had been the victim of serious racial profiling and harassment by the police.

Recall too the research that accents the importance of collective memory. Many African Americans are taught by relatives and friends a strong collective memory of discriminatory events. When discrimination happens to them, they often share the narrative of events, including resisting responses, with close relatives and friends, at times as a lesson for the next generation.[22] In contrast, most of the Asian Americans we interviewed do not seem to regularly discuss and pass along personal incidents with white discriminators, and they seem to possess few collective memories of past anti-Asian racism. Their older relatives and friends apparently have not passed along significant information about the white-generated discrimination they have faced or the counterframes or countering strategies used in dealing with racial discrimination. Somewhat in contrast to our findings, researcher Nazli Kibria reports that some of her Asian immigrant respondents had taught their children about discrimination and ways of dealing with it. However, what Kibria in her analysis of immigrant interviews terms "race socialization" seems to be more about parents accenting their Asian origins, cultural practices, and achievements than about direct ways of fighting white hostility and discrimination. We might note too that Mia Tuan's interviews with third-generation Asian Americans, noted earlier, were similar to ours in this regard. Three-quarters of her respondents reported no instruction about racial discrimination from older family members.[23]

As a result of this relatively weak collective instruction, a great many Asian Americans seem to lack adequate preparation for dealing with white discriminators. They are not well equipped to deal with everyday racist events, in part because they do not have this collective knowledge of antidiscrimination strategies and in part because they have not honed a strong counterframing to the white racial frame of Asian Americans. The main content of the collective racial memory of many Asian Americans appears to be that they are "model minorities," with the imagery of no discrimination and significant prosperity. Acceptance of this view by many Asian Americans often works to further strengthen the racist framing and treatment they face in everyday life.

Discrimination in Other Public Places

Discrimination while Shopping

Public spaces are an arena where, like most Americans, Asian Americans spend much time. In the accounts that follow, women and men are trying to lead normal lives while out in their communities. Unfortunately, white discriminators rarely take a break, often engaging in racial profiling and other forms of discrimination in public settings.

Joel, a Hmong American, lives in a West Coast city with a large Asian population. Whites in this city tend to view people of Hmong descent negatively, indeed much like they do black Americans. Joel manages recurring discrimination and struggles consciously with internalized racism, which has periodically involved a distancing from his "Hmongness." Joel shares his experience with whites in local stores thus:

There are so many incidences.... One was during my senior year in high school.... I went to [a drug store] and, like I said, [the city] has this negative perception of the Hmong people. So, I went to [a drug store] and ... one of the employees was there watching me. So, I walked into another aisle and that individual was walking behind me. And so I knew that they were basically profiling me, saying that, "Oh, he's going to steal something." ... So I went to test that theory, because I was kind of like, maybe they had to put something away, or something. I walked to the next aisle, and I realized they were following me. And I could see that they were looking at me like, "Oh is he going to take that?" But, I think that was definitely a huge point in my life where I realized that was definitely going on. Often times we think that it doesn't exist, and people will be treated equally, but then the whole notion of profiling exists. And that was one of the prominent incidences.

Although whites are the majority of shoplifters in the United States, white clerks are frequently more cautious and fearful of shoppers of color, an experience of discrimination often reported by other people of color.[24] Once again, the respondent was initially unsure about discrimination but, like many Americans of color, he did a little checking and found it was likely that he was being treated differently. This event was enlightening for Joel, as it increased his awareness of racial discrimination. Previously, as he notes elsewhere in his interview, he had expended much energy trying to conform to the white framing of Asian Americans, but his many negative experiences in public spaces began to steer him to critically reflect upon his experiences.

Joel offers an account of a subsequent incident involving white sales clerks as he was getting ready to attend college:

Another incident was when I was transitioning to college and I needed to buy a desk. We went to [an office supply store] and it was my parents and I, and we were walking and we asked a representative if we could have some assistance because we had some inquiries about an adapter. He said that he couldn't help us, but he could find a representative to help us.... But then the representative came by us and just passed [by] us to the white folks who were behind us. So we were thinking, wait, what was going on? We asked him to find someone to help us. Why would this person just pass us to go to the white folks? So it was kind of like that instance was like, what's wrong with this picture? We asked for assistance; they [the white people] didn't ask for assistance. And I turned around and looked at them. I think he asked them if they needed assistance, and they said no. So it was like, what the hell was going on here.... I guess he just thought that these people were just Hmong people and they are probably just looking, they're probably not going to buy anything. So, it was kind of like, I just got very irritated with that and just told my parents that we needed to leave because that was totally wrong.

Again there are significant costs to not being white. Whereas some of our other interviewees consider such negative events as Joel's to be mistakes made by ignorant individuals and use excusatory language for their oppressors' actions, Joel has developed out of his numerous negative experiences with whites a sense of fairness and an ability to dissect such interactive events carefully. In this case he was certain that his Hmong family was being racially profiled by white employees, and he actually left the store in protest. Following these events and others like them, Joel became active in Asian American student groups at his West Coast university.

Lin, a Chinese American, is head of an Asian American center that attempts to find resources and promote a sense of community for Asian American residents. She has been outspoken on behalf of Asian Americans and has been politically involved in her community. In her interview she discusses an incident concerning a staff member:

> One of my staff went to a car dealer intending to buy a car for his wife. [My staff member] is an Asian immigrant and is not fluent in English. The salesman persuaded him to put down [a large sum] as the down payment for the car and asked him to sign the papers for the transaction. He didn't know any better so he signed the paper and saw 16.95 percent interest rate at the bottom of the page. He was supposed to come back the next day to pick up the car after the loan was processed. He came back to the office and talked to me about the interest rate. I have never heard of a 16.95 percent interest rate for a car loan … that sounded ridiculous to me. I was very skeptical, that's not an honest deal, and so I advised him to get his money, not to buy a car from this place and withdraw his loan application, and to look somewhere else for a car.

Lin then took action. She called the salesperson herself and told him she was sending a staff member to pick up the check:

> When [my staff] member came back from picking up his check, he looked terribly upset. His face was pale. I asked him if they had given him back his check. Do you know what he told me? I was shocked! He walked into the door, and the salesman was on the phone. When the salesman got off the phone, [my staff member] asked for his check back. The salesman just

looked at him and said nothing, crumbled something up, and threw it on the floor at my staff member. [My staff member] did not know what it was, thought the salesman was throwing a piece of trash, and ignored it. He did not pick it up. The salesman waited a while and got angry. He walked over [and] asked … "Why didn't you pick this up?" The salesman picked up the crumbled paper and handed it over to [him]. He realized that it was his check that was crumbled and thrown to the ground. [My staff member] was so humiliated. He was so angry and was choked up with tears and he had to run out of the salesman's office. I was also choked up and so angry, all my staff at the center was upset as well. That salesman targeted him because he is Asian, because he looked and spoke like an immigrant from Asia!

Later, Lin followed up and called the salesman's supervisor, the general manager of the dealership. This supervisor apologized profusely and took responsibility for the behavior of his salesperson. He promised to speak to him, but with no promise of disciplinary action. This was enough for Lin; she said she was "touched" by the general manager's "integrity" when he said that "It is my responsibility and I have failed my staff. I did not train them well. I will talk to them." However, the manager's accenting this event as a training issue and not as a discrimination issue is noteworthy. In the position of influence that Lin holds, she could have taken further action but was satisfied with the white general manager's response.

The next account was provided by Helena, a second-generation Korean American. Her father worked on military projects, so her family moved every few years, finally settling in a western state. Asked about racial events, she starts this way:

I never really faced any overt racism. Well, once I did, and it really bothered me. When I was in high school, and it was Christmas time and I was shop-ping for Christmas gifts, so I went into one of those [stores that] sell the sausage and the cheese … and I was laughing at their meat, meat Popsicles … like a lollipop size; it's like a smoked sausage on a stick that they just sell for like 50 cents. And I was just laughing at it, and I had my little brother, who was like five, with me. And then I noticed that the woman who was this, you know, rich, well-dressed older woman was like aghast that I was in the store, and then I saw her turn her back. She was white, yeah, I saw her go on the phone and I turned around again a little while later, and there was a security guard standing there, just like staring at me, and so I was looking around in the store but I felt so uncomfortable with him obviously watching me. So, I left the store and then I saw her go, "[sigh] Oh, thank you" to the police officer, security guard guy, and I was just so pissed, like, "Yeah I'm gonna bring my five-year-old brother and we are gonna rob you or something." I didn't know what to think. That was in [a western state], I was fifteen or so. I didn't have like gang signs or you know, I was just going Christmas shopping and I was laughing at the meat, the meat things, I don't know. So, needless to say I didn't shop there. That was really the most overt racism.

Although Helena calls this incident the "most overt" she has endured, she also reports in her interview *long years* of racist slurs and other racial hostility while she was a child in school. Numerous respondents seem to have a threshold of tolerance for white children acting in an openly racist fashion toward them, but when white adults become discriminators such behavior is more likely to be critically assessed as racist. Still, these racist actions by white children are usually known by the young perpetrators to be wrong, and a few researchers have provided evidence that white children who get away with such actions may well continue these behaviors and feel a sense of entitlement atop the racial hierarchy.[25]

Numerous respondents reported hostile surveillance and other discriminatory treatment in various shopping settings, though some indicated they were uncertain about the reality of discrimination by white salespeople. For example, Ming Huei, a Chinese American with two graduate degrees, resides in a southern metropolis. She grew up in a large Asian American community and attended racially diverse schools. She had positive things to say regarding her experience in school and initially dismisses the likelihood of racial hostility directed toward Asian Americans. Yet, she eventually discusses this incident:

> It's hard to be sure. I went to a car dealership with my parents to buy a car, and the salesman on the lot was extremely rude to us. He was noticeably trying to rush us and seemed annoyed to have to serve us. When he was dealing with us, he looked disinterested and was saying, "Well, are you going to buy the car or not?" And I don't know exactly now if it was about race, or about me. And I actually saw my parents get upset. So, I don't know what it is about us, but that's a time when you can't be sure. I needed help on my water heater a couple of months ago and had a similar experience with the repairman, and I don't know what's what. So, I don't know if that could be when I am being discriminated against or I could be oversensitive or maybe it's prejudice, I don't know.

As we have suggested previously, the everyday reality of stereotyping and discrimination targeting Asian Americans adds the additional emotional and energy burden of trying to assess whether one of numerous recurring incidents has to do with whites' operating out of a racist framing of Asian Americans, or with their just "having a bad day," as some respondents put it. They often seem afraid of being accused by whites of, as some also say, "pulling the race card" when they have legitimate complaints about recurring racial mistreatment.

Incidents at the Movies

Discriminatory incidents take place in many public and private settings, and discriminators come in the form of strangers and acquaintances as well as friends and loved ones. One Chinese American respondent, Charlotte, reports being in an interracial relationship. However, the fact that her white boyfriend had made the decision to date an Asian American woman did not guarantee that he would be free of traditional white stereotypes. She discusses one experience that occurred in a movie theater:

> When I was a college student, I had a boyfriend that I was dating at one point and time who was white. And I remember going to the movies with him, and a bunch of people who were Chinese were standing behind us in the theater in the movie line, and they were speaking Chinese to each other. And he was just getting really upset with the fact that they weren't speaking English because they lived in America.... I promptly told him that I thought that was kind of a silly point of view, because if he went to Europe and was there with a bunch of Americans, he certainly wouldn't be speaking German to them. So I thought that was really silly.

Her white boyfriend feels comfortable in stating his nativist opinions about Chinese-speaking strangers. The message of Charlotte's boyfriend's action seems to be that Asians are tolerable as long as they conform and speak only English. Charlotte thus is "acceptable" but the Chinese Americans in line are "unacceptable." Charlotte adds that her boyfriend would get upset even in her home when her parents spoke in Chinese because he was afraid they were talking about him! Indeed, he would continually ask Charlotte to translate for him. Charlotte later married a Mexican American and reports that, even though their families speak different languages, no one is so paranoid as to always want to know what someone in the family is talking about. This concern or fear about what other-language speakers are saying seems disproportionately strong among white Americans, as recent research on Latinos has indicated.[26]

Another incident at a movie theater happened to Lena, a Taiwanese American, who provides this account:

> We were at the movie theater and we were paying at the box office and one of the African American employees said [a racial slur] to me and I went straight to his manager and said, "You need to talk [to] your employee, such and such person, about the racial slur that he just directed at us." I don't think that young man was employed there later. I just basically let the behavior go, it doesn't bother me because I know it's their problem. But I also don't let things [go] if there is something I can do about it. In the case that it was a business, I will let that person's boss know.

Lena avoided direct confrontation but did take countering action by going through proper channels to address the racial slur. In this example, another person of color used the racial epithet against her, a situation that can make such incidents more difficult to deal with. The reality of *systemic* racism means that there is a white-generated racial framing of all racial groups, a framing that to some degree gets drilled into the heads of virtually all Americans no matter what racial group they may be part of. Most major racial slurs and racial stereotypes targeting subordinated groups in the United States were originally created by whites as part of this racial frame and have long been taught for generations by means of the media, schools, and other institutions to all Americans. Thus, when an African American uses a common slur against an Asian American, or vice versa, such negative actions are often shaped, at least in part, by the larger societal context of centuries of white-generated racism.

In addition, the central racial hierarchy of the society, firmly maintained by whites, greatly isolates racial groups from each other and makes it hard to break out of the white-imposed framing of various racial groups, even for members of subordinated groups. Possibly because of this, Lena may have been viewed as a stereotyped "model minority"—as a threat—by the African American employee. Legal scholar Frank Wu contends that

> the model minority myth does more than cover up racial discrimination; it instigates racial discrimination as retribution. The hyperbole about Asian American affluence can lead to jealousy on the part of non–Asian Americans, who may suspect that Asian Americans are too comfortable or who are convinced ... Asian American gains are their losses. Through the justification of the myth, the humiliation of Asian Americans or even physical attacks directed against Asian Americans become compensation or retaliation.[27]

African Americans have been the targets of oppression at the hands of whites for many generations, and the "model minority success" of Asian Americans, so exaggerated and stereotypically framed by many whites, may incline some

African Americans and other Americans of color to categorize Asian Americans as "allies" of whites. Asian Americans thus can become targets for hostility from various non–Asian Americans.

More Mistreatment in Public Settings

Bars and restaurants can be difficult settings for Asian Americans. Peter, a dark-skinned Asian Indian American, notes in his interview how he has been mistreated in bars, including when he was mistaken for a Middle Easterner following the September 11 attacks: "I've been yelled at [at] a club before. I had a guy yell in my face, 'Just get the fuck out! Get the fuck out of here!' It was like a month after [September 11]. Just pointing for nothing. I'm serious, for not doing anything. So what else would it be? Because you can pick a random drunk fight over anything."

Today, many years removed from September 11, individuals from the Middle East are still stereotyped as particular threats to the United States. Peter, though Asian Indian, is often mistaken as Middle Eastern. If another similar terrorist attack occurs, individuals like Peter will likely have to endure yet more harassment just because of the way they look.

In addition to dealing with their own mistreatment, Asian Americans have the added burden of fearing for how loved ones will be treated in various public settings. Amanda, a Filipino American, discusses one such incident:

> I remember being at a restaurant and my waiter, our waiter, complimented my mother on her English. On how, "Oh you speak such good English, you don't have an accent at all." And I was probably like sixteen or seventeen, and I'm like, Why? I didn't think anything of it then, but now that I think of it, it's like, is she supposed to be an immigrant or is she supposed to be a foreigner? She's been here for twenty years. My dad still has a bit of an accent, and ... at stores, the cashiers would make faces because they're obviously trying to struggle to understand what he was saying. Whenever I was with my dad I felt uncomfortable for my dad.

Amanda has worried about her parents' mistreatment in various public situations. She notes in her interview that when she was younger and more uncomfortable with her racial and ethnic identities, she was sometimes ashamed of her parents and their accents in such settings. She did not want to be considered "foreign" by whites.

Similarly, Ann, a Vietnamese American, shares her experiences with feeling fearful in public settings such as restaurants and malls:

Going through high school, I was very shy and hesitant to be seen in public with my own parents. Because it's just we are that more of a sore thumb when we go out to restaurants and when we go out shopping in the mall and stuff like that.... I didn't like that we turned heads more than once. I was always afraid that someone [would say something to my dad], especially with my dad's thicker accent. I was always afraid that someone would say something to him. I didn't want him, I didn't want us to get publicly embarrassed or publicly harassed. The idea of being mistreated, not getting the service we wanted ... I don't know why I would think like that, I still don't. It was just always there. Growing up I just knew that I looked different and that I would be treated by default differently—and then tack on any accent or poor grammar, forget it! I was just very nervous that we would be harassed. I just wanted to avoid any of those situations.

Once again, there is a profound concern on the part of a young Asian American that an Asian accent would be taken as a signal for mistreatment by whites who themselves likely speak English with a distinctive local or regional accent. As Rosina Lippi-Green has emphasized, "Not all foreign accents, but only accent linked to skin that isn't white, or which signals a third-world homeland, evokes such negative reactions."[28]

Numerous older respondents note that language mocking and other racial harassment in various settings have continued for a long time. Henry, now well into his sixties, recalls that his problems with whites have gone on for decades. As he struggled with the English language when he was younger, he was incessantly harassed by whites as he walked through his neighborhood: "It was rough because I didn't know any English. They always laughed at you. Because I was Asian, they made fun of you. They picked at you when you were going home. They tried to make fun of you. They made faces and pretended that they were Chinese. I got in fights with them and got angry." Henry would retaliate when he was in middle and high school, but as he aged he eventually stopped resorting to aggressive defenses. When asked if his physical retaliation waned because his white peers were treating him better later on, he replies, "I would say not that much. They pretend on the outside to look pretty good, but underneath, it's still the same. I go into the bar, like a pub, and they will still make fun of you, because you are Asian. There is not much I can do, what am I going to do, start a fight? I can't. I just have to turn and walk away."

Because of his age, aggressive fighting back is now out of the question. Henry is resigned to the fact that he now is relatively powerless in ending the racial discrimination. Judging from our respondents, Asian Americans, like other Americans of color, often feel hopeless and powerless about being able to do something to improve discriminatory situations.

Hostile Neighbors: More Racial Profiling

One place that should serve as a place of safety is one's immediate neighborhood, especially in and around one's home. Neighbors do have disputes, but Asian Americans should feel free from racial assaults near and within the walls of their own abode. Unfortunately, this is not always the case, as we saw in our opening account from the first author's youth. To take another example, Fareena, a Bangladeshi American, discusses the changes that took place in her white neighbors after the September 11 attacks:

> My neighbors, I would baby-sit their little blond children, and I wasn't baby-sitting them for a while.... And then the father of the children came up to me one day and said, "Does your dad support Saddam Hussein?" And this was at a time when Saddam Hussein was not—it was Osama bin Laden that was being talked about. And you know, my dad, a businessman, he just became a citizen. The first citizen of our family, you know, we all went to the ceremony, tears, pride, everything. He put American flags, two hundred of them, at the border of our lawn. We have lawn competitions all the time. A huge American flag draped over our fence. He painted his business, painted it with American flags. He just didn't think that people would stereotype him that way. The whole country was in a frenzy of American flags and patriotism, and he was one of them. You know people thought that was a front, to be safe, and we didn't even realize it at all. They said, "Why is your dad putting up all these American flags?" And I am like, "The same reason you are."

After the September 11 attacks, Fareena and her family were no longer seen as trustworthy by local whites who knew them. In one day, Fareena went from taking care of her neighbors' children on a regular basis to being a possible supporter of the Iraqi dictator, Saddam Hussein, who was too dangerous to babysit. Fareena's family is from a South Asian country that is *not* in the Middle East, but many white Americans are so geographically illiterate that they do not understand that reality. The fact that she, her father, and her brother are darker skinned than most whites likely plays a role in their mistreatment. One might consider the contrasting case of Irish Americans. They are not harassed, targeted, or profiled as possible terrorists, even though many individuals in Ireland have directly engaged in violent terrorism. When Irish Americans appear in public, including in the mass media, they are not questioned about possible alliances with terrorists, and their patriotism is not called into question. Yet in Fareena's case the proud patriotism of her father—who does not even come from a country with a history of recent terrorism, who has worked hard to become a U.S. citizen, and who has lovingly displayed U.S. flags—was questioned by white neighbors, probably because of his (incorrectly) assumed national identity.

Alice, a Japanese American who lives in a state densely populated with Asian Americans, recalls certain problems with a white neighbor:

> I'm trying to build a house in this predominantly rednecky type of area in [names state], there are still some that exist, and we have this neighbor that harasses us. My boyfriend's Indian, and he stands on the lot a lot. And I think she thinks that he's, like, Middle Eastern and wants to cause trouble. I don't know what. Well, it has to do with this easement. It's like her husband's a lawyer and she wants to use part of the property, and it's not overtly racial, but another Asian moved in on the other side of her, so I think she's sort of freaking out. So we stopped talking to her. We just talk to the other Asian.... She's [white neighbor] so rude. But she did tell somebody, "I don't like *those people* living next to me." So I think race is still a problem. Who knows why or what? Now we have a support system, and if you have money you can fight it. If you don't have money, you can't.

The presence of Alice, her Asian Indian boyfriend, and other Asian neighbors has generated what Alice concludes is racial stereotyping and hostility on the part of white neighbors (whom she stereotypes as "rednecky"). Reflecting on her dispute over an easement, she raises a key point about struggling with whites in such situations—access to economic resources. Such resources can help people of color, but they do not guarantee freedom from racial hostility and discrimination.

Recent demographic research suggests that there are other related neighborhood issues that involve racial stereotyping on the part of white Americans. In some neighborhoods where there is a large and growing number of Asian Americans, white Americans are leaving, thereby creating a new type of "white flight." In this case, many whites fear that in areas with heavy Asian American concentrations their children will not be able to compete academically with students stereotyped in "model minority" terms. As has often been the case for African Americans over the past half century, whites are again moving out of residential areas as they worry about an "invasion" of families of color.[29]

Conclusion

Ronald Takaki, a distinguished University of California scholar and professor, has shared details about a visit to a major East Coast city during which a taxicab driver congratulated him on his good English and inquired how long he had been in the United States. A surprised Takaki told the driver that his Japanese American family had been here in the United States for generations, indeed since the nineteenth century.[30] Across the country, whites and other non-Asians often ask Asian Americans, "What are you?" or "Where are you from?" Honest answers such as "American" or "New York City" may irritate such questioners. No matter how long Asian American families have been in the United States, non–Asian Americans often treat their members as somehow foreign, alien, or unwanted.

The numerous accounts of everyday discrimination in neighborhoods and other public places reveal a harsh reality of racial hostility and discrimination. Asian Americans' often significant educational achievements and job performances do not bring them consistently fair treatment from white and other non–Asian Americans. Asian immigrants, together with their children and grandchildren, frequently pay in humiliation and degradation for their achievement of elements of the American dream—in great contrast to the experiences of most recent white immigrants and their children, who are generally welcomed and not aggressively stereotyped.

Most of our respondents adhere strongly to the "American dream" of individual and family success, socioeconomic achievement, and material acquisitions. As in other recent studies of Asian Americans, most view the United States as a land of opportunity where hard work is supposed to achieve the fabled dream.[31] This rosy view may be one reason why most of our respondents initially hesitated in replying to our interview questions asking if they had encountered racial discrimination. Eventually, however, all later revealed that they have faced the reality of white hostility and discrimination. Many were concerned that they cannot predict where or when such discrimination will occur. White hostility or discrimination can occur during a quick trip to the store, when dealing routinely with store clerks, when trying to relax and attend a movie, when getting a meal in a restaurant, or while traveling to and from these and other places. Some of these Asian Americans report being shocked when they are blindsided by serious racist incidents, while others have come to expect it and have taken various defensive measures to protect themselves.

Much discussion in the mainstream media and in some scholarly analyses emphasizes that the United States is now safely nonracist, especially in its public settings. Unfortunately, this commonplace notion of a "post-racial" United States is regularly contradicted by our data, both in this chapter and in subsequent chapters.

CHAPTER 3

EVERYDAY RACISM

ANTI-ASIAN DISCRIMINATION IN SCHOOLS AND WORKPLACES

Early Schooling: Learning Your "Place"

"We just want a safe environment to learn and make more
friends. That's my dream."[1]
—Wei Chen, 2010 President of the
Chinese Student Association of Philadelphia

On December 3, 2009, fifty Asian American students were attacked on and
around their South Philadelphia High School campus. Thirty of them sustained
injuries serious enough to warrant a hospital visit. These Asian American students were targeted, and school officials had ignored their complaints of bullying and pleas for protection for years. School days were rough for these Asian
American students, as their classmates routinely hurled racial epithets; pelted
them with food; and beat, punched, and kicked them in school hallways and
bathrooms. The students finally had enough after this day of massive attacks,
and they staged a boycott for eight days. Media outlets highlighted the racial
tensions between the mostly black student attackers and the Asian American
victims.[2] Lacking in the media discussion was an analysis of the ways in which
media stereotypes of Asian American students as "model minorities" could
facilitate a lack of cultural understanding in this particular school environment.
As noted in Chapter 1, whites have historically used Asian Americans and their

"model minority" status to shame and blame other people of color for economic and educational inequality.

Systemic racism regularly creates *alienated* social relations on four different levels: (1) between whites and people of color; (2) between different racial minority groups (i.e., black-Korean conflict since the 1990s); (3) within a racial/ethnic group (e.g., colorism); and (4) within an individual (internalized racism). While one can argue that some types of racism exist in other countries in the absence of whites, racism is a white-crafted system here in the United States. Racial meanings typically stem from our white-racist foundation, and the students at South Philadelphia High School are part of this society. Systemic racism and its white racial frame are embedded in our educational institutions, and they can cause racial strife even in environments with an absence of whites.

In the public mind Asian Americans are often synonymous with academic excellence, in part because their group scores on standardized tests and their college enrollment levels often exceed those of other groups, often including whites. One study found that whites, African Americans, Hispanics, and Native Americans perceived Asian Americans to be superior in college preparedness, motivation, and expectations of future career success.[3] These perceptions of academic achievement come with a price, however, as Asian American students are also portrayed in the media and in much private discussion among non-Asians as robotic overachievers in the classroom who are nerdy, passive, or inept on a social level.

Yet this racial stereotyping misses the discriminatory character of many U.S. institutions. While their participation in sports, student government, and clubs compared to their white counterparts may not be as extensive, this is often not for lack of trying. Mostly white spaces like these may be uninviting or hostile, keeping Asian American students from wanting to participate.[4] As we have seen in the opening account and will see throughout this chapter, Asian American students frequently endure blatant acts of racism in their schooling environments. Several respondents have tried to view racial teasing and taunting as normal, as a "fact of young or adolescent life." The language used by respondents to describe school experiences implies that they must endure a certain standard level of racist teasing and taunting. This incessant mistreatment has driven many to choose all-Asian or mostly Asian friendship groups, yet they frequently seem to lack the concepts to explain why such decisions were forced and how they were made.

Racism as "Elementary"

Social science research indicates that children are not born with racist interpretations or proclivities but learn racial interpretations and racial framing of the world as they are socialized. As children attend child-care facilities and elementary school, they are gradually introduced to racial socialization in peer groups. Young children's racist behavior is often excused by adults on the grounds that children are naïve innocents and often slip and fall in the realm of social behavior, yet the assumption that children's racist comments and actions are innocuous is incorrect. Based on extensive field research in a large child-care center, Debra Van Ausdale and Joe Feagin concluded that the "strongest evidence of white adults' conceptual bias is seen in the assumption that children experience life events in some naïve or guileless way."[5] Children mimic adults' racist views and behavior, but that does not mean they do not understand and know numerous elements of the dominant racial frame and use its stereotypes and interpretations to enhance their status among other children. Children perpetuate and re-create society's racist structures in their minds and playgroups. A few researchers have noted, albeit briefly, the racist taunting endured by Asian American children, although to our knowledge none has critically analyzed the role of white children as perpetrators.[6] When Asian children become targets of racist actions by white children, a particularly strong impression is left in their minds. Early on, they learn their subordinate place in society's racial hierarchy and that white children exercise power from the top. White children, in turn, learn early in life that they are at the top of that racial hierarchy.

Charlotte recalls that she was the only Asian in her school and had to deal daily with an onslaught of racist insults from many white classmates:

> I remember in fifth grade specifically ... I went home every single day in tears because people made fun of me every day. And it probably didn't help that I didn't have siblings. I wasn't particularly tough at all. But I would go home every day in tears because I just felt different, and somebody made fun of me.... I felt that I was inadequate and unable to do anything because I was Asian. It was just the little things that kids would say.... And I would be well aware of the fact that I was different from them.

Charlotte recalls the extremely painful character of this racist taunting, although she has tried to repress the memories. She had no preparation for the racist treatment she would experience at her school, and there was no one to instruct her in how to manage her white peers. Although harassment by children is frequent during school years, things like clothing, hair, and weight can be altered, but racial characteristics (often physical, but socially constructed) are difficult to change. Many respondents have tried to alter their appearances to appear "less Asian" with little success and with much consequence to self-esteem. As we will see in the next chapter, Charlotte learned to cope with mistreatment in an unhealthy manner; even though she tries not to remember specific details, the pain of the memories remains. In her interview she further notes that she was cognizant of being at the "bottom of the pecking order," in her case beneath the white, black, and Latino children. She did not experience any "model minority" advantage in her school. Since there were few Asian Americans, she had no collective support from peers that were like her.

Helena, a Korean American, always felt like an outsider because of being Asian and because of her academic achievement. White classmates made school very hard, as she notes with some pain:

> I'm really smart. I took some IQ tests in kindergarten, and they promoted me to first grade. I was actually a year behind everyone, so I was younger. So I felt weird because I was younger.... I never quite fit in so, everybody had their own friends already and then there was just me.... At least I didn't have a Korean accent, then it would have probably been even worse. And then I was smarter than everyone too.... A couple times when I was growing up, they would say, and you know they were girls, saying stuff, "You are just too smart. I hate you!" That kind of stuff, but it made an impact over time, when all you hear is the negative instead of the positive, so I always felt like the outsider and I was teased for just being Asian, the pulling the eyes down. They always thought I was Chinese.

Helena provides an example of how Asian Americans are often classed together by others. Some white classmates did not bother to find out that she was Korean. When discussing such events, Helena, like other respondents, is still in pain from them and has a difficult time making eye contact. She keeps her head down and speaks softly, crying a few times as she recounts painful memories. She was not accepted for being the smart, high-achieving youngster she was, but was ostracized for her intelligence and identity. Helena fit the "model" myth because she was a standout student. Frank Wu explains that the myth is important because it "is useful, even if it is not true. Its content assuages the conscience and assigns blame, a function that is psychologically needed and socially desired."[7] In this otherwise savvy comment Wu never clarifies whom the myth is useful for and does not specifically name whites as the central culprits.

Similarly, Phan, a Vietnamese American, notes that she endured ridicule and racist name-calling from white classmates on a daily basis. Lunchtime became nerve-wracking, as it left her feeling foreign:

> The kids ... I guess they probably thought I was really different. I mean, I remember them making fun of my food. Like all the food I brought from

home—my friends wouldn't eat it. You know, my parents weren't rich or anything, and they were working class, so my mom would make me this sandwich every day. And it was this pork patty sandwich. Which is just really nasty. It was two pieces of bread, sliced pork, and then onions and hot sauce. Which is a very odd thing for some five-year-old kid to be eating. Everyone else has PBJ sandwiches, and I get like pork patty, meat, and hot sauce. Which really makes your breath smell good, I imagine. I hated it and I had it every single day. And I was the only one. I stopped eating at one point, and my mother was wondering why I did it. Because it made me nauseous, and I got really so [self] conscious, that's all I got to eat.

Here physical difference is webbed with cultural difference. The power in peer discrimination is such that a five-year-old chooses to not eat her (probably lovingly made) lunch for fear of ridicule. Phan references socioeconomic class as the reason, but the white children's peanut butter and jelly sandwiches were also inexpensive, so this is not likely a factor. Actually, the taunting was probably because white children considered her food indicative of her Vietnamese heritage, which was negatively viewed, and because they thought she lacked knowledge of "normal American" lunch items.

Most school systems seem to allow much racist teasing. Respondents who protested to teachers were usually told not to take racial taunting seriously. Young Asian Americans are told to thicken their skin, while white and other non-Asian children are often allowed to continue. The parents of tormented students are frequently fearful about complaining of racial taunting and teasing and do not want to "cause trouble" or generate white retaliation. In this era of school multiculturalism, many administrators encourage teachers to celebrate diversity in classrooms, and this superficial "be happy" multiculturalism may sometimes reduce their ability to see the impact of such racist treatment on students of color, as well as the underlying reality of institutionalized racism in their educational institutions.

Charlene, a Taiwanese American, shares an example of a well-intentioned classroom assignment:

When I was in the third grade we [did a project] ... to get to know other people's cultures. And I think I did my project on Canada or something, but there was another [white] girl in my class who did her project on Taiwan and before that, I didn't realize that I was different, I knew that I was Taiwanese, but I didn't really know what that meant, and the implications in that. And her project was all about Taiwanese people don't use forks, they don't use knives, and they poop into holes in the ground, and she was doing this project in front of the whole class. And I was just crying and I cried. And I don't even remember what happened but I, it was traumatizing. I remember sitting down with my teacher and the other girl and the teacher said, "Don't worry, don't get your feelings hurt. It was just a project."

Her teacher's advice was a routinized "just a project" and "don't get your feelings hurt," which requires a seven-year-old to depersonalize something that is indeed personal and painful. This white teacher is missing the point of how disturbing what was in effect cultural mocking can be on a young Asian American. Note too that the presenting child's work was apparently not critiqued or contextualized by the teacher.

Ann, a Vietnamese American, recalls an early incident in her life where she was made to feel different. She grew up in the Northeast and endured bullying from a white classmate regarding her Asian features.

Growing up, my school was very white. It was very noticeable, even in the second grade, [that] the bridge in my nose is very, almost, not nonexistent, but it's very, very, very, very short and it apparently [makes] my face look flat.... One of the bullies in my second-grade class called me "flat face," and I didn't get it at the time. All I knew was that, as a bully, that's just a mean thing to say, but I didn't realize or recognize why he was calling me that. He was like, "You have no nose. Your face looks so flat." No one else really ever said anything, and he was just the one that did it, but that was my first, you know, very much so blatant "I'm different, you're picking on me" type of stuff.

Numerous respondents signaled similar pain and the difficulty of being often lost in a sea of physical and social whiteness as a child and as an adult.

When asked how she reacted to this brutal and stereotyped teasing, Ann responds with a detailed account:

I got really mad. I remember yelling at him, and saying like, "Why are you calling me that? Don't call me that." Little things, I was in second grade, I was like maybe seven or eight. Then I remember, I got so mad because he teased me at recess so much that I eventually started crying. And so the teacher asked, "What's going on?" I told her and after then, of course, after that I got bullied even more because I was a tattletale now. All I know is that she kind of scolded him, but she also, I don't think, realized or even knew what to do either. I don't think she realized the implications for being an Asian American in a very, very white class. How was she to educate seven- and eight-year-olds about race and racism? All that, so she just scolded him "that that's not a nice thing to do and don't do it again."

Again we see a typical white teacher's response to racist actions—the treatment of such acts lightly or like any other meanness among children. This worsened the tormenting for Ann. Clearly even minor discrimination can have lasting effects. Although Ann seems to have exculpated her teacher by noting the difficulty of teaching about racism, research studies show that not only do children as young as three or four understand and carry out racist comments and actions, but also that young children can be taught that racist actions are harmful. Historically white schools and their officials have rarely made serious efforts to teach about racist stereotyping and actions, but such teaching is not difficult, and major resources are available for teachers and schools.[8]

Another respondent, Eve, first identified herself to us as an Asian American. Later she revealed that she was half Chinese, one-quarter white, and one-quarter Mexican American. She grew up in a metropolitan area that was very diverse. Replying to a question about memories of racial mistreatment in school, she responds, "No, yeah, no, I went to an all-white high school. It's a private school, and it was fine. Then in middle school, I went to private school, and it was all white. I was a loner. I was an awkward kid. Elementary was fine, and then middle school. It's been fine. I am awkward and weird, and people like me because I'm awkward and weird, that's what I hear."

Eve sways back and forth as she gives her initial response about her racial memories, changing her responses between "no" and "yes." Although she clearly remembers the whiteness of the schools, she at first says she is unsure about why she was treated differently. Later in the interview, she explains that the first middle school she attended was "rough," and because of this her mother placed her in a private school. She attributes problems she faced to the fact that she was "awkward and weird" but does not yet indicate that it was because whites saw her in racial terms.

However, replying to a question about what was challenging at her first middle school, she explains that she had to be sent to a new middle school:

I was sent there because my mom said I got into too many fights in middle school.... Kids wanted to pick on me because they thought I was some other girl. It was odd. I was walking home one day and someone was like, "Oh do you remember the other day?" And I'd be like, "I don't know what the hell you're talking about!" Then she'd start beating me up. (And I have all this rage now.) It happened another time, and I'm like, "I'm not this girl." Everyone thought we looked alike.

Eve next notes that she was confused by whites with a Mexican American school-mate. Her classmates apparently could not differentiate a person who was wholly Mexican American from someone who was one-quarter. As the dominant racial group, whites do not need to take time to differentiate people of color. The latter are often confronted by whites who, carelessly and stereotypically, believe that they "all look alike." Eve's first interpretation was that the difficult events were isolated, with no link to the way whites viewed her racial characteristics. Yet, her later comments did recognize the racial targeting, a slow shift in the interview that happened with numerous respondents.

Alice, a third-generation Japanese American from the West Coast, recalled for us many negative memories of her schooling, from elementary school to the university level. In her interview she indicated she was very cognizant of her place in the U.S. racial order, beginning with early experiences in school and today in her professional career. She explained that she had always felt like an outsider in predominantly white spaces, a condition that was aggravated by her knowledge of the very negative experiences with white racism that Japanese Americans, including her family, had during the World War II internment camp years. In her early years she was segregated from whites in school and her neighborhood. Growing up in a predominantly Japanese neighborhood on the West Coast, she also had black neighbors. In her interview she discusses elementary school with detail:

> I remember we were, our school, we got bused. So we paid for a bus to pick us up; I guess my parents did. And they bused us from all these different parts of [names city]. One time, there were eggs thrown at the bus by some black kids. I think this is like after the riots, maybe '66, '67, somewhere in there. And then another time, which was more dangerous, a bottle was actually thrown . . . and the bus driver got very nervous about it. So he kind of stepped through, made sure all the kids were okay. Which we were, and we continued from that.

Growing up in the 1960s desegregation era, Alice and other Asian Americans were often in an in-between position as racial tensions peaked in towns and cities. Whites were resisting change in traditional segregation patterns, and blacks were protesting the racial segregation and lack of change. Alice says in her interview that even as a child she did not feel animosity toward the black kids that threw things at her bus, as she understood—likely because of the Japanese American experience with white racism—some of the complexities of a racial order where whites controlled school segregation or desegregation.

More Discrimination: The High School Asian Experience

When our respondents moved from elementary and middle school to high school, the racial problems did not cease, and new types of problems arose, usually from white antagonists. They faced yet more self-esteem issues, now coupled with puberty issues. This was especially problematical for those left out of the social networks or the dating process in school settings that were mostly white. In addition, the model minority stereotype was still in operation in many minds, such as in white teachers' expectations, and this put continuing and heavy pressure on Asian students.

Ann, a Vietnamese American in the Northeast, shares her struggles with self-image as she moved into high school settings:

> School was really hard. I'm not gonna lie. It was, you know, I wasn't comfortable in my own skin. I really resented the fact that I was Asian, you know. When the dating phase started kicking in, I never had anyone up until my senior year of high school. And all my friends in high school, even in middle school, had boyfriends or what have you. Middle school is more like, "Let's hold hands" and stuff like that. High school, it got a little more serious, and they were dating each other for a long time. And I was always third wheel or fifth wheel, never had a date, never had anyone, and it was a very painful, high school was very painful.

After noting her great discomfort in "her own skin" in a sea of white bodies, Ann explains with great insight and poignancy the social reality of being a young outsider in a very white space:

> Well, Proactiv [acne medicine] wasn't invented by the time I hit puberty. I had a lot of acne at the time and that didn't really help at all. Also ... I was one of the faster developing girls, but also one of the least noticed throughout high school. It was hard because all the guys I always had crushes on never had a crush on me back. They always had crushes on all my other friends around me. I kept thinking after so many crushes and so many letdowns, it had to be because I was Asian. It didn't make any sense, like, why wouldn't [someone] want to be with me? I'm thin, and I'm smart, and fun. Everything was there.... Eventually I gave up. It has to just be because I'm Asian. There's no other way to explain why I don't have a date to any dance. No one would ask me. It's always I asked them, or one of my friends would convince someone else to go with me—and that didn't

ever feel good either. That was eighth grade through junior year. In junior [year] I almost didn't go to my own prom. We don't have a senior prom. We only have a junior prom. I almost didn't go because it was getting crunch time, and nobody had asked me. And at that point everyone was paired up, and I didn't know who to go with. I didn't have any other friends outside of my high school.... Finally, one of the guys in our group was like, "Oh, Ann doesn't have anyone yet? Then I will just ask Ann if she wants to go to prom." But he ended up ditching me for another girl in the middle [of the] prom anyways, so that didn't feel good either.

While white friends had no trouble finding dates, Ann faced consolation dating, including being chosen at the last moment. Later in the interview Ann notes that in her senior year she started dating a boy whom she met at work. However, similar to being chosen as a consolation date at school dances, her boyfriend admitted that he had chosen her too out of "convenience," for his last girlfriend, also Asian American, had moved away. Ann became a logical choice because she lived nearby. In a later chapter we will discuss this problem of partnerships.

Ann also reports difficulties with students and teachers in the classroom because of their model minority expectations, which signaled that they did not recognize her as the distinctive and well-rounded individual she was. Although she was rarely recognized for her significant involvement in important extra-curricular activities, people did associate her with academic excellence. While performing well in school made her feel like an outsider, she worked hard for academic success as a defensive mechanism. She explains thus:

> It was just the little things like, even my teachers sometimes, when you think about in high school or even in college we get pinned as "model minorities." I hid behind my books because I was so frustrated with the fact that I was almost ashamed of being an Asian female because nobody, barely anyone besides my close-knit friends, I didn't feel like anyone really recognized me. As a result I studied a lot, and even the teachers would turn to me. My classmates would turn to me, "Oh, of course Ann knows the answer to that question," or "Ann wants to answer this question." ... Teachers were shocked when I got below an 80 on a quiz or something like that, or if I got less than a certain grade. They were like, "What's going on?" I don't think they understood that it was hard. I felt that like from then on there would be these high expectations of me and I had to meet them because it's a small school; teachers talk.... From 8th grade and on, it was just these high expectations, and I felt kind of pressured to meet those standards. It was parental pressure too, to get the good grades and to do well in school.

As a rare Asian American female there, Ann was invisible and nonexistent to white peers. Although hard work in academic subjects helped Ann to cope with social isolation, high expectations sometimes made her the unwanted center of attention:

> It was a science course, and the teacher said something, made a comment. We were doing a quiz or something, or we were all just goofing around, and we weren't paying attention necessarily. And she wouldn't let us move on or go to the next class or something weird, something really bizarre. She said that we couldn't move on until someone gets this answer right. When she said that, everyone turned to me. Lo and behold, I actually didn't have the right answer for once in my life. Actually, one of the girls that you would almost least expect to get the answer right, got it right. That was huge.... It raised awareness with me when everyone turned their heads to me, that they all expected me to get, to pull everyone through, grade wise. That was the hugest moment that I can recollect right off the top of my head.

Once again, Ann's classmates expected her to bail them out. This incident still sticks out in her mind and indicates the immense pressure that Asian American students feel in school settings where they are the special "model students."

In spite of her high-level academic success, Ann, like many other Asian Americans, paid a price for coping thus. She offers this poignant note:

> The students in my class would start saying things. I remember freshman-year English. We all had to write a huge paper. And one girl was *so* mad and upset by her grade on that paper, and she just started asking people what they got for grades, like out loud and I didn't want to share, but she saw my paper and she said, "Oh, of course you got a 90, that's no surprise." Where she got something like a 70 or 75 or something. Those are all with the cool kids, or popular kids that didn't excel in school, but everyone knew their names. And whereas the smart kids, the ones known as the nerdy people that are seen as bookworms, were stereotyped. I got pinned on.

By performing well, she reinforced the model stereotype in the minds of teachers and students and got mistreatment from the "cool" white students who were academically weaker. Teachers paid special attention to her issues when they were academically centered, but when she was being brutalized and called racist terms, they typically dismissed her pain and concern.

Ann felt then, and feels now, unrecognized for yet other important accomplishments:

Like when my peers didn't recognize me.... I played a lot of volleyball, and I did some tennis. You know, even though I was cocaptain one year, they didn't "see" me. The school didn't recognize me as the cocaptain. They didn't even know. They didn't even recognize that I even played volleyball, whereas my cocaptain, who was the girl-next-door type of look, every guy wants to date her, every girl wants to be her—she was my best friend at that time—got all the attention for the volleyball team. In that sense, I wasn't recognized by anything except for, I'm the honors-track kind of girl. It wasn't until senior [year] that people really saw me as a volleyball player. OK, now the team is doing really well, after four years, then they started recognizing everyone on the team, actually.... I don't even think my teachers recognized that I played volleyball, sadly, until senior year of high school.

Her cocaptain was white and thus received much favorable attention from other students and adults. Notice the implicit power illustrated in this example. Once again whites got to decide what accomplishments would be rewarded and for which racial groups. This is a commonly reported experience for Asian Americans of all ages, this being ignored or not seen—a type of social *invisibility* generated by racial difference that has long been reported by African Americans as well.[9]

In his interview, Josh, of Chinese descent, indicates that he grew up in the North. Initially he said that he had not experienced any racial mistreatment. However, when talking in more detail about his life, he contradicted this overview comment. He recalls racial stereotyping and taunting by white members of his high school baseball team, including painful experiences with their mocking his Chinese name with the word "dong" (slang for penis):

I guess if there was any point where I was mistreated, where I got kind of annoyed with it, was when I was in high school.... I probably played baseball for three years, and my friends—I guess they were my friends, yeah, they were my friends—would take my baseball hat and draw penises on my hat because, like, it was the whole Dong thing. And actually, most of the time I didn't mind it. But eventually, after a while it just kind of like, they would escalate things, thinking they were funny. And ... I know they weren't trying to be mean to me; like, they were just having fun. And so they would like, draw a penis on the underbelly of the hat.... And then, like, it would eventually move on to other things like notebooks, or it would be someone, like, use White-Out to draw a giant phallic symbol. And I would take a lot of it in stride. I didn't think it was a big deal. But sometimes it was like, that's enough. I think I definitely at one point said something. And I think at one point I maybe even, like—not physically assaulted somebody but maybe like, put them in a headlock and then told them to stop it. But other than that, I've never actually said, "Stop it."

Josh refrained from saying anything to his teammates about their racist hazing until pushed to his limit. He views his teammates as not trying to be mean, yet in fact they were. The mocking and teasing use of his name involved common white stereotypes pointing out the "foreign" character of his Asian name and visage—and probably white stereotypes of weak Asian male sexuality. Josh initially demonstrates uncertainty over whether the perpetrators were "friends," but then asserts that they in fact were. This demonstrates a poignant aspect of the reality of those who are not white in this society: they often have a complex relationship with whites, wanting to gain their friendship and approval even at the cost of humiliation. Josh did his best to control his anger but still remembers the teasing. We see his pain in his strong if belated reactions and sense it in his narrative voice.

In addition, Josh reports that his family never openly discussed discriminatory incidents they faced. Thus, not until some years later did he hear a story from his sister about a racist incident involving her:

My sister when she was in high school … would work on yearbook staff, and some parents' little kids would call her like a "Chink." I was shocked when I heard the story later because I've never heard of anyone being called a Chink, like, among my friends. I always considered that word, that like it's a funny word in the sense that it's an awkward word today. In the sense that I don't feel any particular like negative stigma with it because I've never experienced negative stigma.… When my sister was telling me the story, I didn't think anyone actually used that word.… So she mentioned it one day a while back and I remember thinking like, ha! Apparently, it wasn't like an adult. It was some kid calling her "Chink." I think he was younger, could have been a year younger than junior high. I think she was kind of like me. She didn't take it to heart at all, but I think she was like shocked because it even came out of this kid's mouth, number one. This kid was younger, way younger. And number two, … our family has never, like we never associated the word "Chink" with negative. It just came out of nowhere. So we were kind of like, what? People say that? That's weird. I think she was offended, I mean, I guess I would be offended in a weird way but I wouldn't be like angry. She wasn't either.

Josh indicates a certain disbelief on his part and his sister's that such a thing could occur. In his interview he says that he had never been associated with a negative racial stigma, yet at the same time he reports racial harassment targeting his name and other racist incidents faced by his family. Seemingly, he thinks "Chink" is rarely used, although numerous other respondents indicated that they have heard it frequently. Noteworthy is that Josh's sister never confronted the parent or the child about the racist epithet and did not share the incident with family until years later. Typically, silence about oppression hurts the individual and also prevents the development of a collective memory of white oppression. It teaches whites that if they call Asian Americans racial slurs, they will not suffer any negative responses or consequences for such actions.

In the family responses to racist incidents here, we see some similarities to what has been reported in past research on how African Americans cope with racism. Some earlier studies during the legal segregation era indicated that many African Americans were encouraged, from a young age, to rigidly control their anger and rage over discriminatory incidents affecting them.[10] Historically, it was very dangerous for African Americans to unleash their anger about racist attacks. In earlier decades, black parents taught their children to remain even tempered in the face of extreme Jim Crow oppression, which silence demonstrably had severe effects on self-esteem and mental health—as it likely does in the case of African Americans and Asian Americans today.

In recent decades, numerous school systems have become increasingly attentive to the mental health needs of students and provide more counseling services. However, such mental health counselors may often be ill-equipped to deal with students of color. School counselors with heads full of conventional racial and ethnic stereotypes can be a problem. Violet, a multiracial Asian American who is part Latino, is a member of one of the few Asian families in her city. (Her state does have numerous areas densely populated with Asian Americans.) She reports being invisible as an Asian American and that she has often been grouped by local whites with Mexican Americans. A white counselor at her high school attempted to "reach out" and help students of color by taking them for one visit (and only one) to a local community college for a tour to "inspire" them to go to college:

> She gave these really condescending spiels about how minorities have a lower higher-education [attendance] rate and how she wanted to change that—single-handedly, I guess. And it's really bad. And so we were going to get to spend a whole day, we got to miss school, and it was just really horrible. I was fuming at this point because she made it sound like we didn't know how to read or write. And then I ... told her, "Are you kidding me? This is ridiculous!" And she goes, "Oh Violet, don't worry. You're going

to get a free lunch." And I just got angry. I looked around. I knew another girl in there. She'd gotten into an Ivy League school. We couldn't believe what she was doing, our dumb counselor. So we got up, left. I was so mad. She was angry that I left and embarrassed her in front of the counselors.

One of numerous talented students in her high school, Violet resisted her white counselor's efforts, feeling insulted by the condescension. Her protests about the counselor's comments were not even taken seriously, and her counselor apparently did not realize why students might be insulted. One reason for the counselor's insensitivity may have been a racial framing of people of color. The largest group of color in Violet's city and school was Mexican American, and local whites reportedly often stereotyped Mexican Americans as "lazy" and on welfare.

In Violet's view, the white counselor, although likely well meaning, showed little understanding of the structural obstacles that students of color face daily. In the interview the counselor was described as "clueless" because she appeared to believe that just one day-trip to a junior college could counter the real economic and other resource barriers that kept many from considering college. Violet's view seems to be this: the counselor thought that just because they had never been inside a college, they had not thought of attending—and not primarily that they faced major institutional barriers. In addition, such motivational efforts by white counselors and teachers eerily suggest the role of the white "savior" of people of color, one that is often showcased in major Hollywood films.[11] Being overly helpful to individuals of color, treating them as though they are unable to help themselves, typically involves a condescending framing and problematic stereotypes.

Yet More Discrimination: The College Experience

As our respondents moved from elementary, middle, and high schools to college and university settings, anti-Asian discrimination did not disappear. Their white peers were mostly young adults, although the maturation process did not always result in the development of open-mindedness and nondiscriminatory treatment. The racial stereotyping and framing that respondents experienced in colleges and universities were, in fact, often reminiscent of grammar school. For example, aforementioned incidents like the Alexandra Wallace "Asians in the Library" viral YouTube video indicate that universities are often not safe havens for Asian American students.

To take another example, white college students and other college-educated whites in California, home to the largest Asian American and Pacific Islander population in the United States (about 5.6 million), reportedly use stereotyped language in discussing Asian American college students and certain state universities. Thus, common white nicknames for certain California universities belittle or express a racialized anger about large Asian American student populations there. For example, the University of California at Irvine (UCI) has been nicknamed by whites "the University of Chinese Immigrants," and the University of California at Los Angeles (UCLA) has been nicknamed "the University of Caucasians Lost among Asians."[12] Often the West Coast is viewed by many Americans as a more accepting place for Asian Americans compared to other regions, but these barbed nicknames suggest that numerous West Coast whites are not positively oriented to the academic achievements of young Asian Californians. One need only reflect on the *lack* of any such racially oriented nicknames when whites were most of the (or the only) students at these same universities to conceive how harsh and racialized these stereotypes really are. In addition, researchers have found that white college students in numerous other states also engage in racial mocking of, joking about, and sometimes attacks on Asians and Asian Americans.[13]

Thus, Asian international and Asian American students at U.S. colleges and universities report receiving a great array of stereotypes and discriminatory actions from their fellow white students. Richa, an Asian Indian student, describes some incidents at her prestigious southwestern university:

> I've heard from a lot of people, Indian students who are doing engineering … [or] in the architecture department. If there's an Indian student who just cooked, and then gone to the office, and he's smelling like curry, professors have actually singled people out and told them, "Why don't you shower?" And "why don't you spray some cologne or something before you come to class because you smell like curry all the time," and I found that very funny, but at the same time very demeaning as well. I wasn't aware of this until very recently, about a year ago, when I heard it through somebody that this is how Indians were characterized, that we smell like curry. You know, there's no way you can react to that besides saying that it's a very weird stereotype.

Richa recognizes the insult and laughs at its absurdity. Demeaning stereotypes about people being smelly or dirty are a centuries-old part of the racial framing of people of color, and these white professors perpetuate them in barbed comments and other discriminatory actions in the offices and classrooms of such institutions of higher learning. Professors have powerful positions in regard to the self-esteem and careers of their students, and such actions likely make a strong impression on students, signaling among other things that it is acceptable to stereotype in this harsh fashion.

Another respondent, Ming Huei, provides some insight into the exclusionary character of campus culture. She explains why Asian immigrants might feel left out at a historically white institution:

> In college, predominantly white colleges, I don't know if people are as accepting. Not in general, "Oh, Asians are great." So, I don't know. Because at [my university], it was predominantly white. I had Asian friends and stuff, but they weren't accepted. I mean, one in particular, and he was immigrant himself—he wasn't born here. Because he was kind of more Asian than, say, us. He didn't have as much to talk about, football and things like that. He wouldn't consider any white people his friends because he didn't have anything to talk about.

Asian Americans and Asians frequently feel isolated in a white-centered world, which has its own distinctive norms for conversations. The cultural provincialism of whites is here suggested in the centrality of U.S. football as a topic of conversation, especially among male strangers. Those who do not know this unique U.S. sport often remain isolated. Still, Ming Huei seems reluctant to name as racist certain informal norms in her university environment. To her, her friend's inability to converse about U.S. sports and relate to white interests was the stated reason for his alienation. As we observe in other accounts, whites frequently deem Asian Americans as odd, foreign, or unacceptable because they do not understand U.S. popular culture, do not speak a certain white-accented English, practice different religions, eat strange food, have strange names, are too smart, or are too passive.

A Japanese American respondent quoted earlier, Alice, reported that she has had difficulties with whites since elementary school. This discrimination was evident in her experiences at a major historically white university, where she suffered much isolation or exclusion in white-dominated classroom spaces. Although there were numerous Asian American students there, they were unable to change the racial climate. Alice discusses some experiences:

> I stayed there six years. I got my master's there too. And by the time I got my master's, I think I had—even the teachers told me, you know, "You have a lot to add. You can't be afraid to say what you think." And that was such a novel concept because even in [my] high school, all girl's Catholic school, and so there's a lot of discussion in class. And you felt comfortable because

it's all girls, and we're all sort of in the same boat. But when you get into a white [college] environment, I rarely did anything else, like participated in class ... because all the previous exposures I had to white people were none too pretty.

Throughout her interview Alice speaks of white-dominated environments that had debilitating effects on her, including when she was in classroom settings. Asian Americans have often been criticized, especially by whites, for being introverted or too academically focused. Alice pinpoints *why* she was quiet in white-dominated environments and found them intimidating. White privilege constantly means that whites do not have to change elements of mostly white or all-white environments that are hostile to people of color. Indeed, whites often purposely set up such environments to keep racial outsiders isolated and at bay.

Alice notes specific college experiences that made her feel this painful hostility and social isolation:

It would be really hard to have Caucasian friends [at the university], because they don't want to have anything to do with you.... Most Caucasians, at that time again ... a lot of times I get really resentful, because what they would do to get a ticket in a football game, you had to be in a [sorority] rush line, and this was before lotteries and anything. And what they would do is they would save like 1,000 seats even though you get there at the crack of dawn, they would interject the rest of the sorority, and then all of sudden if you were second in line, you would be like 100th because all these [white sorority] people would cut in line ahead of you. And they seemed to have a certain clout and be much more a part of student government and all of that.

One might read this discrimination as just involving students involved with influential fraternities and sororities, and not a matter directly involving race. However, Alice's experience with much other mistreatment by white students indicates that there is likely a racial dimension. When asked to explain why whites felt it was okay to skip them in line, she responds thus:

They knew Asians really wouldn't do anything. I mean, now it's different, but back then, in the early '70s, '60s, Asians were seen as kind of docile, and then it was true. Why would you go and hassle when there's a majority? So we were taken advantage of, so it was more they just pushed their way in line, and you just knew that's what they were going to do, and nothing you could do or say would prevent it because there was just too many of them. So, like okay, that's the power structure there, and you began to understand that's how it works.

The unwillingness of Asian American students to resist assertively overt discrimination was used by some whites as a stereotyped reason to discriminate further. Note too that almost all campus sororities and fraternities on historically white campuses when Alice was in college were all-white and openly discriminatory in choosing members, as indeed some still are today.

In further comments, Alice adds some thoughts on how she became adept at reading social signals emanating from affluent whites:

> The cues were obvious.... These girls that came from [names wealthy city] and really wealthy areas of [city where university was]—they kind of snubbed their nose at people like me, who really were working their way through college and didn't have a lot of money for nice clothes. And you know, they always have the nice designer boutique clothes, and we just had jeans and T-shirts. And actually the Asians, there were a couple of clumps of places in the library where Asians would hang out; and we knew that the white folks would give us weird looks, but there wasn't any huge confrontation about it. But we know about [their] rules. Sometimes we would hear a comment, "Oh, those people, du-du-du-du, those state-supported people on scholarship."

The exclusionary discrimination was frequently coded in class terms. Alice reports that she and her Asian friends were not fooled by this socioeconomic coding and knew that white language and looks were often cover for racial prejudice. Indeed, recent analysis of contemporary white commentaries on other racial groups suggests that many have become skilled at talking "nasty about minorities without sounding racist."[14] Alice's mention of the dominant "rules" that Asian American students understood in dealings with whites on campus reminds us of W. E. B. DuBois's discussion of the "double consciousness" about their lives that African Americans have developed.[15] They must understand not only how they internally see themselves but also how whites see them. Asian Americans know what types of behaviors are acceptable in white-normed spaces and what subordinated roles they need to play. Alice and her friends knew that there were scattered places in the library where they were almost quarantined, and where they would get dirty looks from white passersby.

Interestingly, like some other respondents, Alice tries to play down contemporary racism by claiming that things are now different, even though throughout her interview she describes recent incidents that show she is viewed as an outsider by many whites. Alice still faces discrimination at work and in her neighborhood. Noteworthy in her comments is her use of the past tense when referring to the stereotype of Asian Americans as "docile," yet as we demonstrate throughout this book, the racial stereotype is still commonplace.

Violet, who lives in an area with a substantial Asian American population, was enrolled in a prestigious undergraduate program. Later, in law school, she became an officer in the Asian law society, an organization that welcomed students from all racial groups. When some of her society's members discovered that the student representatives hired for an important bar review course were once again *all* white, in spite of the large numbers of students of color on campus, she went to her dean to challenge and eliminate the discrimination, but the dean did nothing. In her interview Violet comments that this "was especially surprising because law school is really diverse, and no one is really blatantly racist at all, or even covertly so." Thus, Violet found it hard to believe that such discrimination could happen at her law school, again suggesting an assumption indicated by some respondents, as well as many other Americans, that attending colleges and universities necessarily lessens whites' racist practices.

Another respondent, Jessica, had a similar experience at her prestigious university. She is a member of the Asian American student group that wrote the first detailed report ever about Asian Americans' facing discrimination on her large campus. One obvious sign of discrimination at the university that the group cited is the fact that, although nearly a fifth of students are Asian American, not one was a member of important student government bodies. After the report was released, white administrators seemed mildly concerned but took no action, while white students generally said nothing. Indeed, the strongest negative public commentary came from some other Asian American students, who were upset that the report aired the "dirty linen" of campus and were thus afraid of a white backlash. Reflecting on all-white representation in key student government bodies, Jessica comments thus in her interview:

> But who says they [whites] represent the student body, because they don't. I mean there's been one Asian American president in the whole history of student government. One. Our population is very great. There's a reason why Asian Americans are not represented there, because they don't want [us] to be there. That's just the way it is, right? And, yeah, ... then let's break it down by ethnicity and see how well represented we are. I mean, come on, where are the Thai students [in student government], where are the Bangladeshi students, where are the Laotian and Cambodian students? Where are they? They're not here, and there's a reason. Why don't we look

into that? But we don't, because our failures are masked by the failures of other ethnicities, and it's pathetic that that's what the university shows us: "Look, you know, we're doing our part, we're catering to your community. Look how many students apply and attend this university."

Jessica is skeptical of what the officials at the university are saying about the lack of involvement by Asian Americans in student government. As she describes it, the lack of Asian representation in student government has to do with the campus being historically white for many decades of its history. She keys in on the campus being "white space," as Alice did earlier, and accents the total absence in student government of numerous Asian groups (Thai, Laotian, Cambodian, Bangladeshi) and the token presence of one or two Asian students from other groups. She amplifies this latter point:

> It's not inclusive space. So the students that are in student government, I mean if we break down the students of color that are in student government that actively work within their communities and are a part of their respective communities, it's few and far between. Those who are, are stars; it's so commendable, but it shouldn't be that way. It should be that there is a link between student government and students of color, but it's not. It's very hard to find these students, and it's by chance. . . . They are traditionally, historically white, privileged groups. . . . Just running for student government, it requires like thousands of dollars you have to raise. This is ridiculous. This is student organization. . . . Why do they have to raise thousands of dollars to put people into office? That automatically puts people out of the race. I mean, there is so much privilege that comes with being able to run.

Insightfully, Jessica points out that the few students of color who do enter into the ranks of student government must be campus superstars. She broadens her view to include African Americans and Latinos as well as Asian Americans. As overachievers, students of color who do make it into student government frequently must work alongside many less-qualified whites. Asian Americans enter the white campus and often have, as a group, high rates of educational attainment, yet they too are blocked out of much campus activity by overt or covert racial barriers.

Throughout U.S. history, government offices at all levels have been structured so as to keep them mostly white, especially at or near the top. Thus, white government officials have the power to reproduce again and again old structures of racial inequality, including those central to U.S. schools and colleges. White students benefit from attending schools and colleges typically provided by these officials with more educational resources. Then they generally score higher on standardized college entrance tests that cater to them, then move on to more advantaged universities, and later enter the workforce where they typically have good (white) networks to better jobs. Whites as a group have been educationally, economically, and politically advantaged for all of U.S. history.[16] Moreover, in the event a person of color manages to enter educational or job settings populated heavily by middle-class whites, he or she often has to overachieve to stay there, as well as endure the marginalizing realities of most such white-dominated environments.

A Bangladeshi American, Fareena, whom we met in Chapter 2, reports that at her college she moved in with white roommates. This all-white environment proved to be very challenging; indeed, her home life became a battleground:

> I just moved in with three white roommates. It was a last-minute thing, and they've never lived with a nonwhite person before. So there are issues with cooking; there are issues with dating. "Why do you date a black guy?" It's like, "Am I supposed to date a white guy?" Who am I supposed to date because all their partners are white? And then different stupid questions about "do y'all worship this, and do you support Saddam Hussein" are always there.

Fareena continues with more detail on her recurring roommate problems:

> Gosh, there are so many issues. And I was sleeping the other day, and her boyfriend was verbally attacking me, making curry jokes at me. Making fun of the fact that I like to lock the door. And saying, "Oh, we didn't lock the door, then Fareena is going to be mad because a bunch of crazy people are going to come inside the apartment," and all these sarcastic comments when I am right there! I was sleeping on the couch and he came in the apartment with her, and [he said] ... "I smell curry. I smell curry in the house. Someone must be here." And I have never cooked curry in the apartment yet.... So, it has become a very racially tense house, but the racial things were first thrown at me. I buy Asian food every day. It has to be something Asian or Mexican ... something with flavor. And they think that it smells bad, and it smells like dead carcasses, and they're like, "Well that's just the type of food that you eat." And oh yeah, one of the girls kicked my dog and slammed the door on it. It's an itty bitty little thing, a Pekinese. Yeah, things have gotten really tense, really bad. Every day I have a story to share with my friends.

Fareena cannot find peace even in her home setting. She is questioned about her religious affiliation and her patriotism. Her food choices are like "dead carcasses," which invokes common stereotyped notions of Asian cuisine being unrefined when compared to European American fare. Luckily for her, Fareena has a group of friends who are supportive and willing to lend an ear. As with numerous other Asian Americans, they often deal with racial mistreatment in silence.

Ann, a Vietnamese American, went to a major university. Like many schools in the North, hers had the reputation of being liberal. Yet she insists that, in spite of that reputation, they had significant problems with racism, sexism, and heterosexism. One series of events was so upsetting that it made her afraid to cook in her dorm. She explains the events:

> Every year, you get hit with, there is always a homosexual or racial comment that goes on. But one that really, really, really will always stick with me was—I was a freshman and food for me is huge. As a freshman, I went to [names university], that's only like forty-five minutes away, so every so often my mom would visit, and she would bring food up. All I would have to do was warm it up and eat it, and not eat the crappy dining hall food. Then, I don't know what semester it was, there was a hall and some dorms have suites where it's a common living room, a common kitchen, and a series of bedrooms, like dorm rooms. And one of the Asian females came home one night to a note that said, "Stop cooking your dog food and stinking up our hall!" That made huge, absolutely huge news on campus, of course, and huge discussion.... For me, when I heard that happened, and it also affected ... a bunch of Vietnamese people.... I knew a handful of them that lived on that floor and that lived in that hall.... The culture events, and the fact they used "dog food," and the woman that received the note was Asian—and here I am a lowly, new freshman student. My first reaction, for the next couple of weeks I was just terrified that here I am warming up my Vietnamese food in the common kitchen, maybe I would get bombarded with this message too. I was just so scared to warm up my food for a week or to cook anything, because I was so traumatized.... It didn't really help that I knew the girl, or ... that they were kind of attacked. It was horrible. It really made me feel self-conscious, and it really made me feel threatened.

The strength of her memory is notable. This happened her freshman year and remains one of the strongest of her memories of racist incidents. Note her words describing the incident and her feelings: "traumatized," "horrible," "self-conscious," and "threatened." Stereotyped comments scribbled on a piece of paper had an intense impact. Although not a physical confrontation, the emotional effect was great.

Then Ann explains why the term "dog food" was particularly significant in this incident of anti-Asian hostility:

> The fact that they used "dog food," because you always hear, you know, both China and Vietnam are Communist countries, that you hear these horrible things about. I don't know why, especially with Vietnam. I hear it sometimes, that people say about it in China too, but especially for the Vietnamese that they cook dog or that they eat dog. It just correlates with the Vietnamese for some reason. It made that even worse that of course they had to use "dog food" and not just "food," that they have to tack on "dogs" to it too.

One white stereotype of Asian Americans, especially of those of Chinese or Vietnamese background, is that they are uncivilized people who eat lots of dogs, the favorite pet of many Americans. As children and as adults, many Asian Americans have had to endure pointed questions from whites about whether they participate in such a culinary practice.[17] This negative stereotype insults and distances Asian Americans as odd, uncivilized, and un-American. Historically, indeed from the earliest decades of European colonialism in the fifteenth century, a central element of the conceptual framing of non-European peoples has been a casting of their cultures, including foods and food habits, as savage and uncivilized. In contrast, Western food habits, such as killing and eating calves and cows on a huge scale, are not seen in the same questioning framework. The ethnocentric stereotyping of Asians as uncivilized in dietary practices helps to reinforce the framing of white superiority versus Asian inferiority.[18]

Ann later speaks more about the discrimination she observed in her college environment, incidents that had a significant impact on her own life: "There were a lot of racial incidences. There was one after 9/11. There was an Arab American student, granted he was drunk, but he was walking by a frat [house], and yelling things. And the frat brothers threatened him, beat him up, called him a 'towel head.' You know, those types of things. There's always been, every year . . . there's one huge racial incident." While these common racial incidents often involved other students of color, Ann indicates that they had an effect on her, such that she never really felt free or safe on this major historically white campus.

Fareena, the Bangladeshi American who faced self-image issues at her all-white high school, adds that her problems continued during her college years:

I had more overt incidence of racism my first year in college, which was when 9/11 happened. That was my first semester in a community college. And that's when I remember the first time actually getting angry. It was the morning of 9/11, and we were in a sociology class.... We were watching it on TV. And I couldn't figure out what was going on. I didn't even think "terrorism" or anything [like] that word would emerge at that time, but the professor and two other men in my class ... started talking about Middle Eastern people, that they were behind it. And then the next week we studied religion in class. And we were looking at a graph of how many Christians exist in America, how many Buddhists, how many Muslims. And so we were looking at the very small percentage of Muslim people that are in America compared to Christian people. And the professor said something to the effect of, "By looking at the stats of, you know, how small the Muslim population is you'd think we would be winning the war against terror, but they're infiltrating everywhere."

Hostile stereotypes articulated by classmates and a professor felt like personal attacks on her national origin and cultural identity. Appalled at the stereotyped generalizations, Fareena continues by describing her own reactions:

And at that time I identified as Muslim American; I practiced it in a sense. I didn't really give it a lot of thought, but at that time I felt really defensive and I remember speaking out in class. And then all these class members were like, "Why don't you cover yourself up like the other women do? We have been watching how Muslim women are supposed to be, you're not even a real Muslim woman." And then I felt like, damn, I need to read the Koran and find the section of the Koran that says women don't necessarily have to cover their hair. And that's more of a cultural practice than a religious one. I felt the need to defend so many things, and I felt like I needed to defend that I was a good person and that my family was [good].

Note the risks of speaking out against such racial-ethnic stereotyping, for here that generated more verbal attacks that articulated yet more stereotypes. This is a common report from Americans of color who do speak out against the commonplace stereotyping and discrimination.

Fareena then describes how her brother was targeted by the university police. After a fistfight involving several people at a fraternity party, he was the only one who had a warrant out for his arrest after the incident and taken into custody:

He was treated very badly, and like he had to stay in jail. We couldn't afford to get him out for a while. And then we still had to pay fines. We're still paying the bail money. And then I talked about what had happened in [my] class: about when our lawyers had asked the judge to be a bit more lenient because it was a very short, brief fight and it could [jeopardize] his status in America.... He could get deported; and the other side, the other lawyers, were like, "Well now this is a matter of national security. Look at him he's an engineering student, a threat. I'm threatened by him. And I think he should get a harsher sentence." The whole [university police department] not communicating at all, and then not being available for questioning or [to] even ask them why do you treat students this way? Why do you shackle them? Why do you not even let them know that they're being investigated? Or that there are warrants out for them? And the [police department] in the past few years, if you look that different, you will be treated differently.

The reactions of the university police and prosecuting attorneys here involve substantial stereotyping and overt discrimination. Fareena's brother was an excellent student with no prior record, yet he was a dark-skinned Asian American whom these whites perceived as "foreign" and a threat to "national security." This latter view revealed significant ignorance of geography on the part of these whites. He was shackled and taken to jail for getting in a brief fight, although the others in the fight were not. His dark skin likely contributed to the police discrimination. In her interview Fareena notes that both her brother and father are often assumed by others to be "black," while her mother is often taken "for white." She herself is often mistaken "for Latina." She indicates that this variation in the way whites and others perceive members of her family has created diverse racialized experiences for them. Yet one thing they share is an inability of others to see their Bangladeshi American identity. Even though Fareena and her family have been in the United States for some years, and her father has indeed become a proud U.S. citizen, they are still sometimes treated as "dangerous foreigners."

The discrimination reported in our respondents' narratives varies in severity and type, but each discriminatory action was recalled with some pain. Memories of past discrimination still evoke significant emotions; there is even some reliving in the telling of these accounts. Time clearly does not remedy or heal the wounds. Racial memories accumulated during college and unfortunately continue to increase as the respondents have moved into jobs and careers in an array of U.S. workplaces.

Workplace Discrimination

Asian Americans are often viewed as generally successful by non-Asians not only in their educations but also in their jobs and careers. They are frequently viewed as holding stable and lucrative careers, especially in professions such as engineering, law, medicine, and physical and computer sciences. However, these stereotyped views mask the significant unemployment and poverty rates of numerous Asian American groups, especially Vietnamese, Cambodian, Thai, Bangladeshi, Laotian, and Hmong Americans; even groups such as Chinese Americans have a greater unemployment and poverty rate than do white Americans.[19] Indeed, the great recession of 2008 only worsened the unemployment and poverty rates for Asian Americans. Not only do these common white stereotypes contrast with the socioeconomic hardships of many Asian Americans but they also involve an assumption that workplaces for Asian Americans are relatively problem-free.

One interview study of a few second-generation Asian American professionals found that they did not report any job discrimination, which led the researchers to uncertainty about whether they face discrimination in their workplaces. Additionally, a recent (2012) Pew Research Center survey found about one-eighth of their Asian American respondents did think that discrimination was a major problem for their group, with 48 percent indicating it was a minor problem. However, researchers in both these studies apparently did not allow their respondents enough time or opportunity to relate the discrimination they and their peers probably have faced. As we have noted previously, many of our respondents did not initially talk about the discrimination they faced, only discussing it in detail later in their interviews. Thus, our respondents' accounts strongly indicate that Asian Americans do face workplace discrimination in professional and technical jobs, as well as in numerous other job categories. Some other recent research does corroborate our more substantial findings of discrimination. For example, one important survey of professional employees in government and nonprofit workplaces found that a majority of Asian American male professionals and a near-majority of Asian American female professionals reported racial, gender, and other discrimination in their workplaces.[20]

This workplace discrimination follows on the heels of school discrimination. What some may view as minor "kid stuff," such as the racist insults often hurled by white children at Asian American children, is seen in a new light when we observe that Asian American adults endure anti-Asian epithets and discrimination throughout their lives. Being surrounded by (mostly white) adults in workplaces does not prevent them from encountering racial discrimination. Such discrimination ranges from overt to subtle to covert forms, and most respondents do note and understand when they are treated as different, unwanted, inferior, or unfit for moving into certain jobs or into higher-level positions at their workplaces.

Language Discrimination

Mei emigrated from an Asian country several decades ago and reported that she has endured anti-Asian racism ever since. Working at a medical clinic, she candidly states, with certainty in her voice, that white supervisors regularly discriminate against her because of her Asian heritage. Although she has been employed at the clinic for many years, white supervisors still complain that her language skills are seriously lacking. They mainly have in mind her accent. We note here the ethnocentrism of her supervisors, for indeed *all* Americans speak English with an accent, including those supervisors. Mei has been in the United States for a long time and, if they did not find her particular accent problematical when they hired her years ago, why would her white supervisors view it as a genuine concern today? Interestingly, Mei notes that the clinic's clients—many of them white—*never* complain about her accent.

She reports too that matters of billing cause conflict with her white supervisors. She finds mistakes in their billing efforts and tries to correct them for customers, but her supervisors complain. Mei was even *scared* to talk with us, believing that her white employers would find out and that she would be fired. After explaining that her identity would be protected, she became more at ease. Mei discusses her treatment thus:

> It's not really a good idea to let people know the ugly face at the health center now. I will be in real trouble now; I don't know how to say it. It's really hard. The first time I got here, it's OK, now, maybe I am foreign.... It keeps getting worse and worse ... and worse and worse. Right now it's really worse.... I probably will be losing my job pretty soon. When they ask me to do something, they don't really ask me. When they tell me to do something, I have a question, "I say this is not really a good idea to do it this way." But they say, "Well ... you have to listen to the supervisor." You know it's hard to talk to them, they think they are right. They think I am wrong, if I say anything, I am still wrong. No matter what, it's wrong. Even if I do the right thing, they still think I am wrong.

Mei lives in fear that she will be fired and is constantly stressed by recurring mistreatment. The energy Mei wastes dealing with the racially hostile work environment has accumulated over time, a cost that workers of color must pay for living in a racist country. For months after her interview, we received phone calls from her saying that things at work were still unbearable and asking if there was anything we could do to help. (We directed her to some relevant organizations and websites developed for reporting bias and discrimination.) Significantly, Mei says that she is viewed as "more foreign" *now* than earlier. A resident in the United States for decades, she, like many other Asian Americans, feels increasingly alienated and targeted as a foreigner. There is likely a cumulative effect here, for the longer a person of color lives in the United States, the longer she or he is exposed to everyday racism.

Discrimination in Business

Another respondent, Henry, emigrated from China a half century ago. Coming to a major West Coast city as a child, he suffered miserably through constant racial taunting and other discrimination, especially in high school, where he was the only Asian. After graduation, he attempted to join the workforce but could not find suitable work. He believes that he was often turned down because of his racial characteristics. (At that time, the Asian immigrant population in his city was growing rapidly.) When he finally found a menial job, it was not permanent, and he switched occupations many times.

Reflecting on his long years in U.S. workplaces, Henry describes some of his everyday experiences with racist whites, especially when he was a skilled cabinetmaker:

> If you are Asian, they always pick on you. It doesn't matter how good you are. I used to have a boss, and he would come to the shop and make fun of me, like talking in [mock] Chinese language. I would just walk away. If you say something, he would say, "I was just joking." I know he wasn't. . . . I think whites get a lot of ideas from the movies they see, and they pick that up. A lot of stuff they pick up from the Asian movies. The way Chinese carry the water buckets, the clothes they wear, and their long ears. They use this, this is the way they insult you. You don't hear them making fun of the whites, do you? If you make fun of them, then they will get angry. The whites. Why would a white do that to an Asian? They do that to insult you. Why do they want to make fun of you, because that's the way the culture is, because they want to make fun of Chinese culture because of the movies they see. Take the N-word, they banned that word, but they are still calling the Chinese "Chinamen."

Language mocking is a problem for many Americans of color, now including Asian Americans and Latinos. Over his lifetime Henry has been ridiculed by white supervisors and coworkers, and he views many whites as unwilling to treat him as an equal. When called out on their racism, whites often use the strategy of "I was joking" to try to excuse actions. Observe that Henry puts a great deal of responsibility on the mainstream media, especially the movies, in shaping racist stereotypes. Recall from Chapter 1 the numerous times that commentators on television or in movies have portrayed Asian Americans using mocking language or other racialized imagery. In addition, television commercials have periodically portrayed Asian Americans in roles where they are humiliated and ridiculed. For example, a cellular phone company recently had an elderly Asian couple wrestling pigs.

Henry eventually opened up a business but still faced discrimination: "We used to have a sign shop. I had it for twenty years. Just because you're Asian, they took advantage of you. I have been ripped off left and right. That's the way the world is." In his view whites' racist actions just have to be endured as part of life in the United States.

A Japanese American respondent, Alice, notes too that her father suffered discrimination in dealing with a white partner that he worked with: "My dad was reserved to this white guy that he had as a partner, and ... that guy was the front guy for all these Asians, Japanese Americans, that were building this furniture [for the store]. And the guy owned the furniture sales outlet, which was a storefront. And my dad always felt that the guy had cheated him, always talking about the 'paddy guy' [the partner was Irish American] who had screwed him, and all of that stuff."

Alice recalled that as she was growing up, she would hear many stories of discrimination. Her father, a young adult when forcibly put into a U.S. concentration camp during World War II *just because* he was a Japanese American, lost his business as a result. Like many Japanese Americans of that time he turned to alcohol to deal with the extreme oppression he faced from whites. Although he used mildly stereotyped language to describe his Irish American partner, the father's deep anger was legitimate and rooted in discriminatory experiences with whites before, during, and after World War II. Such experiences led him to view many whites as untrustworthy. Especially before and right after World War II, Japanese Americans had to find white partners in order to own or operate a business because of state laws that intentionally discriminated against Japanese Americans seeking to enter businesses on the West Coast. Note too that many Japanese American families lost much family wealth, which could have been passed along over the generations to the present day, when their businesses were closed down and their property often destroyed as a result of their being forced by racist white authorities into U.S. concentration camps during World War II.

Discrimination in Hiring and Workplace Climates

In addition, Alice reports that, when she entered the workforce, she found herself up against discriminatory whites:

> We [Japanese Americans] were not even part of the equation.... I tried to go get even a secretarial job or an assistant job in the seventies.... I went to [large media corporation] and they said, "No." They were looking for a videotape librarian. And I had worked six or seven years in the L.A. public library system, and it was strange because they just said, "No." Then everyone tells me about the [company's] culture later: very conservative, and this and that. That's why one of the groups I supported early on, and I worked for them as staff for four or five years of my career, was [names company], because they were Asian Americans working to create Asian American media. And I just thought that was so important to do, so here with my master's degree, I'm going to starve and work with these guys as a nonprofit, but it was really a good experience.

Alice was more than qualified with her previous experience, yet was unable to find work at a white-owned company and was not given a reason for the rejection. She had to take a meager salary to find a workplace where she would be accepted.

Alice eventually earned a graduate degree and began to teach at the college level, where she again faced racial and gender obstacles:

> Being a female professor that is Asian, I think there is some statistic that they have a bias against you because you are a woman. You don't even need to open your mouth. There are some really good teachers out there, but because you're Asian, you're inscrutable, you don't joke around, you have your own style. It wasn't an easy way—an easy journey at all. And it's hard to find community. So, where do I go for food? Most of these small towns have no—[only] Chinese food, but it's really bad.

Already at a disadvantage as a female professor, Alice had to also deal with racist stereotypes and other aspects of a hostile workplace climate. Reportedly, a commonplace "Dragon Lady" image was invoked, and she was not received as just another professor, but stereotypically as "inscrutable" and "too serious." Higher education is by no means free of anti-Asian racism, in this case gendered as well.[21] Alice had to take teaching positions in areas of the country far from her hometown, which increased her feelings of isolation. After a few years she gave up her university position to move back home.

Some type of multicultural emphasis has become a staple in many corporate settings, and numerous corporate diversity organizations have been created in recent years. Yet, many of these efforts showcase white insincerity or ineptitude in dealing with diversity issues, as Indira, an Asian Indian respondent, notes from her significant experience:

> I worked with a diversity consulting company, and I was reviewing the curriculum ... but I noticed certain things. I was looking at all the pictures, so all the pictures. This is a curriculum for a company that does corporate diversity training, so I'm looking at pictures. And all the white people in the pictures are wearing suits. All the black people are wearing suits. And [the brown people]—I say brown because brown could be South Asians or Latinos ... and anybody of Asian descent [are] wearing "ethnic clothing." ... This is corporate diversity training. Now why is that? And they thought that they were being diverse. I'm like, "It's exotifying." It's not like we are talking about global culture here, you are talking about corporate culture. So if everybody else is wearing a suit, I need to do one of two things, have everyone in suits throughout these pictures.... I don't see white men in kilts in these pictures, you know. I don't see Conan the Destroyer in these pictures. Why do I see a man who is half-naked, who looks like a Buddhist priest, in these pictures, why? They're inconsistent.... Things like that and it shows kind of how people, just "Oriental is alive and well." And people don't even see [stereotyping] when they are performing it, so to speak.

The reality of differential treatment even in a company that does diversity training is seen in something as subtle and symbolic as the way in which employees are dressed in company publications and curricula. Putting Latinos and Asians in distinctive "ethnic" dress makes them appear exotic, in line with an old white framing of such groups. These attempts at being culturally sensitive actually further "othering" and accent the foreignness of Asian Americans. Today, most whites would understand that it is stereotyping and offensive to put African Americans in tribal warrior gear, but the same level of understanding is often not reached for Asians and Asian Americans.

At the university where she works, Indira recalls how Asian Americans have been treated by whites as exotic and foreigners:

> So the university has what they call "cultural rooms" for each racial and ethnic group on campus. The funny thing is that the African American room is really nicely decorated; it's modern with some contemporary art, with a picture of MLK [Martin Luther King, Jr.] on the wall. The Latino

room is the same, with these portraits of these great Latino leaders like Cesar Chavez. The Asian room, when you walk in you see pictures of pandas, geishas, and religious figures, like a Hindu god. It's ridiculous! Here we are supposed to have a cultural room ... and the African American and Latino rooms are decorated like that, and we are exoticized and tokenized!

Like the officials in the company she mentioned earlier, the white university decisionmakers who set up these campus cultural rooms do not seem to understand that they perpetuate racial stereotypes even while they are trying to be inclusive. This cultural stereotyping adds to feelings of abnormality and isolation among Asian Americans. To further explain the persistence of this misrepresentation, Indira adds,

APIDAs [Asian Pacific Islander Desi Americans][22] are treated as the stereotype and the assumption is that APIDAs won't push the issue, so they [administrators] delay it, whereas black/Latino folks are "feared" because of the strong political connections and faculty/staff support. APIDA faculty/staff tend to participate in the "don't rock the boat" ideology, and with little political support outside [the university] APIDA issues get ignored. It is not just an issue of the rooms either, this is actually still very alive right now on campus.

Indira further notes that Asian American students on campus have periodically protested to the administration about these insensitive and offensive depictions, but years later "their" room remains clad in pictures of pandas and geishas.

Discrimination: Stereotyping and September 11

One Asian Indian respondent, Peter, discusses the impact of the attacks of September 11 on him and a club where he worked:

I was supposed to start getting work, my first week of work, at the [club name] in September of 2001. And when 9/11 hit, they wouldn't work me for a month because some guy in [gives city name], ... some Indian guy got killed [in a] hate crime. They just wanted to make sure, just in case.... The week after it hit, I was doing a show at [another club].... It was like their Fat Tuesday Night, and ... she introduced me, she introduced me as, "This guy had nothing to do with 9/11." ... That's how she introduced me. She didn't have my name at that point. She butchered my name.... So I go up there, and it's groans right away. And you fight through it.

The white woman who introduced Peter at the second club had likely hoped to be funny, but Peter and the crowd did not receive it as such. Peter further reports that some years after September 11, he is still viewed by geographically challenged whites and others as being Middle Eastern. He seems hopeful that he can just "fight through" these encounters, yet he cannot escape how his skin color triggers negative and stereotyped associations, especially in the minds of many whites.

Another South Asian respondent, Ahmed, reported that a friend has suffered similar problems with getting a job. In his interview, he comments thus about the persisting impact of September 11 even on those who are not of Middle Eastern origin: "But like, some jobs, I heard from a friend, he was telling me about them. His name is Mohammad. And before 9/11, he had a good job. After that, he applied many, many times, never got one. He changed his name to Joe, and the same week he got a job."

Coworker Stereotyping and Discrimination

Coworkers are frequently a problem for Asian American employees. Ann recounts a story of less blatant discrimination that her mother endured at a workplace:

> I know in her work she has a couple people that are blatantly rude to her. Part of it is that she is a very good worker, but also because, um, maybe it had something to do with the fact that she is an Asian woman. That per-haps, predominantly the white workers were not excited to be working with her or they were not happy with the fact that she was within the company.

She then describes one white female worker's actions and reactions:

> One woman in particular was just very, very rude to her, and [regardless] of how or whatever the situation was, whether it was a passing by in the communal kitchen, or if it was something work related—they didn't really work together because they were in different departments—but my mom could always sense this huge tension. She eventually deduced [that] she is treated that way probably because she is Asian.... If they worked together it might have been a different situation, but [the coworker] would give my mom dirty looks every time she walked by. And she would make comments about my mom. My mom would hear through the grapevine a comment made by this woman that was targeted to her. So, that's how she knew that this coworker was very much so not on good terms and didn't think highly of my mom, or anything like that. She [my mom] just read it as, "Well, I don't work with you. I don't do anything to bother you, why are you from day one so angry at me? So hateful towards me?" Eventually, she just had

to conclude that it was her race. That didn't really affect her. She worked hard, she's just there to work and do her job well.

Perhaps because workers of color are often deemed "paranoid" by whites when they assert that such mistreatment is discriminatory, Ann's mother tried to find another reason for the mistreatment. But, after exhausting all other options, she could find no reason but her racial identity. The great energy that Ann's mother had to exert just to decipher and counter her coworker's discriminatory behavior cost her dearly, and she worked hard so as not to let it significantly affect her duties. Interviews with other Americans of color have often revealed that they too pay a heavy energy price in dealing with discrimination at the hands of white employees and employers.[23]

Another respondent, Fareena, reports that her mother has not only had to battle serious illness but also had to endure serious mistreatment from a white supervisor:

> The boss just treats her really badly. She's going through cancer. She's been going [for medical treatments] since 2003. But her boss doesn't like her taking off work for treatment because her boss is never there. She plays hooky from work all the time. So my mother feels like she has to be there.... When it comes to the stereotype of Asian Americans working so hard, and they don't need to go home because they just love their job, and they're so good at it. That's what [the boss] tells my mother: "You're one of those people that needs to do this; otherwise, you will get bored. You like doing it. You're so good at it." And she is afraid to say things, and she also feels that because the [boss] is playing hooky all the time, if she's not there ... the [names organization] is not going to run, and which it doesn't. So, I remember, like, she still has all these stitches from getting her tumors removed, and I would have to drive her every day to work during winter break or something, so she could do enough work, because the [boss] ... didn't do the paperwork because she knew that my mother would pick up the slack. So, that's how the system of power was placed, you know. My mother applied to ... other programs to become a higher administrator to get into her Ph.D. program, [and] she needs a letter from [that boss]. And every single year [the boss] has "accidentally" forgotten it because she needs my mom. And so, my mom just feels stuck. I think she's pretty upset about it now.

Fareena's mother is in a difficult position. Ill with cancer, she still wants to please her supervisor in hope of getting a letter of recommendation so she can leave. This hard work feeds the racially framed stereotype of the hardworking Asian American that her supervisor has already projected onto her. This administrator is taking advantage of Fareena's mother's willingness to do more than her share of the work because of her position of authority.

Fareena's father also has encountered discrimination at work. The treatment he has received from various people since coming to the United States and becoming a citizen has significantly altered his views of the country. Fareena explains,

> A lot of people ... think he's black. And he is in an area where there are a lot of lower-class white people, so there is a lot of resentment toward his business. You will see slurs being painted. You will see his shop being broken into. And all of the people that work for him are also people of color.... They work with him. And he doesn't hire white people on purpose. He's become very resentful in the sense that they will somehow cheat him. And he grew up in Europe.... And he grew up all around the world, actually, so he never had these views where he would ever exercise discrimination policy, but now he does.

Her father has traveled across the world, and his negative views of whites did not develop until he moved here and faced discrimination from U.S. whites. A dark-skinned Asian, now U.S. citizen, Fareena's father is treated as a black man by many whites operating out of the conventional racial frame. He came from a well-off class in his home country, yet now identifies with working-class people of color in the United States because of the white discrimination he and they face. Fareena herself reports that she did not face serious self-image issues until she encountered whites in an all-white school. These significant changes in the lives of Fareena and her father are a profound statement about the power and pervasiveness of U.S. racism.

White coworkers can also have an impact on the families of Asian American workers. Whites constantly impose racialized identities. Even if they acknowledge the Asianness of those they target, they regularly do so by invoking racial stereotypes. We see this in incidents reported by Ann, a Vietnamese American, who recalls some childhood experiences:

> Well, [this town] is very white oriented.... My dad's a carpenter, self-employed, so he doesn't really work with many people, but my mom works in a high-tech company, and she would bring me in to work. When I was a lot younger with the Christmas parties, I remember [white workers] saying, "Oh, your daughter's so cute! She looks like a little China doll." ... Of course, I didn't recognize anything at the time, but looking back, ... it's not like they knew my ethnic background, they did, but it's just the idea of I look like a "doll." I look Chinese. I was so young at the time, I

was just like, "Oh, thank you." That was the very earliest that I could ever remember being recognized as anything other than as a person—that they pointed out my racial difference.

At a very young age, Ann was the target of stereotyped remarks. She took these as compliments at first but later realized she was being differentiated as a racial "other." Ann was not just a "cute little girl" but a racialized "China doll." Over time she has realized that such whites ignore her real Asian (Vietnamese American) identity as they act out of a racial framing that assumes "all Asians look alike." In research on second-generation Chinese and Korean Americans, Nazli Kibria has described similar incidents in which whites tended to ignore or confuse national origins, treating people of one Asian nationality background as though they were of another. Kibria terms this common social process a "racialization of ethnic labels."[24]

Contending with the Glass Ceiling

In U.S. workplaces Asian Americans often find that the positions available to them are not as good as what their educational and experience records should secure. Research studies show that these employees frequently receive a lower rate of return on educational achievements than similarly educated whites. They often face as well a glass ceiling that limits promotion and career advancement. Although they may be hired into certain lower-level or middle-level white-collar positions, many find significant promotions, especially to higher management and upper professional levels, to be unlikely. Thus, in a pioneering book, *Glass Ceilings and Asian Americans,* Deborah Woo reports on research at two important workplaces, one at a high-tech company and another at a higher education institution. She shows, using an array of data, that there is a strong glass ceiling facing Asian American employees in such U.S. workplaces. Numerous other recent research studies have corroborated her findings.[25]

At first Mylene, a Filipino American, had a difficult time recalling incidents of racial mistreatment. Like most of our respondents, she reveals a strong sense of U.S. patriotism and is reluctant to discuss discrimination. Eventually she discloses that she had rocks thrown by whites at her school bus. As the interview moves to issues of West Coast workplaces, she shares this story:

I hate to say it, but I think there is some prejudice against minorities in general by the Caucasian class. It's not organized, but I noticed that all the presidents and all the top CEOs and executives are Caucasians.... Caucasians can be Jews, German, Canadian, so that's a big field. You say

Caucasian, and that could mean anything. I feel that many of us Asians and minorities, in general, are held back at a certain level because there's this thing called "Good Ole Boys Club." They will keep their people in, and keep whoever's not their kind out.... That still happens. And even though I'm happy to be an American no matter what, I still feel that when they say "equal opportunity for all," it's not necessarily true.... I've seen it, I see it, I know it. And sometimes when you go interview, and sometimes you feel like, "Do I even have a chance against all these ... Caucasians and what not?" But still, the higher jobs will go to the Caucasians. Nothing against them, but ... you can have a coach who is a minority, but somebody on top will be a Caucasian. Nothing that I would have, but that's the way it is.... I like to read a lot. I see it.

Mylene is nervous in speaking about the "glass ceiling" in workplaces, as she "hates" to share her thoughts about how whites discriminate. Eventually she becomes confident enough to cite the racial disparities she has seen, but then attempts to excuse the lack of representation of employees of color. Interestingly, in her interview she uses the term "Americans" for the "Caucasians" who are heads of U.S. corporations—thereby downplaying her own citizenship and ignoring other people of color who are American citizens. Data on U.S. corporate executives indicate that in fact they do not represent the diverse racial or gender makeup of the United States, for they are very disproportionately white and male. Indeed, currently, some 96 percent of the CEOs of Fortune 500 companies are white, and *93 percent are white men.* Yet the latter make up less than 31 percent of the U.S. population.[26]

Frank, a Korean American in a western city with a substantial Asian American population, is employed in a high-tech industry. Significantly, he began his interview praising his own ability to conform to the white framing of the world, noting explicitly that he generally "thinks white" and denying the reality of racial injustice. Yet, just as other respondents change their tune as they describe concrete life experiences, so does Frank:

I was at the lower management area, and I kept on climbing to upper management. At the time, I reached the vice president position, and I was competing with a white person. I felt something, but I kind of discounted it. And also I accept my Asian heritage as a handicap. I accepted it as a fact of life. I didn't look at it as any other issue. As you go up the corporate levels, and when you get to the vice president level, the number of people who occupy that position of CEO or DOO or CCO level, I find is mostly white people, and I was the only one—Asian guy—who's occupying one of those positions. Also another experience I had was when I went on a business trip to [names Midwestern city], I was working for what they call an industrial company ... and I went over there representing a division ... and I was wearing a normal suit with white shirt with a tie on it, and I went to the cafeteria. And I was shocked because almost 99 percent were white people, and a sprinkle of African Americans.... And I was lining up to get some food. I was the only Oriental guy with a white shirt and necktie on the line. And everyone was, I thought was, looking at me. They treated me very, very nice, but I did feel something. Then I knew the Midwest was very different. And when I started my own ... company, and I went to meet people on the East Coast, I went in there, I felt the same thing. Almost every upper position was occupied by a white person.

Frank's observations of feeling out of place were initially difficult for him to discuss, but he soon becomes quite detailed in discussing the harsh reality. Conspicuous in Frank's comments is the word "handicap" for his Asian heritage. This racial handicap was, and is, at the front of his mind, and he knows well the severity of anti-Asian discrimination in the workplace. He also notes the geography of corporate America, that on the East Coast and in the Midwest he seemed to be the only Asian American employee, while on the West Coast there are more Asian American employees, but at lower corporate levels. When asked about the reason for the lack of Asian Americans in higher management positions, he responds thus: "I think the main thing is that even whether you are very capable or very well educated, there is always a white person who is equally as well educated and what I call capable. And it seems like Asians have to do a little more than a white person does. They have to have a little different, more edge to become, to get that kind of decisionmaking process position."

Frank identifies the need for employees of color to be better than whites, indeed to be standout performers in order to obtain a position—a workplace reality reported frequently by other middle-class Americans of color. As we noted previously, Asian Americans and other Americans of color often get a lower return on their educational attainments than do whites, because of overt and subtle discrimination in workplaces.[27]

In his interview Frank further suggests that the invisibility of Asian Americans, their lack of visibility in the public sphere and media, helps to explain racial disparities in higher management. He also argues that the few Asian American women in the mainstream media made it because "they appeal to white males. Sex appeal." Previous researchers have made a similar point, that Asian American women often serve the sexual fantasies of white men.[28]

In workplaces our respondents face an array of problems related to racial, ethnic, and nationality issues. Amrita, an Asian Indian American, describes being successful in reaching upper management at her corporation. In her interview, she notes the problems that the outsourcing of certain jobs at her corporation has caused:

> We had moved a lot of our call center work to India, and we were having some problems. This has been published in the newspapers and stuff like that. And, where, you know, being employees, their language, the way they talked, people were not able to understand them, a lot of satisfaction issues. But what was interesting to me was that a lot of the decisions and the key strategies and the leadership was here in [names city]. We had some leaders in India, but you know pretty much looking from direction of [this city] because of protocol central. And I was part of a lot of the discussions and meetings and things like that. I remember being the only Indian person in the room.... I think what was interesting was that we were talking about India and Indians. And I have to say it's hard when you're talking about personal attributes, personally their language is not well understood, or whatever it is. I have to say that I did feel like maybe there should be more Indian people in the room. Similar to when we are doing business in China, you just feel like, why am I the only Indian person? Maybe there needs to be an Indian voice. More Indian people kind of saying, hey what's going from their end? And I know that [names corporation] has come a long way and changed a lot ... but I think there's a big opportunity, just my perspective, to companies in general ... to make sure they have a good mix of people or their customers in their own groups—that ... if they're doing business in China, it's a good idea to have a good mix of Chinese executives and managers and employees, right, to give you the right perspectives.

To Amrita, it makes business sense to be inclusive in higher-level executive meetings about important job issues. If Asian employees are to be a topic, she believes that some Asians should be there to give input. Historically, when people of color have been used to displace white Americans from jobs, they have often become targets of white employees' anger—instead of the top-ranking, white executives who usually made corporate policy changes in order to use overseas labor, thereby make more profits, and thus enhance their own incomes. Later in her interview Amrita notes that, to help with this lack of Asian representation, she has joined a corporate task force seeking to diversify leadership ranks in her company and encourage Asian Americans to pursue management positions. Numerous firms have set up similar task forces so that they appear to be concerned, yet unfortunately continue with discriminatory hiring and promotion practices.[29]

As we have already seen, discrimination comes not only in the form of overt and direct mistreatment, but also in the more covert form of "good old boy" networks that generally favor whites and frequently exclude Asian Americans and other Americans of color from being considered seriously for many employment positions. Whites thereby clone themselves from one managerial generation to the next and thus maintain their positions of power. Lin, a Chinese American, explains why Asian Americans are frustrated by the glass ceiling in work environments:

> We still [do not] see Asian ... provosts, vice presidents, or presidents, [or those] representing the executives, at the executive level, at the policymaking level. Yeah, we are good enough to be engineers, scientists, but we are not good enough to be policymakers.... I think that there are many, many reasons and I can talk about some of them. First of all, the environment was created, we are still foreign, because we look different, many of the Asian immigrants speak with an Asian accent [and] an Asian accent is not acceptable, but Italian and French accents, they're sexy, right? People want you to talk like the European accent; the English accent is supposed to be the blue blood, right?

Lin sees through the conventional façade of "equal opportunity" rhetoric. Americans of Asian descent are still viewed as unacceptable and foreign by many white decisionmakers, yet foreignness is not a barrier for those who are white and hail from prized European countries. Even with advanced degrees and significant educational achievements, Asian Americans face channeling by white executives into certain, often stereotyped, positions but rarely are promoted into higher-level management or corporate leadership positions.

Sometimes it is hard for an Asian American employee to retain a corporate position, even if overqualified. Another savvy respondent, Charlene, describes her father's experience: "I guess looking back, I can definitely see that my dad could have been definitely mistreated. He has so many advanced degrees, he has three master's, a Ph.D. in engineering, and he can never hold a job. He is always laid off, and I wonder, I wonder why, why that is?" Charlene might not have viewed her father's employment misfortunes as involving some discrimination if it had not been for her exposure to Asian American issues and racial discrimination issues in her college days. Attending workshops and taking courses about Asian Americans have opened her eyes to racial inequalities and the history of racial oppression. In her interview one sees the impact of her understanding, for she now takes a deep and critical look at her and her family's past, present, and future in the United States.

Another respondent was excited to talk to us when she heard about our research. In initial correspondence she stressed that she found the research important and that she had much to share. When the interview begins she readily discusses that she had suffered through much work discrimination in her life. Unfortunately, in dealing with specific workplace questions she is too frightened to share the *details* of her discriminatory experiences. All her statements are very general, such as, "I have experienced incredible discrimination in my profession and have been bypassed on many occasions for promotions because I was not seen as a viable candidate [or] as a leader. It did not matter that I may have been more productive than the colleague that was awarded the promotion." Her work evaluations by white supervisors often included "poor" performance ratings, but according to her nothing factual was ever cited. She is unwilling to share specific details because she fears for her job. Even though we assure her that her identity will be protected, she refuses to elaborate.

This poignant example is very revealing because it shows the tremendous psychological power of white racist actions inside and outside workplaces, as well as the impunity this society frequently reserves for white perpetrators of recurring discrimination. This woman was terrified that her employer would find out that she had talked with us, yet she was initially very eager originally to talk. Once again, we see how Asian Americans are often stuck in a racialized limbo—working extremely hard to achieve the American dream, yet enduring many racial obstacles whose impact is made worse by the fact that most have little social support for open confrontation with discriminatory whites.

Discrimination from Clients

In August of 2013, a fifty-two-year-old white woman entered a Chinese restaurant in Seattle, Washington's international district. Shortly after entering, she doused patrons with chocolate milk and soy sauce, began flipping plates and throwing food on customers while shouting, "Go back to China!" The woman even spat on an Asian American man in the restaurant and poured soy sauce on him and his baby.[30] These racially motivated actions happened in an international business district of a racially diverse city. Seattle has a large number of Asian Americans, yet even in known business enclaves racial minority business owners are not shielded from racialized hostility and violence from whites.

Many Asian Americans work for themselves, usually in small businesses. For example, Mei's parents opened a restaurant when they emigrated from Taiwan and mostly have dealt with white customers:

Sometimes a customer [thinks] ... they have a right to ask for anything without paying, you know? Otherwise, sometimes, a couple times they aren't customers, they [are] just talking to you in a public place, just doing [it] without asking you to do it. Or sometimes they cut your flowers [in parents' garden] without asking you! You already know it if you are Asian, if your parents have a business in the United States, you probably know those things. Asian people say, "Well don't say it, we'll be fine." You know, ... don't ask them to leave or just give [it to] them, and they will go.

Mei's parents have taught her that ignoring pushy or hostile whites and being nonconfrontational will produce a better outcome. Her parents have allowed customers and other strangers to do what they want, and have hoped that somehow they will "be fine." Being caught between wanting to trust whites and following your own intuition that many are not trustworthy generates a constant struggle for Americans of color, as numerous other research studies have also shown.[31]

Ahmed and Jasmin Suri, Pakistani Americans, own a small computer business. During their joint interview, Ahmed discusses how they have been harassed because of how whites perceive their racial identity:

It was still scary, like anybody can come to us. A car would pull up. These people are going to think something, and people can arrest you. That's scary also. Before, that was not happening. It was not like this. But, you know, it happened for a while [after] September 11. We were a business; we were dealing with business people making software. And if you don't make good software, say your software is not working, and [a customer] wrote an e-mail: "Oh, I'm going to tell the police you are terrorist, you are those people." I said, "Go ahead, do it. We are here legally. We are not here illegally. We came through proper channels. We are doing a business here. We are not stealing money here. So go ahead, go do it." That's what happened. That's people taking advantage of these things.

White customers, likely thinking in terms of an anti-immigrant frame, sometimes made very serious threats because they were dissatisfied with the Suris' product or services. The tragic events of September 11 are still periodically used by ignorant white perpetrators to justify discrimination against South Asian Americans such as the Suris. Yet, in the United States, killings by white mass murderers do not lead to society-wide stereotyping of whites. They are not perceived as people to be routinely feared as natural criminals or as highly threatening. As we have seen in several respondents' accounts, as well as in recurring media reports, over the years since the events of September 11, 2001, many individuals who look like the Suris have been stopped or detained by various U.S. police agencies. This is despite the fact that most of those detained are legal immigrants and hardworking U.S. workers and businesspeople.

Significantly, even after providing numerous accounts of the discrimination that they and their friends faced, the Suris still find it difficult in the interview to call out and specifically name these acts as racially discriminatory. The psychological costs of being a person of color in the United States have forced them to make certain emotional and other psychological adaptations just to survive.

Conclusion

Once again, the numerous accounts of white discriminators reveal the troubling reality regularly faced by Americans of Asian descent. Our data do not stand alone, for a few other researchers have reported schooling, workplace, and business discrimination. In Kibria's pioneering analysis of the experiences of second-generation Chinese and Korean Americans, her respondents sometimes described discrimination in schools and the job market. However, like most such researchers, Kibria rarely uses the word "white" to describe these active discriminators.[32] If we are to develop a full understanding of the everyday reality of Asian Americans, we need to examine well just who these discriminators are, how and where they discriminate, and what impact they have on the lives of their targets. The often substantial educational and workplace achievements of Asian Americans do not protect them from white discriminators, who are from many different age, gender, and class groups. Again we see that Asian Americans pay a heavy price in routine degradation just to secure elements of the American dream, including creating a safe environment for families.

From their earliest years of development, Asian Americans experience racist events targeting them as individuals, families, and communities. Our childhood accounts are similar to many others. Racist teasing and taunting are often reported in personal accounts and biographical statements by Asian Americans. For example, in a law journal article on Asian-Pacific American identity and political struggles, law professor Chris Iijima notes when his six-year-old son was first taunted with "Ching Chong Chinaman" at schools, "I was expecting it, but it threw me off-balance nevertheless. He said it hurt his feelings and asked me for answers. I, of course, had none. I thought about what the appropriate response was for a six-year-old whose new consciousness of racism had begun to alter his vision of himself and the world around him irrevocably and forever."[33] He continues with some reflection on why whites do this, and then adds yet another account of a young Japanese American friend of his son who was excluded by young white girls from a playgroup because her eyes were not blue. Clearly, even before school starts, Asian American parents usually realize that their children learn, in streets and stores and from television, that they are different and must endure racial mocking, ridicule, and worse. Our respondents sometimes excuse this omnipresent childhood teasing and taunting as a rite of passage for children as they go through lower grades of school. Yet, as they continued their own educations through high school and college, they usually faced yet more discrimination at the hands of whites, and thus felt ever more like racial outcasts.

Our data show clearly that U.S. workplaces do not provide protection from racial discrimination. Workplaces are *not* the bastions of merit and fair treatment that the standard U.S. ideology suggests, for our respondents report a great array of racialized barriers and mistreatment at their places of work. Whether an interviewee had a college degree or not, advancement to higher levels was usually out of reach. They may be stereotyped, mocked, or marginalized. One recent experimental research study discovered some of the factors that lie behind anti-Asian discrimination in job hiring and advancement. Using role-playing scenarios, the researchers assessed how white evaluators viewed comparable résumés for Asian American and white candidates for employment in terms of their competence and social skills. Judging the two sets of identical résumés (except for names), the white female evaluators discriminated in favor of the white candidates in hiring and promotions for positions that necessitated social skills. The researchers showed that stereotypes of Asians' not having social skills played an important role in these white evaluators' job discrimination.[34]

Moreover, as local businesspeople, Asian Americans frequently must endure not only racialized abuse from white customers but also discriminatory decisions by white business and political leaders. For example, studies of urban businesses in California by sociologist Leland Saito have demonstrated how Asian American business interests are often ignored as whites, although a minority of the local population, impose their own interests. In one city development near Los Angeles, as Saito notes, "Rather than reflecting the city's current and future position as a major node for Asian-themed businesses, the shopping center was remodeled to provide a place where whites could shop and 'feel at home.'" Saito and other scholars have demonstrated that business decisions about several urban development and historical preservation efforts in California cities have been dominated by white leaders, with anti-Asian framing in their public commentaries (e.g., "Chinese invasion" language). They have imposed their development ideas over those of local Asian and African American leaders and communities.[35]

In the next chapter, we discuss the many costs of discrimination for Asian Americans. Racist incidents add up, and unlike many African American communities where people are more likely to share the burden of this accumulation,

Asian American communities, and families therein, do not so readily and healthily cope with continuing and accumulating racist events. Many Asian Americans lack a substantial knowledge of the history of anti-Asian and other U.S. racism and of the methods of resistance used historically by Americans of color. Among Asian Americans, racial discrimination at the hands of whites is usually treated as a personal and internal matter. This individual battle with discrimination thus takes a heavy toll on them as they often erase memories, cut off emotions, and are pushed to their limits with great stress.

CHAPTER 4

THE MANY COSTS OF ANTI-ASIAN DISCRIMINATION

In March of 2013, a white University of Southern Indiana student, Sam Hendrickson, posted a video on YouTube entitled "Why I'd hate to be Asian (totally not racist)." Among the ten reasons why he would not want to be Asian are that "most Asians look alike," "if I was an Asian man, chances are I'd probably be with an Asian woman and guess what: I don't find Asian women attractive. Kill me," and that he would have "double chink eye" if he were high on marijuana. He goes on to say that Asian men "aren't good in the bedroom," because they have "small equipment." The video went viral and this student did not understand the backlash, insisting that his video was "just a joke." The racist stereotyping of Asian Americans, rooted in the white racial frame, is exemplified by the video.[1] These racist constructions of Asian American men and women are widespread and perpetuated in the media, but as we demonstrated in earlier chapters, our respondents face racial taunts and discrimination in their daily lives. This racial mistreatment takes a significant toll.

In a penetrating commentary on the impact of racial hostility and discrimination, one of our interview respondents, Charlene, insists that "being in white spaces is kind of like being connected to a low-voltage circuit. Every time somebody says, 'Oh, so what's it like being Asian?' It's like *eh, eh, eh!*" As she made these sounds, she jerked her arm back repeatedly like she was being shocked by electricity. Writing about black Americans, psychiatrists William Grier and Price Cobbs have suggested that the "reality of being alternately attacked, ignored, then singled out for some cruel and undeserved punishment must extract its toll. The penalty may be a premature aging and an early death in some black people. To be regarded always as subhuman is a stultifying experience."[2] Asian Americans, at least in part because of the constant intrusion of racial hostility and discrimination in their lives, are plagued with relatively high rates of depression and suicide, attention to which has so far been minimal among national public health policymakers. Indeed, relatively few Asian American leaders have yet attempted to press publicly for aggressive solutions to health problems linked to anti-Asian racism, the latter an omnipresent reality that few have dared even to speak about. Racial inequalities in health and illness patterns are not new but have persisted for many decades because racial hostility and discrimination have generally been systemic for Asian Americans and other Americans of color.[3]

Extended and accumulating exposure to everyday racism is always burdensome and harmful. The overt, covert, and subtle forms of white-generated discrimination that Asian Americans face in the everyday world take a toll whether the costs are realized immediately or later. Our respondents shared details of their physical, mental, and emotional turmoil. Some immediate physical costs were noted in Chapter 2, such as when respondents have been victims of assault. However, the long-term physical and psychological costs of stress and anxiety from everyday hostility and discrimination are frequently not immediately apparent.

In this chapter we examine the sociopsychological costs of white hostility and discrimination. As we show, some respondents report having gotten openly angry about racist events, or have worked collectively to respond, but such overt responses are relatively rare. Instead, our respondents mostly seem to manage discriminatory incidents internally and individually. This personal battle with hostility and discrimination often leads to feelings of isolation, sadness, disillusionment, or hopelessness. Serious consequences flow from such emotional reactions, frequently including drug and alcohol use, psychological or social withdrawal, and/or suppression of memories of racial hostility and discrimination. Seeking out professional assistance appears to be relatively rare for these respondents or their families. Moreover, when a few have tried to find significant help, they usually have not known where to turn or have been misunderstood or rejected by those whom they contacted.

We see here Asian Americans struggling with their externally imposed and self-constructed identities. They frequently note being caught between two worlds. At times, they feel much at home with their Asian heritage, background, and community, yet only rarely do they feel fully accepted in U.S. society. Some do report feeling fairly comfortable and accepted if they have thoroughly conformed to important white expectations and norms. Sometimes they feel like strangers in regard to both social worlds. Other researchers, such as Nazli Kibria in her research on second-generation Chinese and Korean Americans, have reported similar findings of people being caught "between two worlds," but these researchers tend to accent just the tensions between the Asian culture of immigrants and "American culture."[4] As our data demonstrate, the problem is more than one of tension between two cultures—because of the added pressure of anti-Asian hostility and discrimination pervading the culture and society of the United States. This sense of being caught between worlds is a common experience of people of color in societies with systems of oppression that target them.

Additionally, the anti-Asian hostility is expressed and carried out within U.S. systems of gender and sexuality. In the racist YouTube video we opened with, the white student targets a specific racial group, Asian Americans, but he also challenges Asian American masculinity by insisting that Asian American men are inadequate sexual partners and do not physically measure up to a constructed marker of manhood, penis size. He also evokes the idea that boundaries exist on which women Asian men have access to and the notion that white women are the ideal models of beauty by saying that, "If I was an Asian man, chances are I'd probably be with an Asian woman and guess what: I don't find Asian women attractive. Kill me." Racial oppression is being carried out through systems of gender and sexuality. This intersectional oppression affects how Asian American men and women construct their own identities as masculine and feminine, and as sexual beings. So, when Charlotte describes being Asian in the United States as like being shocked by electricity, she is accurately describing the personal toll involved in dealing with these white-imposed identities.

Responding to Everyday Racism

In this society, model minority imagery is omnipresent and dangerous, especially because it forces unrealistic and unobtainable expectations on Asian Americans. As noted previously, in the 1960s white social scientists and journalists began to use the stereotyped concept and phrase "model minority" to accent the substantial educational and other achievements of Japanese Americans. Japanese Americans had been on the West Coast for two generations when during World War II white authorities forced them into U.S. concentration camps because of their racial characteristics. After that war, educational and job achievement became a major survival response to continuing discrimination. Young parents thus decided and hoped to protect their children from future discrimination by having them become model and conforming students and citizens who would not question white-imposed folkways.

Accenting Achievements and the "Back Story"

In their important book *Black Rage,* psychiatrists Grier and Cobbs draw from the clinical records of patients to show that many psychological problems of African Americans are the result not only of present-day discrimination but also of the accumulating impact of years of past discrimination. As they note, "A few black people may hide their scars, [but] most harbor the wounds of yesterday."[5] One advantage that African Americans have over many other Americans of color is many generations of building up a collective knowledge of white racism and of the strategies that enable people to resist it. In contrast, at this point in time, the collective memory of resistance strategies among Asian Americans seems relatively weaker and generally less effective in providing significant protection.

Indeed, a major Asian American collective memory exists in regard to identity construction and encompasses the "model minority" imagery. Because this imagery is stereotypical and relentless, it is highly stress-provoking and does *not* assist Asian Americans in dealing directly and effectively with persistent racial discrimination. Such model imagery serves mainly as spoken and unspoken behavior guidelines for how Asian Americans are supposed to think and act so as to please, or not displease, white Americans. It also provides a stereotype-riddled script for white Americans to follow in imaging, and interacting with, Asian Americans.

A 2010 California study revealed that when Filipino American men confront racism, it boosts their self-esteem. Ninety-nine percent of these Bay Area participants had experienced a racist incident in the past year and when the men in the study dealt with racism in an "active way" by reporting incidents to authorities or challenging the perpetrators, there was a significant decrease in distress and increase in self-esteem. The women in the study did not see the same boost in self-esteem through confrontation and reporting, and their avoidance coping strategies lowered levels of self-esteem and increased distress.[6] This study provides some clues as to how some Asian Americans may benefit from more actively resisting racism, but that benefit varies by gender and other factors. Not surprisingly, the lack of individual and collective action by many Asian Americans is reinforced by the pervasive, white-established "model minority" myth.

The white accenting of the academic achievements of Asian Americans is relatively recent. As noted previously, it was generated substantially as a white tactic to argue against the necessity for nonviolent civil rights protests during the 1960s.[7] Thus, high-achieving Japanese Americans were racially framed in this one-dimensional way by whites as proof that non-Europeans could succeed in U.S. society and that there were no longer serious racial barriers. However, most social science and popular analysts, from the 1960s to the present, have missed the major point here: the strong academic orientations and accomplishments of Japanese Americans during the 1950s and 1960s were often an intentional reaction to the *extreme* racial oppression they had recently suffered at the hands of many whites.[8] Moreover, other Asians who have immigrated to the United States since the 1960s have picked up on the centrality and importance of the model minority imagery, especially in the minds of those whites who control major aspects of their lives. As a result, they too have usually come to feel, and adapt to, intense white pressures to conform to white folkways and images of "successful" Asianness.

Throughout their interviews our respondents reveal the great internal and external pressures associated with conformity to the model minority expectations and to related expectations in usually white-normed institutions. The internal forces include the specific roles that Asian Americans are expected to fill. Asian Americans growing up with these expectations usually work, at least in part, to fit the mold. For example, Asian American students struggle with not meeting these high expectations; they somehow feel inadequate if they are not outperforming most other students. Asians and non-Asians alike buy into this model framing and perpetuate racialized stereotypes, thereby creating external pressures. Family, friends, teachers, and strangers are named by respondents as those who expect the latter to think, act, and become a model minority person. Researchers have shown that such a strong stereotype will often influence a person to try to meet the expectation, whether that expectation is positive or negative.[9] All respondents noted at some point how the "model" stereotypes have affected their daily lives.

Recall that filmmaker Janice Tanaka has shown in her documentary work that the Nisei generation of Japanese Americans was seriously affected by discriminatory internment during World War II. They suffered much economic loss and serious psychological damage, which led over time to problems with depression, substance abuse, and related health issues. The children of interned Nisei, the Sansei, were also greatly affected. Nisei parents mostly dealt internally with the traumatic experience of internment and its negative consequences, and they usually did not discuss much of this with their children. Instead, they pressured their children to be perfect and conforming students, employees, and citizens to prevent future oppression by whites. Our respondents' experiences and commentaries on racism-related matters are often similar to those reported by Tanaka's respondents.

For example, Alice grew up as a Japanese American during and after World War II. She made a film about her family history, which began as a class project that exposed the suicide, substance abuse, and psychological damage resulting from internment during World War II. Like Tanaka, Alice discovered that not only were interned Nisei affected, but their children, the Sansei, were as well. Alice explains,

> I really was aware of this drug problem that was happening with all of these suicides, with all of these drugs that came out, and I happened to go to school with this [Japanese American] girl that became really well known for sending out a lot of messages that she's going to commit suicide. Because she tried like four or five times, and nobody paid attention to her. And then all of a sudden she became successful at it. So, that's what started the thought about, we talk about internment in terms of what it did to the Issei and Nisei. But what did that particular incident in history do as a legacy for generations? You know, you study psychology in college, and the way the Nisei operated after the war had a huge impact on how we operated in the world. Meaning okay, we were interned because we lacked the education, or there was something wrong with us. So we are going to make sure that our next generation has a perfect world that they go into. So expectations were really high. It was really high and it was really hard for Japanese Americans to live up to the standards.

Like other Japanese Americans, Alice accents the protective strategy that the Nisei regularly used. Academic achievement was a shield protecting the next generation from mistreatment, but her research found that the social pressures were great. The use of drugs and suicide were tragic mechanisms some used to deal with the painful impact of persisting white oppression.

Such responses are not new for Asian Americans. Much earlier, from the mid-1800s to the early 1900s, some Chinese American workers became very depressed, turned to drugs, or committed suicide because of extreme discrimination and poor living conditions in California, where they had been brought in as contract workers to do hard labor for white employers.[10] Today, Chinese Americans still face much racial stereotyping and discrimination. Many white and other non–Asian Americans have extended the model minority image to anyone with an Asian face. Thereby, outside forces create substantial internalized pressures.

Charlene's family, which is Taiwanese American, has put great pressure on her to succeed. Charlene's parents have pushed her and her siblings hard to excel academically, with the hope that they will be able to secure the proverbial American dream:

> When my brother was five, there was this child psychologist that came to school and gave everyone an IQ test. And they discovered that my five-year-old brother was this genius, and then my mother was like, "Oh my

gosh, I must train him in math and science." From that, it just opened up the doors to evils. And when my brother was in seventh grade, he was allowed to take the SAT.... So, I was in fourth grade at that time, and my mom was just like, "Well, you'll be [in] seventh grade in three years, you might as well study." And so, I was in fourth grade studying for the SATs until I was in seventh grade. They really pushed me, I remember being in my talented and gifted spelling class, and they allowed us to pick our own words to spell just so that we could challenge ourselves, so I would always pick really hard words. There is this one word, it was "fortuitous," this was in fourth grade. I couldn't spell it for four weeks straight, among other spelling mishaps that were happening in the class, so I got a B.... I remember walking home and I was so scared. I was crying the whole way. [Her parents] said that, "If you can't perform, then there's no reason we should send you to school. You might as well work." That day, I didn't get a gold star in my notebook that you sign off [on] every day.

The pressure for Charlene to excel was extreme even at this young age. Her family viewed her performance as affecting the whole family, and even the thought of disappointing them was very painful. In his career her father, as we discussed previously, has faced job discrimination even though he is often more talented and educated than white coworkers who are better treated. Nonetheless, he has pressed his children to excel in the hope that somehow they will be treated better than he has been.

Achievement Orientation: Adaptation to Racism or Asian Cultures?

In explaining this type of situation, scholarly and media commentators have frequently made the argument that Asian cultures are mainly responsible for these pressures to excel, because they supposedly value education more so than U.S. culture does.

There are numerous problems with this argument. First, it groups all Asian national cultures together. Yet these cultures vary significantly. Some of our respondents note that they come from agrarian Asian cultures where children are rarely pushed to excel in higher levels of education. Indeed, excelling academically in the United States has often alienated them from their agrarian family and cultural backgrounds. Second, assuming that people of Asian descent are culturally inclined to value education tends to be linked by whites to the argument that certain other racial or ethnic groups are culturally devoid of such a value. This argument is frequently used by commentators in assessing the educational attainment of African Americans, which is often less, on average, than that of white or certain Asian American groups. This lesser attainment is then attributed to a cultural deficiency, such as an alleged lack of respect for education, even though numerous surveys and research studies have shown that African American adults generally place a high priority on education for themselves and their children.[11]

Major structural and historical factors shaping family and individual resources must be taken into account. Young Asian Americans like Charlene have educated parents who immigrated since the late 1960s under U.S. laws that replaced earlier anti-Asian laws. The current laws strongly favor the admission of educated and middle- or upper-class immigrants. Thus, many East and South Asian immigrants are middle class and relatively well educated. Unlike early African immigrants, the ancestors of today's African Americans, these Asian immigrants have moved to the United States voluntarily and with some socioeconomic resources, and they have also benefited immediately from the ending of legal segregation and increased civil rights protections that took place in the 1960s not long before they arrived. Many Asian Americans who emigrated since the 1960s have averaged more in economic or educational capital than do average African Americans whose earliest ancestors came as enslaved immigrants many generations earlier—and who themselves, or their parents and grandparents, have only since the late 1960s come out from under the extreme oppression of state-enforced racial (Jim Crow) segregation. Given that social science research shows that the best predictor of a child's educational attainment is the educational and socioeconomic level of his or her parents, it is not surprising that the children of these better-educated and middle-class immigrant parents have often done better educationally than the children of working-class African Americans (and other Americans of color) just coming out from under many generations of extreme racial oppression in the United States.[12]

A third weakness of the typical "Asian culture" argument is that it ignores the very substantial and continuing negative impacts that white hostility and discrimination have had on Asian Americans. As we show in this and earlier chapters, accentuated educational achievement is substantially a protective and survival strategy against anti-Asian discrimination. Charlene notes yet more of the pressure on her as a young child:

> I put sticky tack in a boy's hair, and I was like, "Oh my gosh, the teacher knows, she didn't give me a gold star. I am *so* dead." They put the folders in our backpacks, and I was like, in the mind of a fourth grade child I was like, "OK, if I don't have a gold star I am gonna jump off of our balcony." I really, really thought this through [she laughs] in the fourth grade because I just couldn't go through the pain of being yelled at. I opened up the folder, and I guess my teacher, she had forgotten about the sticky tack incident!

At the age of eight years, Charlene was already considering suicide and making plans on how to execute it. She remembers that vividly to this day. This is a telling example of the psychological impact of trying to live up to the aspects of the model minority stereotype.

In his detailed interview, Frank shares information about a similar experience with competition in his Korean American community:

> Where I live, because the competition is so intense, I live about 4 blocks from a high school, which is one of the top-rated high schools in [western state]. Every year, there is one Oriental kid that kills themselves. They hang themselves on the street or kill themselves in the house. Or something. If you consider the background—I found it out on the news—they got straight As from junior high school all the way, they somehow got one B, and they could not take it, so they kill themselves.

This periodic occurrence of youth suicide is common knowledge in Frank's family and community, yet this information remains mostly hidden to outsiders. High educational expectations or performances, which are supposed to act as a protective buffer from suffering, create such great anxiety that some Asian Americans have mental breakdowns, which may in turn lead to destructive actions against themselves, their families, or strangers. Recall our Chapter 1 accounts of R. W. and Cho Seung-Hui, both of whom faced such excessively high educational expectations.

Many Asian Americans believe that education serves as a great equalizer in their competition with white Americans. John, a Chinese American computer scientist, has this to say about academic achievement:

> Academia is important because, if they don't like you because of the color of your skin, you're never going to have the social networks. At some level there are some people who are never going to like you. But, in academia, right, okay, I get a 100 on this test, you get a 95, I mean the rules are clear. In order to achieve in academia, or in order to get good grades, you study these things. You pass the test. Once you pass the test, then good stuff [happens]—people say nice things about you. And the fact [is] that in order to advance that way, there are clear rules. They're fairly objective, there's very little room—okay you spell this right, you spell this wrong. There is not very much argument.

John accents a meritocratic rationale in arguing why it is so important for Asian Americans like him to do well in higher education. In John's and many other

Asian Americans' eyes, academic excellence helps to improve, if not level, the playing field. Admitting that he appears to be a model minority, John hopes to overcome discrimination with achievement, while conceding that even with such achievement whites will still discriminate and "are never going to like you." He asserts, thus, that in college settings skin color is a characteristic used to exclude or include people by those in control of the most important social networks, who are usually white. He realizes what our respondents demonstrate through these chapters: there is, in fact, *no* protection from racial hostility and discrimination regardless of one's record of achievement.

John readily admits that the work he puts into achievement and his fear of losing it in an unsupportive environment generate substantial stress. In fact, he uses the word *stress* fourteen times in his one-and-a-half-hour interview. He explains his anxiety thus:

> You can lose everything. I don't want [to] lose everything. What can I do? And that's an incredible amount of stress. And you lose hope sometimes. You see, I think that is part of the thing about America, the model of minority myth.... I would say there's a cost of opportunity for the most part.... I think I haven't done too badly. But people see just that people [are] going to Harvard, MIT, but there is a huge back story behind that. It's a unique back story. If you don't understand the back story, you don't understand that the amount of [stress], you don't understand how *stressed* out I am usually.

The Asian American story is constantly one of a hidden "back story" that almost never gets into the mainstream media or mainstream scholarship. In his interview John conveys a continual state of worry and fear that he could lose everything because he is a "foreigner," even though he was born in the United States. He feels on the defensive and that he must work much harder than whites to get fair treatment. When he comments that there is a unique back story to tell about his reaching and holding his level of success, he is quite serious. His family was celebrated in his community for educational achievements, and there was much shame to endure when his sister failed in her attempts to follow in his footsteps at an Ivy League school and then was institutionalized for mental illness likely related to her "failure."

Family Pressures to Succeed

In numerous interview accounts of these intense pressures to achieve, we see the central role of parents, most of whom are trying to protect their children from direct or indirect discrimination in a racist society. For example, Indira notes the immense pressure that Asian Americans often face as they try to succeed in higher education:

> Understand that we aren't coming to schools as [just seeking] "you and your success." Yes, that's a part of it. But what [more] you carry, like for me … the day that I left for college, my mother said to me, "I know that I will be able to die in peace, my daughter is going to become a doctor now." Can you imagine every time I tried to tell my mother that I didn't want to be a doctor, those were the words that haunted me. My mother will not be able to die. My mother will die because I am a failure. When she dies, she will carry that, that disappointment with her, to her grave. That is *huge,* you know.

Notice again that pressure to succeed in a rather proscribed and stereotyped way is often heavy, and typically comes from loved ones. Alex, a Korean American, sheds more light on these intense family pressures on Asian American youth: "I think that families, the older members of the families, that's what they preach when they are growing up, 'Do well in school so you let our family be proud. And then, don't, whatever you do, don't bring shame to our family regardless of your happiness.' That's what they're preaching, 'Don't bring shame to our family, regardless of your happiness.'" For many Asian Americans, he suggests in his interview, a family feels shamed if a young person fails to conform to aspects of the model stereotype, which serves in the Asian American collective memory as an important guide as to what it is to be successful in society. This socially constructed idea of "Asian American success" increases pressures on them.

Why do so many hopes and dreams seem to be riding on the successes of younger generations? As we have already seen, one answer lies in the overt and subtle racial barriers routinely placed by whites in the way of their parents. To take just one example from our interviews, Min, a first-generation Taiwanese American, discusses why she has pushed her own children so hard to achieve in school:

> It's hard to separate from the old world, and that's why I push, push my children so hard. I want my children to be better than me, to do better than I did. My life here, it wasn't supposed to be like this. I wasn't supposed to come here and work so hard for this long. My husband came to get his Ph.D., not have a restaurant. I worked; I worked in that hot kitchen three days before [my daughter] was born and had to go back, had to work three days after. I was still bleeding! [She cries.] I am a failure here. I have

a bachelor's degree in math, I was a teacher before I came here, now, now
I am nothing. I did the best I could, but it wasn't supposed to be like this.

Min hopes for her children to be educationally and materially successful because
she and her husband were unsuccessful in their bid to achieve their American
dream. Her husband struggled with graduate school for some years but, like
many Asian Americans in his generation, did not finish his dissertation substantially because his English was not adequate. His Anglocentric university
likely did not provide the necessary support to deal with his language and other
adaptive problems, as is often the case for Asian immigrant students. Whites at
colleges and universities often stereotype Asian international students as speaking English with accents that make understanding them too difficult; and, thus,
those in authority may force some to drop classes, or revise or abandon their
educational programs, when this is unnecessary. (We should recall here that *all*
English speakers speak with significant accents, but only some of these accents
are considered problematical by those, usually whites, in authority.)

Instead of a prestigious career as a professor, Min's husband ran a modest
restaurant. Now they are of retirement age with no end of work in sight. A college
graduate, she sees herself as a "failure" and wants much more for her children.
Clearly, in such families second- and third-generation Asian Americans have the
great hopes of their parents and grandparents riding heavily on their shoulders,
and this strong reality adds substantially to the stress that they already feel as
Asian Americans caught in the white-generated model minority straightjacket.

Suppressing Memories of Racism

In their work with African American patients who lived under state-imposed Jim
Crow segregation, psychiatrists Grier and Cobbs found that some denied any
influence of that oppression on their very troubled lives. These black patients had a
"determination not to see. They may insist that white oppression has never exerted
any influence on their lives, even in the face of such realities as police brutality,
job and housing discrimination, and a denial of educational opportunities."[13]
We found a similar lack of memory of, or denial of, discrimination among our
respondents. As we noted previously, most initially said they did not remember
any discrimination, yet recanted this view as they proceeded.

Several African, Asian, and European scholars have developed a body of
"post-colonial" thought that critically assesses issues of racial remembrance and
suppression for victims of white oppression. Analysts such as Homi Bhabha and
Leela Gandhi have accented the great importance of remembering the racialized

past, for individuals and communities, even though such remembering is often very painful. As Gandhi has noted, "While some memories are accessible to consciousness, others, which are blocked and banned ... perambulate the unconscious in dangerous ways, causing seemingly inexplicable symptoms in everyday life."[14] Releasing the repressed past can often be therapeutic for individuals and their communities.

Many Asian Americans continue to cope with contemporary racist events by suppressing, repressing, or erasing memories. Michel, a Chinese American from a city with a large Asian population, is matter-of-fact about how he and his family have blocked out memories of racism. This is one interview exchange after he recounts that "whenever we're outside, and my parents don't understand something, [other people will] make fun of them":

> INTERVIEWER: So in those cases, when someone would make fun of them, what was the reaction after that?
> MICHEL: Mostly, we just ignore it.
> INTERVIEWER: You personally, did you ever experience anything?
> MICHEL: If I did, I ignored it too.
> INTERVIEWER: So you don't remember anything in particular?
> MICHEL: Not exactly. I tend to, like, *wipe* things like that.

In this revealing passage Michel is noticeably uncomfortable discussing personal matters such as the racial mistreatment he faced, and throughout his interview he seems to be trying to provide "correct" answers rather than his own understandings and feelings. When asked a question about events in his life, he usually responds, "I don't know, what do you think?"

Moreover, at first, Michel talks positively about his experiences growing up in the United States, insisting he has not faced racial mistreatment. However, he later admits that he has *only* Asian friends because he feels more comfortable with them. He periodically refers to social situations as if he were not "American," as in this statement about his high-tech workplace: "With the growing emphasis from China—the jobs, the market, the way we're heading, the key—like I was talking to our VP the other day, and they said one of the most important languages in our time will be Mandarin ... and with a lot of these jobs moving over there, or the growing power of China, maybe the American view of the Chinese [is] different. Maybe they are worried about *us* taking *their* jobs."

Michel uses the pronoun "us" in aligning himself with the Chinese when he discusses his worries about the future of his career. Although he never specifically articulates a sense of being a foreigner, such statements seem to indicate whom he often identifies with. As he puts it in his interview, he has "wiped" away memories of discrimination that likely influence his decision to identify himself as something other than American.

Another respondent, John, has also learned to block out certain painful memories of racism. As part of the first Chinese family in his hometown, he and his folks have faced considerable social isolation. He was the first person of Asian heritage to attend the local public schools. His memory is a little fuzzy regarding discrimination there because he has intentionally attempted to forget, as he reports in his interview:

> My mother always talked about the fact that they found out the milkman charged us more. I don't know, because I was so young, I can't identify specifically, but there was a sense, oh, there were specific things. I mean, people making fun of us being Chinese. It's actually a *painful* memory, but we just probably *suppressed* it, people making fun of the fact that we were Chinese and telling us to go back to China.... And that was part of the *survival strategy.*

Note the strong and revealing words "painful" and "survival" that are used in rethinking the strategy John and his family have used to deal with discrimination. Throughout the interview, he talks fast, but when asked about childhood events he slows down considerably. At one point, he closes and squints his eyes, places his head in his hands, lifts his head, and shakes it as though trying to shake away the painful memories.

In contrast, John remembers the exact date that another Chinese family moved into his city. Their arrival was a relief to John, thus his clear memory. He explains,

> And I think that goes with the fear that you are five in a group of 50,000. What you need to do is make sure you are not five vs. 50,000, you're in some group, some subgroup that you're seen, that you can *survive* [in]. And for me it feels like a life-or-death issue. If I'm seen as nobody or just neither part of the community, then that feels like I'm just *finished.* And so a lot of how I handle things is to make sure I never get into the situation where I'm the only one against everybody else.

In John's adult life, he expends great energy to protect himself. His words indicate the seriousness of his fear that if he is alone, he might well be harmed or even killed, perhaps by a white group. In his interview, after some careful reflection, he references how difficult it was growing up and feeling out of place and says that when he looks back at his childhood, he uses "filters" to look at the past. When asked to explain what he means by "filters," he gives a vague response that "so anything I say may have absolutely no relation to what actually happened, so I'm absolutely uncertain what happened then." Somewhat baffled by this response, we ask him again to explain. He answers thus:

> Well, first the idea of the minority, right. That one of the things that was, I felt growing up, . . . that we were different. . . . But one of the things that later sort of deconstructed the idea of minority was, is that how come I thought of myself—we did think of ourselves as separate and minorities, just different, right? . . . One thing that really was a part of my life and still is, is the idea that you can't be ordinary. You can't just blend into the crowd because the crowd will always consider you different. The other thing is that—and this was certainly drilled into me—and it was actually a source of *exclusivity*—if you fail, all right, there's no safety net. You have to achieve well because if you don't sort of stay with yourself, then there is no family around, and so at some level there was a fortress mentality—that there was us and them.

Although he never clarifies his "filtering" idea in regard to memories, John does make it clear how difficult it is for him to look back on a past of painful ostracism and other racism. Older, perhaps shared, interpretations present painful understandings of a racist environment—which we see in terms like *exclusivity, the minority, being different,* and *us versus them.* Here is a person who feels he is an outsider in a dynamic of people of color versus whites. One cost of the white discrimination that John has experienced is his realization that he and others like him have had to develop a "fortress mentality" to make it through each day of their lives in the United States.

Moving on, John shares a lesson from his mother that has left an impression on him to the present day:

> I remember when somebody was complaining against mixed-race dating, and they were talking black and white . . . and I heard people say just awful, awful things about African Americans. And I think this is one of the good things that my mother, I think she actually mentioned once. We were talking about women in the neighborhood. Somebody that we knew said . . . how lazy, blah, blah, blah and how uppity they were, how they liked to make waves and just make trouble. And I think my mother at some level said, "You know, all those things that they are saying about African Americans, once your back is turned, they will say that about you." So, I mean that was one thing that really *depressed* me.

John's mother was able to view the stereotyped comments for what they were and to identify the likely racism that her neighbor would direct privately at Asian Americans like them. Indeed, research has shown that whites often do engage in much racist stereotyping and extensive racialized commentary about various groups of color, especially in backstage settings where only whites are present.[15]

John's mother passed on a rare lesson about white stereotyping, but it was a hard pill for John to swallow. Psychiatrists Grier and Cobbs long ago noted that the African American mother "has a more ominous message for her child and feels more urgently the need to get the message across. The child must know that the white world is dangerous and that if he does not understand its rules it may kill him."[16] Recall our point made earlier that a substantial collective memory of oppression often assists African Americans in promoting group survival. This helps parents in passing on lessons to children about how to interpret and resist white racism. However, in our Asian American sample John is the only respondent to report a specific parental lesson about the dangers of white racism.[17] An increase in the teaching of such lessons about white racist actions might well save Asian Americans much pain and stress, as well as, in the case of hate crimes like the murder of Vincent Chin and others we have previously discussed, perhaps their lives. Like numerous others, John now lives with his guard kept up in preparation for racist events. His interview reveals a great deal about how struggles that may appear as though they are created just by "Asian culture" are in fact substantially about "survival strategies" in this still-racist society.

Shutting Down Emotionally

In addition to blocking out memories, some respondents reported a related emotional shutdown in dealing with everyday racism. In a previous chapter we discussed how Charlotte would come home crying from school because of discrimination there. Finally, she reports, she shut herself down emotionally:

> In fifth grade, my mother and my teacher told me that I just needed to keep a stiff upper lip, and I really couldn't go home every day in tears. And I couldn't just cry all the time because it just didn't work. So I stopped crying.... Um, that unfortunately, psychologically, probably damaged me until I was much older, until I was probably an adult, but I didn't know that. And it was probably a survival technique that I probably really did need to have at that time, I'm just not sure that that was the best way of handling it. In order for me to stop crying every day, I just cut off all of my emotions. And so as a result, I had a very difficult time relating to the fact that I had any emotions, and that that was not a very healthy way of surviving, either.

Charlotte describes her youthful solution to episodes of discrimination as cutting herself off from certain emotions. In turn, such painful actions, likely common-place among targeted children of color, fuel the stereotype that they are cold and emotionless. Yet, in actuality these reactions are just part of a necessary survival strategy. Quietly, almost nonchalantly, she states that she probably damaged herself psychologically for the longer term.

Rejecting the model stereotype and resisting the wishes of her parents, Charlotte put less effort into schoolwork. In her further nuanced account she discusses that decision:

> I tried my very hardest to flunk out of school. That's my rebellion, to try not to be Asian.... I was insistent that I was dumber than a box and that I was going to make sure that everyone else knew that I was dumber than a box by flunking out or by barely succeeding, and I did that well. But that's how I kept the pressure off of me with the grades. On the other hand, when I turn around and look at a lot of friends—and I've got to have the highest percentage [of] friends who are all doctors and attorneys who are all Asian and all did extremely well in their class no matter what—and the amount of pressure that's put on there. And does that mean there's any joy or happiness in their lives? I really don't know. And now that we're all adults, nobody seems any more happy or satisfied with their lives. With the paths of their lives, they're all still struggling to find themselves.

To be a successful Asian American is to perform well academically—this view demonstrates how central the model stereotype is to Charlotte's idea of Asian identity. Her rejection of this image for herself involved purposefully doing poorly. Numerous respondents seem to believe that if they and their children conform to the model minority stereotype they will be happy and successful. However, Charlotte describes apparently successful friends who have worked hard to fit the stereotype yet are still struggling to find joy or happiness. The restrictions of the model minority straightjacket do not allow free choices in life, including the choice of a satisfying self-identity.

For numerous respondents, memories of racial events were painful to recall, or even missing, because they chose to suppress them. Either way, the events likely have had a serious and long-lasting impact. Those who recall past incidents carry the weight of being an outsider, a "racial other," a target of white racism. Those who have chosen to forget must deal with the consequences of suppressing important memories on their long-term emotional and psychological well-being. Those who choose to deal with discrimination more overtly and openly frequently must do so without the help of friends, family, or community.

The Absence of Help

Many Asian Americans attempt to achieve academic and economic success whatever the personal and psychological cost. Yet, when they need psychological help for accumulating stress and pain, they frequently have a difficult time obtaining the necessary services. Indira, an Asian Indian professor, describes an incident with one of her Asian American students: "I had a student who was trying to seek phone counseling, she was struggling with the pressure, you know she's like sixteen years old and an undergrad, so she's really [the age of] a junior in high school but is a junior in college.... A [counselor] on the phone started asking, 'How'd you manage that [getting in college]?' She's called to say that she's suicidal, and this person is asking her, 'How'd that happen?'" This stress and anxiety over educational performance can be overwhelming, and white and other counselors who do not understand such intense pressure may fail, often significantly, to help a young Asian American in dire need.

Indira worked closely with school administrators to hire an Asian American counselor at the student health center, but to no avail. As of the interview, the university still had not hired an Asian American counselor, but Indira was holding training sessions for members of her academic community. She continues with this assessment of that effort:

> To me it's shocking. I did a training [of] college of liberal arts faculty because 20 percent of the incoming class was to be Asian. How do you deal with a student who has this mental breakdown in front of you, and they are suicidal because they want to change majors from chemistry to English? And you are looking at them like it's gonna be OK. I am not a counselor, but I believe this. Any time someone tells you that they are suicidal, you believe them, number one. Number two, just because you don't understand the pressure doesn't mean that it doesn't exist. Just because it's as simple as a [college] major thing for you, doesn't mean that's what it is to them.

Judging from commentaries of several respondents, few administrators or policymakers in these institutions of higher education seem to care enough about the serious psychological problems often faced by these students of color to take significant action to deal with them.

This neglect of Asian and Asian American health problems extends well beyond higher education. Those seeking help from public servants often face callous disregard. Recall the case of Ethan, a high-achieving student targeted by an overt act of racist violence. This event dramatically changed his life. Ethan got no assistance from the local police or the district attorney's office in dealing with the vicious attack. After unsuccessful attempts to get the attacker punished by the "justice" system, he chose to deal with the trauma privately, leaning only on his parents:

> Part of it, as a victim, is finding a balance between seeking justice versus the amount of exposure that you want. It's difficult to say you've been a victim of a hate crime, but I didn't feel comfortable going public. I talked about it with my family. I could have gone to the papers or the television stations, but I wanted to move on with my life. I was still in school and I wanted to move past it; I didn't want it to hold me back in any ways. . . . It would be a distraction. I want to be Ethan, not Ethan the victim of a hate crime. You are perceived differently when something like this happens, and I didn't want to be treated any differently. I was not seeking sympathy. I think it might be that way because of my race. Particularly, my parents were not as willing and did not want me to pursue talking with the D.A. They wanted me to move on from this.

Ethan's account indicates yet another Asian American dealing with discrimination mostly by himself, in this case with a little support from parents. Like the Japanese American internees during and after World War II, Ethan's parents seemed fearful and wanted him to move on and forget about the violent attack.

Until the white violence, Ethan reports, he had not really thought much about being Asian American. Now that reality is at the front of his mind. Physically he is healing, but serious psychological and related problems persist: "Not a day goes by that I don't have to make sure that my tooth is still in. It's a constant reminder every day about what happened to me. Not a day goes by that I don't think about it. It was senseless, stupid, and unprovoked, and he [the assailant] is still out there." Ethan is forced to think daily about the incident and its implications, including the fact that his assailant remains unpunished. Ethan has experienced a paradigm shift in how he views and operates in his community and in society generally:

> I am more cautious now when I am out at night. I am much more vigilant, and I am always looking at the environment. . . . I am lucky that this was not more serious. I am definitely more aware, watching and avoiding situations. . . . Also, I am definitely more aware of race. I now know that discrimination is more prevalent than I noticed before. I didn't assume it happened, but now I do. My mind-set has swung the other way. I realize now that racism is a lot more prevalent than most people think, and I am more aware of that. Sometimes I worry that I see things when they are not

there, thinking it has to do with race. I never thought that way before. I always thought those kind of things would never happen to me, at least not to an Asian American.

Reportedly, over his first two decades, Ethan had not paid much attention to racial issues and believed that he was fully accepted by whites in a just society. He apparently thought being Asian American would protect him from difficulties experienced by other people of color. Yet, in an instant he found out that he has no control over the racial order. Now he carefully assesses interactions with others, especially whites, and wonders if he is being treated differently because of his Asian ancestry.

Asian Americans frequently deal with whites' discrimination internally and privately rather than collectively and organizationally. Many Asians immigrated to the United States after the 1960s civil rights movement and have not yet learned the necessary strategies of resistance, especially to subtle and covert forms of discrimination. Often lacking a collective memory of resistance strategies, a great many have not developed the strong community and organizational responses that they really need to contend with contemporary racism.

Gendered Racism: Body Image and Self-Esteem

Long-term discrimination has had serious consequences on the self-images and self-esteem of Americans of color, including women, men, and children of Asian ancestry. Social science research shows that women of color in particular face the double burden of racism and sexism, as well as blended combinations of the two. In research on black women, Grier and Cobbs found that they "have a nearly bottomless well of self-depreciation into which they can drop when depressed. The well is prepared by society and stands waiting, a prefabricated pit which they have had no hand in fashioning."[18]

While both the men and women we interviewed are affected by racist stereotyping, there is a complicated manner in which racial oppression operates through systems of gender and sexuality. It has been well documented, for example, in *Asian American Sexual Politics*, that both Asian American men and women face a gendered and sexualized racism that shapes their daily lives. However, it is difficult to tease out the controlling racist images from the dominant social constructions of masculinity and femininity. We assert and show here that systemic racism persists through gender stereotypes of what it means to be an Asian man or woman. Asian American women are exoticized and fetishized as sexual objects like other women of color, while Asian American men are emasculated and often ridiculed as the "bottom feeders" of the U.S. masculine hierarchy.[19] In its everday operation, the white racial frame is not just a stand-alone racialized frame, for gender stereotypes are regularly racialized in a particular manner to maintain white supremacy. Historically, through "Orientalism" and colonialism, whites have assigned negative values to bodies of people of color.[20] Today, this gendered racism is often more subtle in the mainstream media, but our respondents pick up on these intersecting messages about their race, gender, and sexuality in these media and many other sectors of society as well.

Some of our female respondents are very clear in describing how the dominant physical image for women has affected them. Fareena, a Bangladeshi American, recalls a painful time in her youth: "I had the lowest self-esteem issues ... and so did my brother. I remember *hating* myself. I remember *hating* my features ... and I remember being really excited the one day they had multicultural day [at school], and I got to dress up. But everyone else was dressing up in things that weren't even part of their ethnic identity, so ... I still didn't feel recognized then."

In contrast, when Fareena describes growing up in Bangladesh before her family emigrated, she reports no problem with self-esteem. The timing of her self-hatred coincided with her move to an all-white school in the United States. She is not alone in this, for her brother also has felt the pain of being in a hostile all-white environment. Fareena continues,

I remember I hated myself in the sixth grade. Hated myself. And that was the time I went to [an] all-white, all very rich white [school]. I remember that the type of girls that all the boys started liking didn't look like me, you know, being a brown woman. Issues of body hair came into play. I have body hair that other girls don't have. I have to pluck my eyebrows, and other girls don't have to. It looks dirty on me. And there is this concept of dirt. I had real issues of just wanting to purge, physically purge things out of me. You know, my elbows are darker, my knees are darker, when I scar I leave a brown mark instead of a pink mark that fades. And all that is looked at as dirty or ugly or scarred, and not simply like a part of life. So, I felt very dirty. And I was also curvier than the other girls at the time. I started puberty in the fourth grade. By sixth grade I didn't look a lot different from this [she points at her figure]. And I felt fat. All the other girls were skinny. I felt I didn't have muscles the way the other girls did. I was really into sports at the time. And I felt puny and couldn't athletically compete like them. And there is an attraction with athletic girls. You know, the girl's basketball team or track team. There'd be this camaraderie ... with the boys' basketball team because we had to travel together and do things like that. There are a lot of hookups. No one wanted to hook up with the lone brown girl. And at that time I was really searching for some type of acceptance somewhere.

In the United States the white-controlled media and other sources accent a racialized standard of female beauty, one that is typically blond, white-skinned, and relatively thin.[21] Women of color obviously cannot fit much of this image, yet it is pressed on them from many social sources, as in this school situation. Fareena's troubled self-concept encompassed concerns with "fatness" and "puniness" at the same time. Her early sexual development differentiated her from her white peers, as did her color, hair, and muscle mass. White students clearly perceived these differences as negative.

Jessica, a second-generation Vietnamese American, had a similar difficulty with being a young woman who does not meet the conventional white standard of beauty, as she makes clear:

> You know what people think is beautiful, and you don't know how to be that. I didn't know how to put on eye shadow right, because they only teach you how to put on eye shadow if you only have a certain shape of eye in a magazine. And if you don't have that eye, how do you put on eye shadow? And you try to look for models in the magazine that have your eyes so you can do it like them, and none of them have your eye. It was like, great! And none of the makeup looks right on your skin, and so it's nothing that one student does. It's that you know how different you are from them, and it's hard to reconcile it.... I guess, like, for a long time I didn't see myself as a person of color, because I didn't know what it meant to be a person of color. I knew that I wasn't white. I knew that it would be nice to be white, it's so much simpler.

Jessica's poignant and probing comments reveal awareness of the ways that numerous privileges are routinely awarded to whites that people of color do not receive. White privilege leaves people of color wishing they were white so that they would not have to deal with the stigma and pain of being racially othered by many societal sources. Later in the book we will examine some of the great efforts that some Asian American women have taken to make themselves look whiter and more attractive in terms of this dominant image of beauty, actions that even include major operations by plastic surgeons.

Grappling with National and Racial Identities

Internalizing Racial Identities

From the beginning, our country's racist system has made it very difficult for Americans of color to develop a personal or group identity substantially of their own construction. Writing from the heart of southern segregation around 1900, the pioneering sociologist W. E. B. DuBois probed deeply into the psychological impact of systemic racism. As he described the situation, the black American is

> born with a veil, and gifted with second-sight in this American world—a world which yields him no true self-consciousness, but only lets him see himself through the revelation of the other world. It is a peculiar sensation, this double-consciousness, this sense of always looking at one's self through the eyes of others.... One ever feels his twoness ... two souls, two thoughts ... in one dark body, whose dogged strength alone keeps it from being torn asunder.[22]

A critical insight here is the "twoness" forced on African Americans, a white-imposed racial identity versus an internal self striving to have one's own identity free of that racially imposed identity. Today, as in the past, this double consciousness is a dilemma imposed by systemic racism on *all* Americans of color. From the time of first entry into the United States in the mid-nineteenth century, Asian immigrants and their descendants have been positioned, most influentially by leading whites, somewhere on the racialized ladder well below whites.

Some of the identity struggle of new immigrants of color has involved struggling and trying to define themselves in ways that counter the imposed white definitions of who they are. At home, with friends and relatives, a person may be able to identify just as she or he wishes, but usually does not have the power to resist a contrary white-imposed identity in white-dominated workplaces or in dealing with white officials, teachers, and other decisionmakers. Non-European immigrants and their children often face a white-imposed identity that conflicts, to varying degrees, with the self-identity they prefer. Until recently in U.S. history, the identity whites imposed on Asian Americans was only an extremely negative one, as the "Chink," "Jap," or "Gook," as a greatly inferior and dangerous racial group. Like other Americans of color, Asian Americans have long had to struggle against this imposed racial identity in order to assert a positive self-consciousness and self-identity.

In recent years, certain (but not all) Asian American groups have been singled out by whites for a new "model minority" identity that appears on its surface to be positive but still stereotypes and targets Asian Americans from a white perspective. As we have already seen, this model imagery is often coupled with older stereotypes of Asian Americans as socially or culturally odd, foreign, or threatening. The model minority identity, which some analysts often inaccurately describe as "honorary white" or "near white," is yet again one that has been *imposed* by whites, and an imposition against which Asian Americans must struggle to establish an internal identity that is not stereotyped and destructive.[23]

There is much exaggeration in mainstream media discussions and scholarly analyses that suggests that numerous Asian American groups are now viewed by white Americans as "nearly" or "already" white. Recall from Chapter 1 the research project in which we gave a questionnaire to white college students asking them to place a long list of U.S. racial-ethnic groups into "white" or "not white" categories. Substantial *majorities* of these white students classified all listed Asian American groups, including Japanese Americans and Chinese Americans, as *not white*.[24] These well-educated, mostly young, whites are operating with the traditional U.S. racial-status continuum in mind when they place various groups into racial categories. For most, all groups of color seem to be viewed as closer to the denigrated "black end" of that white-imposed racist continuum than to the celebrated "white end."

When interacting in white-controlled spheres, such as historically white workplaces or public accommodations, how members of racially subordinated groups view their own identities and goals may have little effect on how they are typically viewed and treated by most whites and others in these areas. How whites view a group's identity often shapes what happens to its members in such societal areas, especially in regard to access to white-controlled resources and opportunities. The white racial mind-set consistently looks at racial identity from a distinctive perspective honed over centuries. Moreover, the heralded identity of "American" is often a white identity in public presentations. Indeed, the word *American* is often taken to mean *white American* in the electronic media and many publications of all kinds, not just in the United States but across the globe.

Initially, Asian immigrants to the United States have usually viewed their personal identities in nationality terms, such as Koreans, Japanese, or Chinese. They are people from societies with important cultures, languages, and religious traditions, and they typically have great respect for their home cultures. The home identity is usually positive, and most seem to arrive with no pressured double consciousness like that described by DuBois. However, once in the United States for a short time, these Asian immigrants come to see that they are socially constructed as something different, especially by those whites with power over them.

Typically, they come to know that their home societies are not viewed as very important and that their home cultures, languages, and/or religions are frequently considered to be problematical, inferior, foreign, or uncivilized. Not being white and European, not speaking English, and/or not being Christian usually mean that whites define your group, and thus you, as inferior culturally and racially and typically as well down the racial status hierarchy and continuum. As DuBois notes, seeing oneself through the eyes of whites—as inferior, foreign, or even as a "model minority" (with an accent on *minority*)—brings a painful and imposed unhealthy double consciousness. For example, one is no longer Chinese and Confucian, but rather not white, not European, and not Christian—that is, forever less than white and forever foreign. One is no longer just Chinese but a person with Chinese ancestry who has been socially redefined by most white Americans for their own purposes, a person who is both Chinese and a foreign "Chink" or odd "model minority." Clearly, for a great many whites such a person is also not really, or not fully, an "American." This is a new, difficult, and very troubling experience. Being in the United States for just a generation or two makes this even harder to endure, because there is often no strong collective memory or well-developed resistance counterframe to draw on, one with clear strategies for dealing with this racial construction of one's life.

Moreover, whites are collectively so powerful that they pressure all new immigrants, including immigrants of color, to collude in the white racist system by adopting not only many white ways of thinking and doing, including a certain type of U.S. English, but also the white racial frame and its view of the old racist hierarchy. Immigrants are commonly pressured to accept that racist framing of society, with its ideology of stereotyping people of color, in order to assimilate into a white-dominated society. They pay a heavy price for acceptance and internalization of this framing of society.

Some respondents are very aware of stereotypes of Asian Americans and other Americans of color that they have internalized. Some report that they are working to remedy the impact of this racist framing. For example, Jessica describes insightfully her encounters with white racism:

> To me, overt racism was few and far between in my own personal experiences. You know there are times when people call you, like, a "Chink" or call you a "Gook," and you don't know what to do. You're so angry. But at the same time there are those little things where your "friends" make fun of you. Like, oh, you know, "you and your little Asian gang," or "your mama likes," you know, those little jabs that are supposed to be funny. But you just internalize all those things, and you know that you're different and you want to be a certain way.... When I was in middle school, I seriously

considered becoming Christian because a lot of my friends were, and I just hate that, and I know it's a little bit different because they don't necessarily go hand in hand, but that religious privilege is very much like that racial privilege where you see it all the time.

These racist epithets tell Asian Americans that whites view their identities as inferior and not fully human or civilized. Jessica, responding to these racialized attacks like numerous other respondents, seems to downplay identity slurs and related mocking as routine and not especially serious. These respondents do not seem to have yet connected barbed racist epithets to the long U.S. history of anti-Asian discrimination—and to the strong racist framing that lies behind anti-Asian discrimination today. Jessica does see the dangers in internalizing views of Asian identity as inferior, an internalization she says she is working on in her interview. Note too her substantial insights into how racial group membership and associated privileges are linked to religious group membership. Most people in the Asian American community in which she grew up are Buddhist, so religious background is another way in which Asian Americans can be different from and stigmatized by the dominant group.

Awareness of the Racial Hierarchy

Another respondent, Violet, indicates that she is very aware of the dominant racial hierarchy and status continuum. Her hometown mostly consists of whites and Mexican Americans, and she recalls that "you would see a lot of racial tension ... but because there were not that many Asian families there—we were probably one of the only ones—we were kind of caught in the middle, so it was like we didn't really have [a clear] identity." She articulates the complexities of her position in the national racial hierarchy in this manner:

> I feel like we're sometimes stuck in the middle ... because with the whole model minority thing, I know that other minorities look at us and say, "Oh, they're pretty much close to Caucasian anyway, and they have it way better than the rest of us." And then ... Caucasians, they see a big difference: "Well, they are minorities so they are with the other group." Sometimes I feel like we are caught in the middle, and maybe there isn't a middle, but there are higher expectations, I think a lot. When you get the whole, "oh, you're Asian, you must be good at math," or "you play the violin," or "you have a teriyaki place," or "you're dry cleaning," or whatnot. So, in the whole U.S., so we're kind of in the middle. We don't

have a gigantic group. Sometimes I don't think we're the minority, and sometimes I do. It's odd.

Violet is acutely conscious of the array of stereotypes that make up the dominant racial framing of Asian Americans and sagely notes that how the latter are viewed in terms of identity and hierarchical placement depends on *who* is doing the categorizing. While whites typically see Asian Americans as "minorities," other people of color often see them as "close to Caucasian," likely because they too have had that conventional framing of the Asian "model minority" drilled into their heads by the mass media and other societal sources.

Where their local community is diverse and multiracial, our respondents often seem particularly sensitive to how Asian Americans fit into the local racial hierarchy. Sometimes this has led them to a rejection of certain aspects of their own backgrounds. Eve, who is half Chinese, one-quarter white, and one-quarter Mexican American, reports that she does not relate much to her substantial Chinese ancestry, though she notes that this ancestry makes her appear privileged. She has decided to deny or play down this ancestry because, she believes, Asian Americans are regarded "too highly" in society, but her rejection may also be due in part to concern about her and her family's inability to meet the expectations of the model minority stereotype: the only time she stutters in the interview is when asked about her father's profession. He works in a service industry, and she seems to be uneasy about revealing that. She discusses her self-identification in this provocative manner:

Yeah, I will say I am Asian, but I guess, like, I don't know, I am not gung ho. I'm gonna do Asian things. People ask me, and I'm like, Oh, I am Chinese and Mexican. I usually don't say that I am white, because there's too many white people. Actually, I say Mexican for the most part. I think it's because, because usually people look at Mexicans differently. But I am just like, whatever, I am Mexican and my mom won't identify with that, even though she is.

In continuing commentary in the interview Eve makes it clear that she understands the privileged socioeconomic position that many Chinese Americans have compared to other Americans of color and is uncomfortable with accenting her Chinese ancestry. She says that she is part of the "counter culture" and prefers to be associated with her (more modest) Mexican ancestry. She does this in part to gauge the reactions she gets from people she meets and to challenge stereotyped ideas of Mexicans. Yet Eve's mother promotes a negative view of this Mexican identity, as she will not allow her daughter to date Mexicans—even though Eve's maternal grandfather has only Mexican ancestry.

Forever Foreign: Othering and Isolation

Some respondents, as we have already seen, reported very traumatic discrimination. Numerous others reported substantial mistreatment of various kinds, from blatant to subtle and covert mistreatment, at some point in time. All recognized to some degree that Asian American identities are not seen positively, or as fully American, by most whites. This reality has caused some to give up on ever being considered "an American." There is variation in dealing with these issues by generation. Let us now look at the views of members of the first generation to emigrate in regard to identity, acceptance, and citizenship, and then compare these views with those of later generations.

Before they come, and often for some time once here, most Asian immigrants believe the United States to be a welcoming place where opportunities and riches are available for those who just work hard. These new Americans arrive full of hopes and aspirations that the United States will be a wonderful home for them, their children, and their grandchildren. Unfortunately, they have subsequently had experiences that indicate they are often wrong in these expectations. Life has definitely not been as easy as they anticipated before they made the long journey across the Pacific.

Systemic racism puts a lot on the line for the first generation because of their treatment as "forever foreign."[25] In his interview, Henry, a Chinese American, remarks, "What can I complain about? Even if I complained, it wouldn't do any good. If you are Asian in this country, you are the minority. You don't think about Asians here." After many decades in the United States, and after living for a long time in a city with a large Asian American population, Henry still feels that Asian problems with racism remain invisible to non-Asians. His views on important racial matters are not considered significant by whites. In his interview numerous comments demonstrate his frustration in regard to how he has suffered discrimination for so long. Similarly, Mei, who works at a health center, has felt the chill of racism's cold shoulder for several decades. When asked about being in the United States for so long, she responds, "I'm getting more frustrated. Why am I here? There is nothing really acceptable because you are alien. You know? Usually I don't have these kinds of feelings. Now I kind of accept that I am really not supposed to be here." These older Asian Americans are veterans of U.S. society yet have resigned themselves to never being accepted fully as "Americans." They fear they will continue to be viewed by whites as unwanted and outsiders. Common too among first-generation respondents is that the longer they have been in the United States, the less they believe in the American dream of unlimited opportunities and fair treatment.

Our interviews, like those of numerous other research studies, show clearly that whites still sit firmly at the top of the racial pecking order. Whites, especially those at the middle-class level and above, have substantial power to decide who gets identified positively, who will be treated fairly or unfairly, and who will be included or excluded. Some respondents have come to this discovery only over a long period of time, whereas some, like Bari, report that they did feel the cultural and racial shock early on:

> I thought I won't have culture shock, but then I realize I did go through culture shock. Not because it [his college] was too advanced or anything, but mainly because this college was too backwards in many ways, the culture of [this college town]. I got quite a shock from it because the media portrayed the American culture to be quite liberal and welcoming ... and it didn't follow through in [this town's] case.... That was the problem.... I was treated well, but ... you can clearly tell that they treat you differently because they think that you don't know how to get on the Internet.

Bari first says that he was treated well but then notes that local residents treated him differently, even to the point of assuming that because he was an international student from a relatively poor country (India), he must not know how to use new technologies. As we noted previously, Asian Americans often deal with a set of stereotypes some researchers have called "Orientalism," the general view that Asian and Middle Eastern countries are somehow unfree, exotic, or primitive. Such stereotypes fuel the white imagination that South Asian international students live in backward countries. Bari continues,

> I will never be part of this culture, and I'll always be made an outsider. I really think I want to go back as soon as I can. One thing I would tell another international student is ... not to think that here is what the media says it is, like most of the television series like *Friends* or the *OC* or *Desperate Housewives,* all set in California or New York.... I used to think that's how the entire U.S. was. And that's such a wrong portrayal of the culture and the lifestyle.... It's very hard to close the cultural barriers. So that's the other thing that I would caution them about, that relationships can be pretty tough. And I think that I would ... tell them to look at, feel that sense of isolation. And that it takes some getting used to the solitary life.

Talking about leaving, Bari feels alone even after being in the United States for some years. He attributes much of his difficulty to the provincialism of whites. He adds that some whites whom he met in the college community were not genuine in their interactions:

> I realized that I made such emotional friendships in India. And, certain friendships [in the United States] when they would say, "Hi, how are you," it was just a greeting. But in India when they ask you how are you, they mean it. And the [American] people talk and smile and talk insignificance.... The way they approach you makes you feel like they really like you, and they want to spend more time with you but cannot. That's all they are. But then they approach others and show that interest. And that's part of cultural fabric, how they approach people. In India, if you don't make a friend, you don't really go and say hello, or how are you or anything. So it took some time to get used to it.

Numerous students that he has met at his historically white university have not shown a sincere interest in really getting to know him and his country. Thus he reports that he lives a "solitary life" not at all like that he expected from watching U.S. television.

Problems of marginalization, isolation, and identity denigration are reported by Asian Americans in all regions of the United States. For example, Alex comments about how a Cambodian woman he knows has been viewed by white coworkers:

> I got into this disagreement with one of my coworkers because we have this person, she's rather old. She's from Cambodia. She is an assembler, so all she does is she comes to work for eight hours, she assembles some stuff. She goes home. Because her English is poor, he wouldn't say she's "American." I say she has American citizenship, she pays American taxes, you know, she does everything to be qualified to be [an] American citizen. His argument is that she doesn't speak the language that well. I tried to tell him ... that's just unfair because she did everything the American government asked her to obtain American citizenship. Now somebody said she's not American. So I started thinking, what is American then? I always thought American, the culture, America by itself doesn't have much culture in my opinion. Rather it's the mixture of other cultures [that] is the American culture. If someone is going to say, "Well, that's not American," then I don't know what American really is. A lot of people, I think, still have that kind of mentality in their minds that, "You don't speak the language, I don't care

what you are doing. You are not American." I wouldn't say the government is actually taking care—or they don't care for Asians that much.

Although he initially said that he saw no racial discrimination, as the interview continued, Alex describes how he feels unwelcome in the society. His conversation with his white coworker has encouraged him to think critically about what the label "American" means. He recognizes that even if an Asian American is a citizen, that person may not be considered as being "American" to many non-Asians. The imposed identity and the personally sought identity again come into conflict, likely creating a double consciousness. In his interview Alex explains that he feels more comfortable with Asian friends, noting that his "closest friends are mostly Asians—Asian Americans. Like some Koreans, Vietnamese, Cambodians, Chinese, and so on." These friends seem to be chosen because they understand the hostility faced by people like him. Note too that the friends are identified in terms of their home countries. Choosing Asians and Asian Americans as friends is one strategy to counter the racist climate.

Asian Americans are often targeted with reasons why they are not good enough to be identified as "real Americans." Despite the energy they put forth to be model citizens, they are confronted with rejection by more nativistic whites. The exclusion and other difficulties that older generations have faced at the hands of whites help to explain why the stakes are high for successive generations, as parents and grandparents hope that at least their children will eventually be accepted by whites because of hard work and educational achievements.

For example, Jessica offers some thoughts about the relative solitude that has affected her immigrant parents. They were initially part of an extensive working-class Vietnamese community in her hometown, but the social demographics of her neighborhood have changed over recent decades. "When we were little, my parents [who have since divorced] had a very strong connection to the Vietnamese community. They went to temple a lot, and all of the aunts and uncles, or the aunties and uncles that you pick up that aren't really aunties and uncles, and they all had babies together, and so that created this great support network for me. But as we got older, they drifted apart and moved to other suburbs, and they got to create opportunities and careers and stuff." Success led to some families moving to the suburbs. Jessica continues,

And so they don't always get together. They don't work in the same factory. They don't sew together any more. So I think it's hard for [my mom] because she doesn't have all these friends to bond with, and she's lonely. And she has her clients that she does nails for. She has, like, two friends ... and I feel bad for her. And, like, my dad, he doesn't really have that many friends either.

They live very different lives, and my dad's much more privileged than my mom, and he has a lot more money. He has a more stable job, and he has a wife. He lives in a real nice area, nice cars. But still he doesn't have a lot of friends. Like, he has tons of acquaintances. And they're both very social people, but they don't have that connection to anybody. Like, if they got up and moved, who would miss them, and who would be missed? It's us, that's all they've got, their kids.

Jessica's parents have secured much of the American dream. As political refugees, they have substantially adopted U.S. lifestyles, yet are relatively isolated now. They moved away from their working-class community and have lost contact with Vietnamese friends. Their suburban lifestyle has not provided them new friends, perhaps because they are not seen as fully American by whites there. Thus, their hopes and dreams now seem focused on their children.

No Longer Asian, Not Yet "American"

As we have seen numerous times, the umbrella group of Asian Americans is actually composed of numerous different groups, which have complex and multifaceted experiences that vary somewhat by generation. What differentiates successive generations of Asian Americans from the first is that later generations are most likely to feel caught between two social worlds. They may feel fewer ties to their parents' or grandparents' Asian cultures, but still have the physical characteristics associated with Asian immigrants, and thus are often treated as such by non-Asians.[26] Our respondents often said they feel lost and unsure of the social world into which they really fit. Even if those in later generations are highly acculturated to the mainstream culture and do not speak the language of their parents or grandparents, first-generation Asian Americans may still expect them to be able to communicate in their ancestral tongue. In contrast, white strangers may be surprised by their solid grasp of the English language, assuming that they are immigrants even if their families have been here, as with some Japanese and Chinese Americans, for four or five generations. Their in-between position can create identity struggles and personal and interactive confusion.

In her detailed interview, Helena, a Korean American, relates that she has always felt she was rejected by whites. She provides evidence for the way she has been marginalized by whites who treat her identity as still "foreign Asian" and not as a full-fledged "American," even though she has so fully assimilated to the dominant culture that she cannot speak the Korean language of her parents. Because of this acculturation Helena can no longer relate well to some older relatives and acquaintances. For some time her father worked overseas, and they moved a lot. One of her father's assignments was on a U.S. military base in South Korea. Some of our Asian American respondents noted that they feel more at home when they are in Asian countries, but Helena does not feel this way because of experiences she had in Korea:

> Some of the other Koreans, this other girl, I don't know why she was going to the American school too ... but her family knew, they all spoke Korean. And her mother actually said that she was not to hang out with us and be friends with us because we didn't speak Korean. She would spy out of her apartment, because they had these tall apartment buildings in Korea and so you could see pretty far and she would watch when we were walking home from school. And so the girl got in trouble because she would walk home from school, anyway, with us; that's where we all knew each other, so it's kinda sad. So there's this point where we would turn and it's like, at this point this mother can see me from the building, so now she would cross the street and walk on the other side of the street from us. So, you know, that affected me.

These incidents with rejection accumulated. Helena was not Korean enough for Koreans in South Korea, but she also reports another language issue in her family in the United States. Her parents decided it was unimportant for her and her sister to learn to speak Korean:

> It always made me sad because I always felt apart. All my cousins, *everyone* in my family, *all* the kids my age, some older, slightly older, they *all* knew Korean. In my *entire family,* it was just us. So, it was really hard and we didn't have a lot of family reunions, but when we did, it's like, ah everybody would be speaking Korean. Me and my sister would sit there.... I had nothing to do, nobody to talk to. So I just, I never grew up with a close family bond, which I regret, but I don't think there was anything I could do about it.... It was kind of difficult too because all my uncles and aunts, their English was usually not that good.... They worked, a lot of my uncles worked, and they spoke English, but their English still was not that good so they chose to speak Korean when they were there at home and around. And so I used to think for the longest time that they didn't like me, but I realized much, much later that, oh, they just can't really communicate with me, so they kind of ignored me.... I think that affected me too, because I never felt like part of the family.

Because of her inability to speak Korean, Helena could not find a place of comfort within her extended family. The issue was not intentional exclusion, but rather the inability of older Korean Americans to communicate well with younger people. Here we may see some evidence of the impact of the intensive English-only pressures of white nativists and politicians in the United States. These pressures lead many immigrant parents to aggressively channel their children away from the Asian languages and heritages into a strong conformity to the English language and white folkways, a strategy that may reduce some types of white hostility or discrimination but may also separate them from older members of their communities.

Several research studies have shown that the different Asian American generations are sometimes in conflict with each other. One researcher examined the views that seventy-three children of Korean and Vietnamese immigrants had about their families. Most of these children had accepted the dominant conception of the "normal" American nuclear family and thus often criticized their parents as too strict or emotionally distant. In part, these children had assimilated an Anglocentric view of the family. However, the researcher found that they also held certain traditional Korean and Vietnamese values, such as important filial values, that were similar to those of their parents.[27] Growing up as an immigrant child in the United States almost inevitably means intergenerational conflicts and significant compromises.

Helena further notes in her interview that she married a white man and that they have a child. Where she lives there is no large community of Korean Americans where her son might have Korean contacts, but she is hopeful that he can eventually develop this part of his personal identity. At the end of the interview, she comments on a question about her own identity:

> I think about it at least every day. I do feel, I really need to learn Korean. I feel that so anytime I see another, especially a Korean, and they try to talk to me in Korean, and I'm just like, "Sorry, I don't speak Korean." Or, I have, I guess a Chinese look about me, so I get a lot of Chinese people coming up to me to talk to me, and at least I can be like, "I'm not Chinese." It's hard enough getting people to go out with me to eat Korean food. I can't even get my husband to go.

Every day Helena is reminded of some pain tied to struggles over retaining her Korean identity in a society that makes this problematical. Helena wants to be more connected to her heritage. Simple things that make her feel at home in her national-origin identity, such as partaking in a Korean meal, are a chore in which even her white husband refuses to take part. Helena's struggle with retaining this aspect of her identity in an overwhelmingly white world may seem to outsiders to be modest if not innocuous, but she also has decades of discriminatory incidents that have accumulated into a stockpile of racialized and painful memories that force her to rethink constantly who she is as a Korean and Asian American in a still-racist society.

Many of our U.S.-born respondents reported being situated in a confusing position when it comes to their national or racial identity. Some never thought of themselves as other than American until they were treated as nationally foreign or racially inferior by white Americans. Many remain confused as to where they belong. They share a substantial lack of control over their own identity. In his interview John, a Chinese American, admits that when he was younger he felt like an outsider because of the way whites viewed his "foreign" ancestry. He is fearful of feeling marginalized and puts forth much effort to fit in. Like others, John is divided in his sense of national identity, as he makes evident: "I hope that I've always been able to do, and for a very large part, be both Chinese and both American. The fear that sort of underlies it is that I am neither. Because if I'm both, then when I am in China I am with the majority, in the United States I'm with the majority.... Okay, I can be a weird ... I don't like the word 'nonmainstream,' but that I'm white in a certain context, in another context I'm Chinese."

John says he is happy to have a dual national identity. In his interview there is no fusion of identities for him, for he never comfortably describes himself as "Chinese American." For him being American means being white or white-like in the U.S. context. He fears not being legitimate in either country and has worked hard to master the Chinese language so that he can "be Chinese" when visiting his family in China. He attempts to fit into both societies, and he never wants to be the "minority" in either place. Indeed, he seems somewhat on edge, clearly stressed that he is neither Chinese nor American enough.

John makes clear in his interview that if you are a permanent minority, you are going to get the "short end of the stick." His fear of minority status seems to be why he equates "white" with "American." For him, trying hard to be white should award him liberties given to white citizens. He makes it evident that he places great faith in U.S. institutions:

There are people who think that you're American because you salute the flag, you obey the Constitution.... What does it mean to be American? I am willing to credit this country. I am willing to support the Constitution, I believe in rule of law, I believe in democracy, I believe in saluting the American flag, I am willing to learn enough English to survive, I am willing to participate in the political process. And it's a civic definition of

America. Okay, given I am willing to do these things, it doesn't matter that I've got black hair or that I speak Chinese to my kids.... This is why I care a lot about law and rule, because I associate—okay, as long as people believe that I am an American citizen simply because of the Fourteenth Amendment of the Constitution. I cannot be stripped of my American citizenship because of the Supreme Court rulings. As long as people obey the Constitution and listen to the Supreme Court and have a system of rule of law and a due process, I'm fine. And that's how I deal with insecurity.

Numerous respondents voiced their faith in and support of U.S. civil rights or civil liberties laws. Such laws appear to serve as a type of security blanket for them and, of course, *should* offer the protection from racial mistreatment that they seek. John explains his reasoning that because he is a U.S. citizen, he is protected by laws. Yet, as he dialogues with himself in the interview, he realizes that he is not necessarily secure because the U.S. government often breaks its laws. He gives this example:

That makes it really tough with all those people in Guantánamo Bay [U.S. prison in Cuba]. That really scares me because I can imagine myself in one of those prisons. There are idiots in any society. If we are treated well enough, by enough people, then it's not our problem. It's the problem of the idiots that are treating us badly. They are not the Americans. I mean, it sort of turns the tables. So we are the true Americans. They are just pretending to be.

John is in internal conflict over what is a "true American" identity. He points out that the government unjustly imprisons people but then moves from institutional oppression to threats from individual "idiots" who discriminate. On this latter point, he holds a view common among our respondents—that anti-Asian racism is mainly about acts of narrow-minded white bigots. In general, U.S. laws help him to feel secure, yet he is frightened that he could "lose everything" and believes that individual discriminatory acts are problematical for Asian Americans like him.

Conclusion

There are myriad ways that Asian Americans choose to deal with the discrimination that they daily face and must somehow withstand. For some, the pain and stress become so great that they more or less self-destruct by turning to drugs or alcohol, or by physically harming themselves and others in their families or communities. Most internalize the pain of everyday racism and thus damage themselves psychologically, to varying degrees, and usually for the long term. Assertive attempts to erase memories of racial hostility and discrimination do not protect them from future incidents.

Subordinated to whites in the racial hierarchy, which is buttressed by the dominant white racial framing, people in Asian American groups frequently find themselves caught between an imposed racial identity that is negative and their own internal conceptions of themselves in more positive and national-origin terms. Few respondents have gotten to a truly comfortable place, to a place of internal peace, in U.S. society.

First-generation Asian Americans often feel overwhelming feelings of racial denigration, exclusion, and isolation. Successive generations still feel this as well but are also challenged with figuring out where they fit between the sociocultural worlds of their parents and the assimilation crucible that is U.S. society. They are racially othered by whites and other non-Asians in a white-dominated world, yet are well-socialized Americans often with weak understandings of the ancestral cultures of the communities where they grew up and may still reside. First-generation Asian Americans, or Asians overseas, may treat them as too whitewashed culturally and thus as inauthentic, even as whites treat them as racial foreigners who do not fit in. In organizational or governmental efforts to celebrate multicultural or multiracial diversity, Asian Americans often find themselves continually "Orientalized" and celebrated, often for nefarious purposes by whites, as "superior minorities" or "model minorities." Their difficulties in responding to racial hostility and discrimination are often exacerbated by a lack of a strong collective memory of the racial oppression faced by Asian Americans and of the resistance strategies coming out of that experience. Few respondents thus understand well the centuries-old, deeply racist past of the United States, and thus most are often blindsided by the numerous racist incidents that involve them, their families, and their acquaintances.

The costs of everyday racism accumulate and, over time, are enormous. In this book, we continually observe the cumulative and substantial impact of white racism on our respondents' lives, often over many years. Everyday racism steals much work and energy from those who are subordinated. In a study of third-generation Asian Americans, sociologist Mia Tuan notes briefly the mental and physical energy her respondents have expended in having to be constantly alert to discrimination, a feeling of vulnerability that restricted their social interactions.[28] Our interviews indicate that the physical and mental energy loss is even greater than this, for it involves many areas of Asian American lives in this racist society, and must be endured for lifetimes. A previous study reported this sage comment from a retired black psychologist about the energy costs of being black:

If you can think of the mind as having one hundred ergs of energy, and the average man uses fifty percent of his energy dealing with the everyday problems of the world ... then he has fifty percent more to do creative kinds of things that he wants to do. Now that's a white person. Now a black person also has one hundred ergs; he uses fifty percent the same way a white man does, dealing with what the white man has [to deal with], so he has fifty percent left. But he uses 25 percent fighting being black, [with] all the problems being black and what it means.[29]

These are costs that whites do not have to pay and indeed usually do not even see or understand. In detailed comments about their lives, our Asian American respondents suggest that they face a similar energy loss problem, as do their relatives and friends. The white-generated hostility and discrimination they regularly face in many areas of their lives usually drain their energies. This reality began with the first Chinese immigrants in the mid-nineteenth century and has continued for Asian Americans to the present day.

Chapter 5
Struggle and Conformity

The White Racial Frame

A seventeen-year-old Chinese American male high school student was brutally beaten by seven other Chicago teens in February of 2012. The beating was captured on video and posted online. In early reports the news outlets were saying that it was likely to have been racially motivated because on the video it looked like the immigrant student's assailants were white, and as they punched, kicked, and robbed him, they shouted racist epithets, repeatedly calling the student the "N word" and making derogatory comments about his speaking Chinese. However, the media began to backtrack on their accent on racism when it was discovered that Asian Americans were among the attackers in the teenaged group.[1]

Nonetheless, we view this attack as racially motivated because it reveals the power of the white racial frame and its pervasive nature. People of color are not immune to adopting the racist stereotypes and ideologies of the white racial frame. As we will demonstrate in this chapter, our respondents often struggle to resist the anti-Asian framing of this white racial frame and, at times, conform to it. The Asian American teen attackers were using physical force to dominate someone they probably saw as "less American" because he was a recent immigrant to the United States. A follow-up video was posted on YouTube with a young Asian American woman saying that there were tensions with the attackers and a group near the school that call themselves the FOBs ("Fresh off the boat").[2] Systemic racism is powerful in creating many alienating relationships, and in this example it created alienated relationships among Asian Americans—and thus what was in part an Asian-on-Asian attack. Quite notable is the repeated use of the "N word" in this case. As these teens physically assaulted the Chinese immigrant, they utilized a potent racist slur used for hundreds of years by whites to demean and attack African Americans. Such white-racist framing is learned, and in this case the white framing was emulated and acted out in regard to a youth from the same racially constructed group as some of the attackers.

This country's omnipresent and systemic racism creates many social contexts in which individuals like our respondents are regularly ridiculed, humiliated, and excluded. As a result, they have developed important survival strategies and significant coping skills. One major strategy involves conforming aggressively to white norms and folkways, not only with the hope of achieving the American dream but also to reduce white hostility and discrimination. To protect themselves, many strive to be as "white" in their orientations and daily efforts as they can.

Everyone in U.S. society lives within the centuries-old white frame, and no subordinated racial group is exempt from its barrage of stereotyped views, images, and emotions. Buying aggressively into the dominant frame is not exclusive to whites, for people of color have often accepted and used numerous "bits" from this frame as well. As we have just observed, Asian Americans frequently embrace racial stereotypes created by whites about other groups, as well as the racist notions that whites have created for Asians themselves. Our interviewees have regularly conformed to white framing and folkways by attempting to change personal and family characteristics in their physical and social worlds—by giving up their Asian names, changing their style of dress, and trying to enter white networks, for example—and in the psychological realm, by adopting white ways of thinking, understanding, and acting.

Striving for Whiteness: A Nuanced Example

Many Asian Americans have gained some degree of acceptance into white social worlds because of their adoption of white framing and folkways. Because of this, an apparently privileged title is sometimes given by whites to Asian Americans: "model minority" or "honorary white," as we have previously underscored. This model imagery may appear to be a compliment, but such stereotyping is, as previous chapters demonstrate, oppressive and damaging. The damage is multilayered: (1) the model minority stereotype is used to insult other people of color, and as a measuring stick to accent their inferiority for not attaining high educational or career achievements; (2) the stereotype is another method by which whites reinforce racial othering and differentiate themselves from people of color; (3) on a personal level, the stereotyping creates stressful and unrealistic expectations, self- and externally imposed, that Asian Americans should succeed in fitting the stereotype or be deemed failures; and (4) the model stereotype creates unrealistic expectations within, and outside, Asian American communities that negatively impact all Asian Americans.

As we have shown in previous discussions, Asian Americans commonly feel like outsiders. To fit in, some make extensive efforts to be the all-American student, coworker, or citizen. As the scholar Frank Wu puts it, this aggressive assimilation "gratifies the ego of whites who are assimilated toward" and is seen as a ticket to the world of prosperity for Asian Americans.[3] To the latter, the image of success has a white face.

Take the example of Lara, a Chinese American who owns her own firm. She exemplifies the multidimensional character of dealing with everyday racism, including conforming to white folkways and to stereotyped images of the old white racial frame. Her life reveals great efforts to adapt to gain acceptance. Her academic and economic success has reinforced the white frame in her own mind. She thus adopts and uses it as a reference in her hiring practices, yet still faces discrimination by whites that she rationalizes as isolated incidents of individual ignorance or prejudice. Her experiences are not unique, for we could provide numerous similar accounts from other respondents.

In her revealing interview Lara notes that she was "quite lucky" to never have endured an overt act of racism. However, over the course of the interview she makes it clear that in fact white-generated discrimination has regularly been a threat. Instead of avoiding white spaces that were unwelcoming, Lara has made it a point to conform to white folkways as much as possible, believing that her conforming and hard work will be rewarded with acceptance. For example, she discusses her high school experience in this way:

> I was in the math club, and the Latin club, and the vocational club . . . I was also a varsity cheerleader. . . . I was the only Asian; there were no African American cheerleaders in my group that I can recall. Um, so basically of a squad of, let's say, a squad of sixteen, it was all white and one Asian. . . . That would give me choices, and nobody would have anything on me, no one would say, "Well hey, well you know what, Asian Americans can't be cheerleaders because they are too geeky." Or I just figured there's never a disadvantage to joining everything. [She laughs.] I have tried so hard to assimilate.

Lara's attempt to be very involved in overwhelmingly white extracurricular activities was one important method she used to try to combat the Asian stereotype. Lara wanted access into high school spaces where young people commonly look down on those with academic prowess. She was motivated to prove that Asian Americans could do anything that a white person could do. She initially stated that her drive to assimilate was just part of her competitive nature to want to achieve and be "the best" in everything. Later, however, she admitted that her extensive involvement in school activities was also a protective measure against discrimination: "I mean, if nobody can say, 'Well, that person's less smart than me, or that person is less successful than me or less socially adept than me, or somehow nerdier than me,' then what can they say negative about the race? It was a *defense* tactic."

Lara tried to obtain the model minority status, where she was smarter and more successful than her peers, and yet at the same time to be socially integrated with whites. Asian Americans frequently find themselves criticized by whites no matter what they do. If they fail to achieve academically or economically, like some other people of color, they may be viewed by whites as inferior. If, however, they achieve more than average whites academically and economically, they may be treated as odd "grade grubbers," "nerds," and socially inferior. Lara puts forth much effort to meet the white stereotype of Asianness and the white standard for everyday whiteness. Shortly after making this statement about defensive tactics, Lara adds that if she had been raised in Asia, she might have done some of the same activities, except that the racial dimension would not have been there.

In reply to a question about what she has tried to defend herself against, Lara replies in this poignant fashion:

> A defense from the potential that there could be a race issue. It's not like I've never had a racial slur. And maybe I have a low tolerance for that type of aggravation or degradation and so I knew that that was a potential, and I tried to minimize it. I don't think it's that I didn't recognize the potential was there, I just wanted to make sure I was ready. Generally, I try not to be reactive. I try to say, let me get ready, I know what could happen, and so I am just going to prepare, so that life goes the way I want it and not how it is forced upon me by other people's actions or thoughts.

The threat of a racist incident is omnipresent in the lives of all Americans of color. Even though Lara has become exceptionally successful, she has often lived her life on "red alert," building her arsenal against racial attacks in the form of an impressive résumé and careful consideration of her defensive responses. Like numerous other respondents, Lara eventually shared with us her experiences with racial discrimination and how such experiences have motivated her to excel. She has overachieved in order to feel in control of her life. A top student in school and college, she later performed well for employers and got promoted, and then opened her firm. Her substantial accomplishments have often been used as defensive tactics in a racially harsh world.

Even when Americans of color attain socioeconomic success, they still pay a heavy toll. In this racist society whites have pressed them to think and act as whites would have them think and act, and thus often against their own individual and group interests. Whites have created social arrangements where those oppressed lose substantial control over lives and livelihoods. They are, to varying degrees, alienated from control over their ability to make decisions about many aspects of their lives. Lara's "choice" to prepare herself for everyday racism by being an overachiever is a survival technique. Although she clearly articulates the purpose of her "defense tactic," to protect her from discrimination, she still tries to convince us that she has not been significantly affected: "I just haven't been very traumatized by race differences. Again, part of it may just be me, the opposite side of me, you know, *ignoring* issues and always just trying to be *better* than the people around me so ... that they didn't have anything over me. There was nothing they could say: 'Oh well, she's Asian, so she's therefore less because of such and such.' I never gave anybody, or I tried not to give anybody, the opportunity to say anything like that." Her admirable accomplishments have required that she work much harder than comparable whites because of the embedded racial barriers. In her view, as long as she works hard enough, she will be accepted and achieve her American dream.

Lara believes her entrance into the white world has been awarded because of hard work, not because she adopted white ways. However, like many Asian Americans, Lara has worked so hard to assimilate to the model minority standard that she appears unaware of the fact that some of her important choices are not really her own. Previously, the second author has described this reality thus:

> Those who are not white, whether recent immigrants or long-term residents, are under great pressure, in the language of much social science and policy analysis, "to assimilate" to the white-determined folkways. The word "assimilate," however, does not capture the everyday reality of the pressure cooker–type demands on individuals to conform to that white environment and white folkways. There is often no choice for those who are not white but to more or less accept, mostly emulate, and even parrot the prevailing white folkways, including the white-generated negative images of racial outgroups, usually including one's own group. People of color constantly resist these pressures to conformity, but most have to accept and adapt to some extent just to survive in a white-controlled society.[4]

Lara's goal is to protect herself from discrimination by achieving a near-white position on the socioracial hierarchy. Yet, no matter how much they achieve, Asian Americans will still be viewed and treated as second-class citizens by many whites because the underlying racist structure of the society has not thereby changed. Like many others, Lara is apparently misled by the widespread rhetoric of the American dream to believe that someday she will be fully accepted into the white world. When she was in school, she attempted for several years to join a highly selective social club of white girls. These were the most popular girls, and the only stated qualification was a good academic record. As a top student, Lara should have been a shoe-in for the club. When asked about why she was never accepted, Lara cited personality differences and her inability to have a connection with club members, not intentional discrimination by the whites.

Lara has committed to the idea of assimilation to whiteness so fully that she admits that in hiring for her firm, she has a certain image of a new employee in mind. Even though her father had difficulty with English and was denied career opportunities because of that and whites' stereotyping of Asians, Lara asserts, "If you do not speak English well, which I was given the opportunity to do, if they don't speak English well, there is probably a *ton* of discrimination. Because even myself, when I am thinking about hiring someone, if they have an accent or if they don't speak English fluently, that affects my thought process as far as selecting them." To most Americans, discrimination on the basis of language, accent, or citizenship seems rational and acceptable.[5] White middle-class English is thought by many Americans to be "good English" and the desirable speaking norm.

When Lara was in elementary school, she used her grasp of the English language and her "excellent diction" aggressively to defend herself against racist slurs and whites' mocking comments, as she noted in her interview: "One time, I don't remember who it was. It was just some random kid, and he saw me and said something, you know pretending to speak Chinese, kind of mocking, and I just looked back at him in the eyes and said, 'Hey, I bet I read and speak English a lot better than you do. So you may as well just cut it out.'" In her mind, mastery of English elevates her status over the white child teasing her. Yet she in her interview does not seem to sympathize much with newer Americans who may have not yet mastered the language.

During her school years she reportedly did not befriend other Asian children and viewed herself as different from them. In her view they were not as involved with school social activities as she was and were, as she puts it, "loners." When asked why she called them that, she responds, "They may have felt more isolated. Again, I did my defensive tactic. Get involved with as many things as you can, just for the heck of it regardless of whether you know why you are doing it or not, and try to fit in as socially well as possible."

Even with all her work to get involved socially with whites, Lara has still faced recurring racist incidents. When she experiences such events, she says that she deals with the person head on. During her younger years she "just wrote it off as ignorance, you know. I think I just thought, well they may, they are clearly stupider than me if they are going to act like that, so therefore I'll just make it up by being their boss when we're both thirty. That's just how I wrote it off, as if 'you know what, they can continue to have those attitudes, and they are stupid enough to act like that then they are just not going to succeed.' And I will just let time tell the difference, I think." Lara has experienced racial discrimination but tends to attribute the events to individual ignorance, and her words reveal a little uncertainty as to whether her efforts will eventually pay off. She shared with us vivid memories of racist incidents, including one that occurred just a couple of years ago. White children at a grocery store mocked her Asian appearance like her white peers did in school. Systemic racism persists, and Lara's extraordinary achievements are not enough to destroy the anti-Asian notions and actions of whites she encounters. Once again, we see that the American dream is chimerical, hypothetical, and in reality for whites only.

The Psychological Impact of Discrimination: Strategies and Responses

Pressures to assimilate into the dominant U.S. culture and society, and specifically to conform to white framing and folkways, are intense for immigrants and their descendants. When Asian Americans become relatively successful, they are sometimes awarded certain privileges still inaccessible to other people of color. Because of this, they may appear to be, as some put it, the "darlings of whites."[6] However, it takes enormous work to be placed even in this "darlings" status, as analyst Vijay Prashad perceptively suggests:

> This puts enormous pressure on migrants, who seek to "assimilate" but find themselves confronted with a forbidding racism. This leads them in at least two directions, either into the shell of "national culture" (that is, retreating from an abandoned "outside society") or else into an intensified desire to "assimilate" and gain acceptance (that is, seeing the earlier attempt as insufficient, as having made mistakes that need to be remedied for a successful assimilation). Many of those born in the new land first try

to assimilate in a one-dimensional way to become "American," discover the resilience of their own "pasts" as well as of racism's present, and then recover the resources within "national cultures" in a process that we may name "reverse assimilation."[7]

Such choices are open to Asian immigrants, and their children and grandchildren, as they attempt to move into the mainstream institutions of U.S. society and compete with white Americans. Here we examine aspects of the option of assimilating in a one-dimensional way; the countering option of reverse assimilation will be discussed in the next chapter.

Like other Americans of color, Asian Americans face additional, often high, levels of daily stress well beyond those normally faced by most whites. This added pressure creates or aggravates an array of significant psychological and physical problems.[8] It means the loss of much physical and psychological energy. Let us now examine life accounts of numerous respondents who have expended much energy to absorb a racist event and to strategize how to defend themselves from such racial threats. This psychological workout translates into a kind of psychological discrimination for Asian Americans, just as for other people of color. From a young age, our respondents have learned about the threats of white racism and put forth efforts to protect themselves, such as by changing their names, friends, and neighborhoods, all attempts to avoid discrimination or pass into a near-whiteness. Numerous respondents even spoke of wanting to significantly change their physical features, just as many Asians and Asian Americans now actually do with cosmetic surgery.

One of our respondents is a Vietnamese American professional who grew up on the East Coast, where she still lives. She recalls early attempts at social conformity:

> I remember when my dad took me to school, the first day of school … the teacher asked, "Oh, what's your daughter's name?" And my dad was like "Fat" because it's the closest to my name in Vietnamese. I remember I was like five or something. I was like, "My name is Phan." I didn't want to be called Phat because I already knew what *fat* meant. I was like, "No, I don't want to be called 'Phat'" and they can make weight jokes and all that stuff, you know? So I was like five years old, like "Don't call me Phat!" And then they called me "Fang" and all this stuff and made jokes about me being Chinese and Vietnamese.

At the tender age of five, "Phan" changed her name; she was already developing an understanding of and defensive reaction to racial ridicule by whites that she would endure because of her Vietnamese name. Conformity to white expectations as a protective adaptation strategy has been reported in at least one other study of younger Vietnamese Americans. Researcher Hung Cam Thai writes that his respondents have tried hard to be "American by acting and being white to fit in with peer groups."[9]

Indeed, children of all racial and ethnic backgrounds often pick up racial concepts and terms much earlier than in elementary school. Summarizing conclusions from an extensive ethnographic study of a multiracial child-care center, Debra Van Ausdale and Joe Feagin suggest that "many white adults still harbor deeply racist images and stereotypes and practice racial discrimination in settings they traverse in their daily lives. Not surprisingly, children are not protected from the reality and pain of this racist context, and their activities often reproduce and experiment with what they observe and understand about that racist society."[10]

In U.S. society, children usually do not live in a protective bubble that keeps them from learning about racial stereotypes and framing from parents, peers, and the mainstream media. If the framing of major social groups in the society in which they grow up is often racist, as it is in the United States, they will pick up and use some of that racial framing. Research such as that just cited shows that in preschool and school settings white children frequently exercise their racial power, and children of color soon learn their subordinate positions.

Phan changed her name early on because she had a better understanding of the racial hierarchy than her father did. She worked to save embarrassment for her younger sister as well, as she recounts at some length in her interview:

> I know I was six, because that's when my sister was about to be born ... and I remember telling my teacher, "Oh, I'm about to have a sister." And you know, the teacher was like, "Oh, that's great. You know, what's your sister's name going to be?" And you know, it's funny because looking back I don't like to embellish and come up with a story or anything about it, but I mean it was obvious that I told her that my sister's name was going to be Jennifer. I knew my sister's name was not going to be Jennifer. I knew my sister's name was going to be Tuyen. I remember telling—I don't remember why it came out of my mouth—I told my teacher, "No, her name's going to be Jennifer." So she wrote ... a congratulations or something like that ... and then she sent it to my parents. So my parents, of course, were highly upset about it, because they were like, "Why did you tell them your sister was going to be Jennifer?" I was like, "I don't know, I want my new sister to be Jennifer. You don't call her an American name." I remember thinking it's going to be awful. They're going to name her Tuyen and [everyone will] make fun of her.

Again at a young age, Phan understood the painful nature of being different, but her parents did not appear to have understood. She was unable to articulate to her parents why she chose to change the name.

In contrast to Phan's parents, a great many Asian American parents see why a child like Phan might resist her Asian name. Many parents now give popular English names to their children. One New York City study, for example, found that the five most common names given by Asian American parents to their baby girls were Sophia, Emily, Michelle, Nicole, and Rachel, and the most common names given to boys were Justin, Ryan, Jason, Kevin, and Daniel. *Not one* of these is a typical name in Asian countries. Clearly, defensive conformity to important white folkways begins at birth.[11]

Jessica's parents emigrated from Vietnam, and she reports that they have had trouble understanding well how U.S. racism works, although over time they have become well acquainted with it. The learning process has been difficult for her to watch:

> It's really hard that my parents *don't get it.* We're foreign. We're on welfare, and so, I guess for me my ethnicity has always been ridiculously intertwined with my class. And I can't separate the two because to me that's a specific experience, being from a Vietnamese immigrant family that's poor. I know it's hard for them. People gave my mom dirty looks because of the few things that she used, combined with the fact that she didn't know English. So it was like, "Oh, immigrants come in here, taking our money." That's exactly what that is. And it was really hard for her. It was embarrassing that she had to use her children to translate for her, and that's why she learned English. She became a citizen, and when she became a citizen she changed her name to "Christine." But the reason she did that is because they couldn't say her name, and they would never remember it. Right? If they can't say it, why bother to remember it. Yeah, and it's weird watching them assimilate.

Having been victims of substantial stereotyping and mistreatment, Jessica's parents have more or less been forced to conform to a white-controlled society that has psychologically assaulted them. In account after account we observe the constant and coercive pressures on immigrants and their children to adapt to U.S. society in a unidirectional way.

Many immigrants of color go through this process to protect themselves from white discriminators, and Jessica admits that it makes sense that her parents would choose to assimilate in these ways, but it is still unnerving. We ask Jessica what she means when she uses the word "weird" for the change in her parents. She replies,

Because it's such a delayed reaction to their own children growing up and having success and seeing that success and wanting to be part of that. And, you know, dressing differently and buying different cars, and learning English and watching the shows that we watch and buying things that we buy. And ... I guess it just feels weird to me, because I'm in a stage of my life where I'm working through that internalized oppression. And working through who I am and what I think about myself, and watching my parents go through what I went through when I was younger and in school. And seeing them just try to fit in and having American friends and having white friends specifically, and it's weird! And my mom, she's been here for so long now. ... It seems so long, and so even she doesn't feel that comfortable in her Vietnamese identity any more. She feels that she is a Vietnamese American. When people say that I'm first generation—and they count me as a first generation—they completely discount my mother, who's been here for [more than] twenty years. I think she counts as an American in this country. How do you discount that? ... So, come on, that's more than my life that she's been here. And so, I can't blame her for wanting to change and grow.

The way Jessica describes her success and that of her family revolves around how well they conform to certain conventional images of success in this consumer society. Acquiring the right kind of car and clothes and watching the right television shows are what she and her parents seem to view as rather necessary to become "true Americans." Jessica's parents hope to gain greater white acceptance by such conforming, but after nearly three decades in the United States, they are still treated by whites as foreigners.

Dealing candidly and perceptively with her internalized oppression, Jessica is aware of the pervasive psychological and other impacts of everyday racism. Yet, in regard to her mother she "can't blame her for wanting to change and grow." Describing this one-way adaptation to white folkways and framing as growth may signal some internalized racism at work, as it implies that the mother's mimicking of a certain whiteness is healthy. The discomfort her mother feels in her Vietnamese identity again demonstrates the powerful imposition of a stereotyped white framing on these relatively new Americans. It appears that Jessica realizes that her mother will never be accepted if she does not make these choices to conform to certain white folkways. The psychological discrimination that Asian Americans experience in a racist system is like an abusive interpersonal relationship: they must succumb to many norms and requests of whites, yet never be on a healthy equal footing with them.

Separating from other people of color, and perhaps from themselves, is a way some Asian Americans try to conform to white framing and folkways. Some respondents recalled that during their school years, they would yearn to look different physically and were often less than thrilled with having Asian American friends. Charlotte thus recounts a high school experience:

> I remember in high school, when we moved to a different part of town, meeting one girl who was Chinese. And her mother was giving me a ride home because it turned out she lived very close to me, and her mother said, "Oh, look, she's Chinese too. Maybe you could be friends." And she and I respectively rolled our eyes, I think, wherever we were sitting in the car, not at each other, and it was nothing personal, and we didn't take it personally. It was just annoying that—"Oh, somebody else is Chinese, maybe you can be friends with them." ... I think that it was just ... we were, I guess ... second generation, but we were the first ones that were born and raised in this country. And they [the parents] just didn't want to lose the cultural identity. I understand that a lot more now as an adult than I did as a kid growing up—where assimilation was the name of the game. I remember she [her friend] and I talked about it, and all she wanted to have was blonde hair and blue eyes and to be named, I don't know, Chris or something like that. And all I wanted to have was *regular* brown hair and *regular* brown eyes and be named Janet. And so, we would just talk about how all we wanted to do was be like everybody else.

Charlotte did not like the mother's assumption that because she and the daughter were both Chinese they should naturally want to be friends. In addition, she sought to be far removed from another Asian because that would draw further attention to the fact that she was Asian. Since "assimilation was the name of the game" in her youth, Charlotte often worked hard to be as far from being seen as Chinese as possible. In Charlotte's description, her desire to be like everybody else specifically means to be like a white person, with the desirable characteristics being "regular" (white-type) hair and eyes. Charlotte and her friend shared an understanding of what it means to be different from "everyone else." While other, usually older, respondents found comfort in common understandings and close relationships with other Asian Americans, initially the young Charlotte did not want to befriend the other Asian American.

When Charlotte was in school some time ago, cosmetic surgery was not readily available and affordable. Today, however, the most frequent Asian and Asian American cosmetic surgeries are procedures to Anglicize their facial and other body features. Recent reports show a sharp increase in cosmetic surgery for Asian Americans, to whom much aggressive advertising is directed now. The most common surgeries for Asian American women are eyelid surgery, nose reshaping, and breast augmentation. The nose surgery usually involves a nose bridge operation that changes a flatter-looking Asian nose into a protruding, more European-type nose. Thus, much cosmetic surgery is directed at making Asian women look more like a common white view of ideal female beauty.

In September 2013, Julie Chen, host of CBS's television show *The Talk*, revealed that early in her career she had cosmetic surgery to change her "Asian eyes." She chose to undergo the procedure because she had become deeply insecure after her boss told her that her "heritage" was "holding back her career."[12] Chen admitted that she was rewarded after getting the surgery and that was a decision she has to "live with," yet one that has helped her get where she is today. Chen admitted that her difficult decision was driven by white-imposed racism, and assimilation through permanently altering her body with a surgical procedure to be "less Asian" was what she had to do to "make it" in her media profession.[13] There is a white-standardized idea of beauty, and Asian American women do not fit that picture. Yet, with advances in cosmetic surgery, women of all racial groups can pay to try to match the white-normed images portrayed in the movies, on television, and in magazine spreads.

While Chen faced this workplace discrimination in the 1980s, this pressure to meet white beauty standards remains, if not growing stronger with globalized media images. In Japan, a woman who changed her name to Vanilla has undergone over thirty cosmetic surgeries, including double-eyelid and rhinoplasty, to look like the "perfect French doll." Vanilla is hoping to look "anything but Japanese" and believes "nobody would say a French doll is ugly."[14] She has internalized the racialized view that her Japanese features are unattractive and is going to great lengths to whiten her features.

Recently, one Chinese American teenager commented critically on countering the pressures from her own stereotyping and from female relatives to dramatically change her facial appearance: "After all these years of wanting to open up my eyes with tape and glue and surgery, I have opened up my eyes to a different definition of beauty, one that embraces differences and includes every girl … because being Asian is beautiful."[15]

Of course, many Asian American women cannot afford to surgically alter their appearances. Some, like Charlotte, seek to surround themselves with white friends, thereby downplaying their Asianness and hoping that whites may pay less negative attention to them. Amanda, a Filipina American, grew up in an area where there were many Asian Americans. She discusses some middle and high school choices: "For a while, I must have had this complex where I felt that I was whitewashed, and I didn't ever want, my choice of friends was never any other Asian Americans. I always hung out with people [who were] ... not necessarily white but almost never Asian American." In reply to a question about her choice to be disassociated from Asians, she responds, "There was just a negative connotation with being FOB ["fresh off the boat"], and I remember that the few Asian American friends that I had, not necessarily from high school, but from church, I remember that we would always talk badly about immigrants. Or even people, like, traveling places or whatever and making fun of them, and how they talked so funny, and how they're giving the rest of the American-born Asians a bad look." In her youth Amanda poked fun at Asian and Pacific Island immigrants, probably to differentiate herself as much as possible from those "fresh off the boat."

In her interview she indicates too that she has been very concerned for her parents when they are out in public, as they are not always treated well by those who do not understand their accents. Her parents have pushed her to conform as much as possible in order to access some privileges they had been denied. As she notes, "My parents wanted, really wanted me and my sister to identify as being American and not as a different kind of American." In this case being "American" means not being a hyphenated "Filipino-American."

Amanda explains that in school she hid her identity in interactions with white and other non-Asian friends, as she recalls in this reflective passage:

> We would talk about ... music and clothes, and everything they would say, I would agree with them. And I would never, never mention anything that sounded even remotely Asian-ish. I would probably *never tell them* I was Filipino. The thing is that *secretly* I was really proud of ... my racial identity. I really was. I'm almost fluent in Tagalog [language in Philippines], and my family is really important to me, and there was no doubt that I really loved my heritage and my culture. It's just, I guess, maybe I thought that my friends wouldn't understand.... One of my closest friends is black, and she is probably like twenty-fifth generation American, or something like that. And how can she possibly relate to immigrant parents? ... I'm trying to think of problems my parents would have, but they assimilated very well.

Amanda did her best to "lay low" in the hope that her Asian identity would not be found out. Even with other people of color, she was worried that they would not be able to relate to her family's immigration experience, so she had to be proud of her national identity in secret. Clearly, numerous respondents have gone to significant lengths to lessen or hide their Asianness for defensive reasons.

Rejecting Asianness

Many respondents spoke of going through a process of rejecting some or many aspects of their Asian backgrounds and characteristics. Those who have chosen to make the effort to abandon their Asianness usually have done so to succeed in white-dominated institutions. They generally believe that this movement away from their backgrounds helps them achieve more and gain acceptance from whites.

Like some other respondents, Joel, a Hmong American, reports feeling a *double* burden from race and class. In his hometown, where there are many Asian Americans, the Hmong are commonly viewed by whites in much the same negative way that they view black Americans. In his poignant interview he points out the impact of this common framing:

> I guess because the fact the Hmong people were a new cohort of immigrants into the U.S. during that time period, there was a more negative perception of them.... There is the whole notion that the Hmong people are on welfare and that they're taking taxpayer money, etc. So I think from my perception, there's a negative perception of the Hmong people because they're new immigrants. And more likely that they weren't getting a junior high education. I chose to associate more with the white individuals so I can internalize their expectations and also go in the same route that they are going.... I got straight As, and then I was one of the valedictorians for our junior high. But then at the same time, I kind of like, I knew that I wouldn't associate with the Hmong people as much, because it was kind of like, they're not doing so well. And I was doing better because this is where my parents want me to go, and this is also where most of the individuals in my class are going. So I kind of turned my "Hmongness" off, and I kind of of more associated with, like, white individuals or those individuals who were doing academically better.

Note the contrast here to the model minority stereotype. Joel himself bought into the negative stereotyping of his Hmong American group, which he associated with a lack of academic achievement. The recipient of racist actions from whites, he decided that academic achievement would shield him from further mistreatment. Just as other Asian Americans have chosen to do, Joel worked to distance himself from his Asian heritage because he thought that was necessary in order to succeed in U.S. society. Later on, Joel notes, he became aware of the impact of white racism on him and the larger Hmong community, as well as of the insidious nature of pressures to hyper-conform.

May Ia, a Hmong American from a heavily Asian area in the Midwest, has not reached Joel's level of critical awareness. She sums up her experiences with adopting white ways thus: "Because growing up, I chose to follow more of the prosperity of the Caucasian culture, the white culture. Therefore, a lot of my thoughts, my attitudes, are more of an American culture.... [The white mind-set] pretty much means individualized, be independent." She associates her own people with economic and racial hardship, and white culture with success. In her interview, however, she never mentioned the role of discriminatory whites in creating severe political and economic problems for the Hmong people.

Indeed, the Hmong were exploited by U.S. government (especially CIA) officials in waging a secret war in Laos against Vietnamese communists during the Vietnam War. This Hmong involvement in helping the U.S. military and intelligence organizations made them targets for retaliation after the United States withdrew. The Laotian government retaliated against them, and those unable to flee or hide in the mountains were very destitute and placed in refugee or reeducation camps.[16] Beyond the U.S. borders, white political and military officials have long exploited various peoples of color to enrich or protect U.S. national interests. Nonetheless, May Ia only blames her own people, who typically immigrated as impoverished refugees, for their economic and social failures today, while she credits white folkways as the necessary route to Hmong success. Her views seem heavily shaped by an acceptance of much of the dominant white racial framing of the Hmong and other Asian Americans.

Frank, a Korean American, formerly a technical worker and now business owner, comes from a city with a large Asian American population. He too has adopted significant aspects of the white mind-set on various societal matters. Recall from Chapter 2 our previous discussion of some of his views. He initially said that he had faced no discrimination but later discussed at length the significant glass ceiling that prevents Asian American advancement. Let us now consider some of his thoughts about assimilation and conformity over the years:

> I didn't feel like I was a minority because they [whites] treated me just like one of them. And also, I assimilated to the U.S. very quickly. At that time, I had a younger brother who was six years old. And he got assimilated even faster. So we became just like they did. Even today, a lot, I have a lot of Korean friends who call me "banana" now. I look Oriental, Asian, in the face, but inside is pure white.... I look like all Asian outside. I am Asian. But inside, and the way I think, and the way I behave, [the] way I approach the problem, the way I approach the government, or whatever, I act exactly like white Americans. I do everything correctly, do step by step as the government requires, which causes far less problems.... I am a conservative and

a Republican. And the way I look at it is, I know that most white people I know, I don't know the exact political affiliations, when I talk to them, we are talking the same thing, the same language, and the same subject. And we both agree on it, so I assume he and I are both [the] same.

Frank seems to relish his stereotyped "banana" identity. He articulates strong views and uses clear language to describe his actions as he conforms to and mimics whites. He argues that the white ways are the "correct" ways, and that contrasting Asian ways are usually "wrong." An interesting part of Frank's societal analysis is that in his view much important "white thinking" and political orientation are conservative and Republican, even though in fact a great many whites are moderates, liberals, Independents, and Democrats. The reason for his false impression may lie in his significant reliance on the mainstream media, such as television networks, several of which have become more conservative in their reporting on U.S. society over the decades of significant Asian immigration since the 1960s. One irony in Frank's views is that about the same time that some Asian Americans shifted their political allegiances to the Republican Party, that party shifted its political goals and efforts even more in the direction of white voters and their political interests. Indeed, white Republican leaders have periodically admitted that they have little interest in actively recruiting Americans of color, especially immigrants of color, into the party and instead prefer to rely heavily on white voters.[17]

At the root of these adaptations by numerous respondents to white thinking and folkways is the view that they are correct and normal, and that other ways of doing things are undesirable if not dangerous to life, family, or career. From this perspective, Americans of color must protect themselves by adopting the white framing and folkways. Recall Janice Tanaka's documentary on Japanese Americans who decided after the World War II concentration-camp experience to conform more aggressively to white ways to stave off a recurrence of that highly racist and destructive process.[18]

Brian, a Sansei administrator who grew up in a community heavily populated with Asian Americans, recounts this experience involving his father, who was put into one of those concentration camps during the war:

It was passed down to us in regards to being raised in an assimilationist household. There's a piece of us [that] was reinforced from the rest of the [Japanese] culture, but there was also a strong push for us to assimilate, to [be] raised to conformist status, and to be as white in America as possible. . . . In essence, he's telling me implicitly that, when he was twenty, he didn't have that opportunity. There's too much racist policies, and mobs

and attitudes, and so one of the only things available to him was gardening.
So he did gardening. I have a lot more options. So that's what I chose. But
going back to where I am, he would do anything to help me assimilate. . . .
So, from not learning the [Japanese] language . . . and then [to] being
involved much like our current millennials, being involved in soccer Little
League . . . and then not learning the language. But [he still taught me to
have] . . . a little cultural pride by knowing some stuff, so it wasn't a total
conformist upbringing. But I don't think it was really a childhood—by
pushing the biracial in regards to knowing and honoring the Japanese side,
and the white and American cultural side.

Brian uses the word biracial to describe the approach that his father used to raise
him during formative years, yet he is *not* in fact half white and half Japanese,
but of Japanese (and Okinawan) descent. Thus, biracial is an unusual term for
his being socialized in many white ways and some Japanese ways, especially in
what he describes as an "assimilationist household." Brian's father wanted him
to have opportunities that he never had because of extreme racial oppression,
and his father, like many of that generation, saw these opportunities as coming
from an aggressive adoption of white framing and folkways.

In a probing interview, Lin, a Chinese American head of a community center,
explains the phenomenon of Asian American conformity:

So many people in the past have worked to make this a great nation, but
we have to really . . . , Asian Americans, have to really take that responsibility and go beyond just to have comfortable homes, two cars, have good
children that grow to be knowledgeable. [We have] to really understand the
struggle of single moms, the struggle of affordable housing, the struggle of
affordable health care, all the basic needs for all people. I think there is not
enough discussion in the Asian American community about all the other
social issues. It could be because we don't think that we have the power to
change it, because, after all, we are disempowered, and maybe it is because
we are so consumed by the busy pace, the fast pace of life. And I think it's
also because we are not being treated as American citizens [that] we don't
think that we are allowed to contribute to the social issues.

By achieving economic stability and acquiring some consumer comforts, many
Asian Americans seem to be lulled to sleep. In her interview Lin refers to
middle-class comforts that many Asian Americans enjoy as "crumbs" that have
been "tossed" to them from whites, crumbs that are often enough to keep them

compliant and grateful. Asian Americans frequently conform, and whites are often idolized in this process. Yet, in a kind of odd Newtonian social law ("with every action there is an equal and opposite reaction"), even conforming people of color are often vilified by whites for not living up fully to various white standards.

While social "laws" are not directly comparable to the laws of physics, there are certainly recurring socioracial patterns in societies like the United States. One of these is seen in what happens when Americans of color adopt the white racial frame in their minds, which adoption binds them closely to the racist system. The latter, in turn, continues to oppress them. Often favored by whites among people of color, Asian Americans who substantially adopt the dominant racial frame seek to gain yet more favor from whites. In his interview, Josh, a Chinese American in a northern city, mentioned that his father taught him to assimilate and fit in with whites as much as possible to be successful. Reflecting on this, he comments thus: "My dad probably adjusted best to America because of assimilation. He just kind of accepted that to survive in America you have to become a little more Americanized. If you hear him talk to any of his brothers, he ends up talking more in English than Chinese. He definitely speaks more English than Chinese now."

When Josh's father reached a comfortable place economically and socially, he encouraged his family to play up limited aspects of their Chinese background, but mainly if it assists in societal advancement. Josh's father has recognized the significance of certain Asian stereotyping among whites and apparently hopes that by playing into that stereotyping he and his family can do better. Josh explains,

> My dad always talks about if he's meeting up with someone who is Caucasian, [who] doesn't have any idea of Asian culture, he will always take them to a specific Chinese restaurant. He knows the entire menu and takes them there. He can just talk about how Chinese and how Oriental and how this has a certain value in the Chinese culture. Like potential patients or potential contacts that can help politically or, like, you know, just people of power. He tries to impress the right connections by *exploiting*, but not really exploiting, like really advertising Asian culture to like everything. Like, he might take up a teapot and be, like, this is a kind of duck [on the teapot], in this era of China. And, like, basically kind of bullshit them. And he would actually use the word *bullshit* when he was explaining it to me. He would just—well you know, people are like, "Aw, that's so interesting and fascinating of Asian culture."... He also would encourage me to do similar things to my college application, back when I applied to schools....

So like, you know, to differentiate yourself from every other person, [not] just from everyone else but also from Asians. Maybe do a different kind of exploitation.

There is a fine line for Josh's father to walk between being substantially assimilated to white folkways and yet being proud of, and using his connections to, Chinese culture and history. Because a weak type of multiculturalism is fashionable in many organizations, Josh's father can sometimes accent or exaggerate aspects of Chinese culture in ways that he hopes may benefit him. Josh uses words like "bullshit" and "exploitation" to describe the technique that his father advocates for certain settings. What seems to be involved here is an attempt to play into white interest in Asians and Asian cultures as "exotic." There is a blending of a type of resistance strategy that involves conning whites ignorant of Asian culture with what is a submissiveness seeking to please powerful whites—so as to advance economically or socially, yet still mostly in white terms. Once again, we see the great power of the surrounding and systemic racism in shaping Asian American strategies of both adaptation and resistance.

Internalized Racism: Yet More Dimensions

Asian American conformity to white folkways and framing usually involves internalizing racism. We have already seen numerous examples of this process. In this section we seek to delve more deeply into understanding how this internalizing works and into some of its important effects. Americans of color are generally forced to adopt many white folkways and at least some white racist framing. This framing frequently creates much conflict with how people of color wish to regard themselves. There is a substantial literature on the negative self-concepts that groups like African Americans have developed in reaction to systemic racism.[19] This research reveals much about how certain groups of color have internalized negative stereotypes of their group from the omnipresent white racial framing surrounding them.

In similar ways many Asian Americans adopt some white stereotypes about Asian Americans. Anti-Asian stereotypes and related sentiments manifest themselves in some of the following ways: opposing the choice of Asian partners, purposely denying a job to an Asian American, discouraging Asian Americans who challenge the racial status quo, perpetuating negative Asian American stereotypes, seeking to change physical characteristics to appear white, and denying one's Asian heritage.

Searching for a White Partner

Before the large increase in Asian immigration facilitated by the 1965 immigration law, Asian American men outnumbered Asian American women, but since the late 1960s the population of Asian American women has grown, and they now outnumber Asian American men. Asian American women are more likely than Asian American men to marry outside of their group. They out-marry more than other women and men of color, and much more than Asian American men.[20]

In many cases, a white racial framing in the minds of Asian American women may intersect with the sexualization of Asian American women in white male minds. One study of Asian-white interracial relationships in the Southwest found that "contrary to popular utopian celebration of mixed-race marriage as a sign of multiracialization, interracial intimacy is still regulated by racial, gender, class, and national hierarchies." That is, the Asian American women interviewed "saw white men as sources of power through which they might transform their marginality" in their communities and the larger society.[21] Asian and Asian American women often see white men as avenues of liberation and mobility from the patriarchal or modest-income realities of their own backgrounds, even as white men are often attracted to them because of old stereotypes of Asian female docility or exotic sexuality.

Among our female respondents with partners, four had married Asians before they immigrated to the United States, and ten formed relationships in the United States after arrival here or as U.S.-born citizens. Of those ten, six partnered with white men, three with Asian Americans, and one with a Mexican American. Among our male respondents, those who immigrated were all single when they arrived. Of those who formed relationships in the United States, four are partnered with Asian or Asian American women, and one with an Iranian American woman. Not one has partnered with a white woman. Our sample thus reflects the higher out-marriage rate for Asian American women than for Asian American men found in other research studies.[22]

One Japanese American respondent, Alice, is distressed by the extent of this out-marriage. In her interview she discusses the resultant "whitening" of her Sansei generation:

> Why is it that Asian women are dating white men three to one over Asian men? And you know, for Japanese Americans, that out-marriage started in the '60s where 50 percent were out-marriage, but now amongst all Asian American women, the statistic is three to one. Ironically, we have three couples that are very good friends, and they are all Asian women and white

guys. And they are all having children this year. So it's like, Oh my God, it's true. But it's a strange phenomenon. And, like, I keep talking with the Asian men, and they get more and more mad as time goes on.... So it's a very strange racial thing that is happening. And now we have a lot of "Hapa" kids. And what are their lives going to be like? You know, there're going to be a lot of women with the half-Asian [children], like Tiger Woods. And in reality, mothers have much more influence over things like culture, over things like values because they spend more time naturally with their kids. But, who knows, I think it's really a dilemma that we're facing.

Younger Japanese Americans are among the most integrated of all non-European groups into numerous areas of various European American communities. What this integration means for the future of Japanese Americans is unclear, but Alice calls out this racial blending in her area as a "dilemma" in regard to the future. Some Japanese Americans view the children of mixed marriages, often called *Hapa* (from a Hawaiian word for half), as definitely Japanese American, with a goal in mind of somehow socializing them into the traditional culture. Analysts like Greg Mayeda have suggested that eventually the typical Japanese American family may be a Hapa family: "Community leaders must recognize this and encourage Hapas and their multicultural families to participate in Japanese American organizations and customs. If given the opportunity, Hapas can unify and reinvigorate the Japanese American community."[23] However, Alice does not seem so hopeful, as there is an undertone of fear that the Hapas will lose important connections to the traditional Japanese culture.

In the nineteenth century Asian American men were commonly stereotyped in an omnipresent white framing as oversexed and threatening to white women, but in recent decades they have been more likely to be stereotyped as feminized and emasculated, a shift that may link to the rise of model minority stereotyping.[24] However, this docility stereotype does not fit with Alice's experience. As she notes, many Asian American women, including herself, have an opposite view:

> You know, a lot of Asian women say from their point of view that Asian men raised by Asian mothers have a lot of macho expectations, especially if they are from China or from Korea or from India, wherever.... Asian men, well ... some of them are really angry.... It's an interesting dilemma to me, because I see the seething Asian man. You have the angry Asian man, and they are so outspoken about why, and so enraged about why. But nobody ever comes to any conclusions except that it's just happening.

According to this interview, Alice and other Asian women commonly believe they will be treated better by a white man and be granted more freedom. Yet there is no empirical evidence to support their claims. Indeed, some research suggests the opposite is more likely—that the inequality characteristic of Asian American female relationships with white men makes these women very vulnerable to significant abuse and mistreatment by their white male partners.[25]

Accepting the dominant racial framing makes white men the desirable partners for some Asian women. The latter are frequently bombarded with messages of white superiority and of the desirability of white privilege, and it is hard for them to combat these powerful influences on their thinking. One respondent, Lee, emigrated from Thailand some years ago. Before she came, she was working in what she called a "secret American factory" in Thailand making "forty times" less money than she does now. Yet those she knew there loved Americans and wanted to move to the United States. Sponsored by a relative, she was able to find work at a U.S. factory, where she met a white man. In her interview she reports that "I married him, white guy, everybody just thinks I am so lucky for that too. Like I said, I always think I like American people. I think they look wonderful. I always like them. Thai love American people." Attempting to clarify what Lee means here by "Americans," we follow up with a question asking if she means all Americans including black Americans. She responds in an interesting way: "Yes. White and black. [long pause] Because [pause] I don't know. Uh, maybe white more than black. [another long pause] I don't know, but I think so. [pause] Yes. I think white, more white." Lee's initial answer was a clear "white and black," but as she thought about the question and began to answer further, she apparently realized that black Americans are not held in such high regard as white Americans. She transitioned from definite, to hesitant, to unsure, and finally to a different certainty about "white."

Lee has a daughter who is white and Asian American. Like numerous respondents, she claims early in her interview to have not experienced racial hostility and discrimination. However, she later mentions that she is "so worried" for her daughter. In reply to a question about this, she reveals that she had in fact been a target of racial discrimination frequently from her white coworkers at a previous job. In addition, she now owns a business, and white customers sometimes treat her badly, probably because of her racial identity. She reveals that she wants to go back to Thailand as soon as she can, and with her daughter. She indicates that she would rather work for the low-paying "secret American factory" than stay in the United States. Marrying a white man has not protected her from racial hostility and discrimination, but that marriage, she believes, will give her increased social status in Thailand. She comments further, "Thai people like American people. I don't know if they like us, but we like them.... My people love American people. That's why I want [my daughter] to go back home, and they're going to treat her wonderful.... Here, it makes me worry." Interestingly, Lee wants to move back to Thailand because she perceives that her biracial daughter will receive better treatment there. Asian American women may gain some white acceptance and respite from discrimination by forming relationships with white men. However, as here, some fear that they will not be able to protect their children from that same discrimination. We might note also that at no point in her interview does Lee actually put *herself* in the important category of the "American people."

If whites are the preferred partner choice for some Asian Americans, then partners of color become an unwanted and unattractive choice. In her interview Amanda (a Filipina American, discussed earlier) recalls her partner preferences while she was attending middle school and high school: "I remember growing up that I always thought the cutest guys were all white. They were all pretty much white." Amanda could not remember where her preference for white males came from but noted that it did change over time as she became much more comfortable with her Asian American identity.

Ann, a Vietnamese American, clearly recognizes the messages she has regularly received from her parents about their preferences of partners:

> I swear to God, if I ever brought, dated a black man and brought him home, I would be disowned by my father. [Regardless] of whether he went to an Ivy League, is a doctor, a lawyer or whatever, he could be the most gentle person, the greatest person on the face of this earth, my father would disown me— because he does, he thinks that every black person is on welfare and no good. Even if I went for a Cambodian guy, I think my dad would think the same way. He doesn't think highly of the Cambodians either. My dad has that idea of that "dirty Mexican," and kind of stereotypic and racist ideals against the blacks and the Latinos. Whites, of course, of course, are better than any Asian person I could ever be with. My mom thinks so too. That she'll be blatant about.

The racially framed stereotypes that Ann's father strongly articulates about black Americans and Mexican Americans are standard ones that whites have long used to describe these Americans of color. He did not invent this hostile white racial framing but has accepted it, probably influenced by the mainstream media and other mainstream sources. Our second- and later-generation respondents often spoke of how their relatives have pushed them to adopt and conform to white standards in regard to dating and partners. These pressures to prefer white partners are commonly coupled with significant pressures to distance themselves from certain people of color.

Some choices result from personal experiences. Josh, who is Chinese American, recalls this experience when he was in elementary school and middle school: "I definitely remember actually half of my girlfriends were minority ... at the time. They were all Asian, or ..., or yeah. I think they were all Asian. And like, maybe one was Indian, and definitely no one was Caucasian. I had friends that were Caucasians but all the girls ... I was in a relationship with were Asian." It is not clear if Josh dated Asian Americans because of his personal preferences or because white females did not consider him desirable.

As he grew older, however, Josh's preferences shifted away from Asian American females. He explains why:

> But I do have a problem, like, last year a lot of Asian American females I end up meeting and talking with, it's no offense to them, but ... a lot of them actually end up like they're trying to be something else. I know this one girl, this Asian girl in my high school, and she would always talk about how popular she could have been. "I could have been so popular. I could've been so popular." She had an *image problem*. "I could be a cheerleader." She just really dreamt of being a popular girl in our class, but it was primarily an upper-class white population. I meet a lot of Asian American females, and not all of them, but some just end up really, not really wanting to be who they are. It's as if they ... are trying to really push toward something really different or really trying to be something that they naturally aren't. And I do end up dating less Asians as a result.

Josh makes an important point about identity struggles that we have highlighted previously. Some Asian American females with whom he has interacted have struggled significantly with their personal identity and have a strong desire to be socially integrated into white-dominated spaces. To Josh, this is not what they should aspire to. Indeed, he describes his sister as being at risk of losing her cultural and family connections because of a partnering choice:

> One thing that's happening with the Asian American identity, I mean, for example, my sister, when she got married, she definitely became less Asian American and just American, definitely by far. Because when she became part of [her white husband's] family it became all about his family. So it's like her race is never anything at all. It doesn't seem to come up with her, or with anyone like the in-laws. But as a result, she also has kind of lost

ties in our family. She is not as well connected. But basically, if you go to her house there is nothing Asian American about it. Nothing. Nothing.

A common report of Asian American women in such relationships is that they are not only distinctively dependent on their white husbands but usually rather subordinate to his white family. The Asian American relatives of the wife often have to take a distant second place in extended family interests and gatherings. Interpersonal connections are reduced, and personal isolation may well increase.

Notice several important issues in these last few accounts: (1) whites are the ideal partners for Asian Americans; (2) there is fear on the part of Asian Americans in interracial relationships that their half-Asian children will suffer discrimination from whites; and (3) out-marriages may disconnect Asian Americans from Asian American traditions, culture, and family connections. Most importantly, whether conscious or unconscious, partner "choice" is affected by the larger societal structure. As an individual creates a checklist of traits they deem desirable in a partner, racial stereotypes and inequality in society play a role. Often there are racial politics involved in partner choice. That politics affects Asian American men and women in different ways. Asian American women are often exoticized and are constructed as sexually attractive, frequently giving them more diverse partnership opportunities, but Asian American men are not constructed in the same way and, at times, find their partner choices more limited.[26] A study of expressed dating preferences online confirmed that the odds favor white men and Asian American women the most, while Latino and Asian American men have the lowest response rates to their personal posts.[27]

Asian-on-Asian Stereotyping and Discrimination

We have already observed how numerous Asian Americans participate in at least some Asian-on-Asian stereotyping and discrimination. Some attribute negative characteristics to Asians or Asian Americans as "natural." Some articulate group-hating views. Some with the power to hire and promote consciously deny people of Asian heritage jobs or promotions. Yet others openly criticize Asian Americans who actively work against anti-Asian racism. Such Asian-on-Asian mistreatment substantially serves the interests of whites and the U.S. system of racism.

Blaming Asians and Asian Americans

Recall from a previous chapter that one respondent, Bari, was a victim of a hate crime while coming home from his college campus. He was the first victim of several street attacks on international students near this university, all of whom were Asian. Bari's incident came up when we interviewed another Asian international student, David, who has served as a leader in a campus association that represents many Chinese students. Asked by a campus student association to alert the students in his organization to the danger of further white attacks, he took no action because he believed, in fact erroneously, that the only students being attacked were South Asians.[28] In his interview he rationalizes the violent attacks on South Asians thus: "I know the people that got beat around that area. They are from India. Maybe for the Chinese, they don't really get into trouble. Maybe because they don't speak very good English, so they kind of get away from the trouble, get away, the Chinese students. But Indian students, they speak better English. They want to argue [he laughs]."

When we explain that the attacks were unprovoked and that the targets included East Asians, he replies, "Oh, really, that's really bad." In regard to informing students in his organization, at first he said that he had not received complaints of discrimination from students that he represented, but after further discussion he did cite numerous instances where Chinese and Chinese American students did report feeling unwelcome on campus. Later in the interview, he has this to say about how other students at the university feel about international students: "People say they don't really care or interact with international students. But still I can feel there is a barrier between international students and American students. They hang around American students, but I don't think many international students interact with that many American students. It depends; maybe it's our problem. We are probably too conservative."

When David refers to "American students" at this large historically white institution, he makes clear that he means *whites*. Other researchers have found too that "Americans" and "whites" are often interchangeable terms used by Asians and first-generation Asian Americans—and apparently for many people around the globe.[29] David's comments about the campus area hate crimes and other mistreatment of Asian students never mention or fault the violent white perpetrators. He specifically blames the divide between Asian and white students on certain tendencies of Asians, such as the latter being "too conservative" in certain styles of interaction. Yet in his interview, Bari, the target of a hate crime on that campus, says that when he first arrived on campus he felt an immediate chill from the white students that made it impossible to make friends with them.

Alex, who lives in a Pacific Coast area heavily populated with Asian Americans, says that he too believes that Asian Americans should take the blame for some of their problems. In his interview he notes that the government pays little attention to Asian issues:

The government ... they don't care for Asians that much. But at the same time, the Asians aren't very good about coming forward with political issues, I think. So lots of times you watch TV, or listen to the radio. When they talk about minorities, they're usually talking about African Americans. They hardly mention Asian Americans. And that's because I think that we as Asians are not very good about putting up the issues in American government. Or maybe other Americans, they don't look at it being an issue, even when we actually do. So actually I think it goes both ways. For example, when I go to Costco, and sometimes there are people, they are collecting signatures to make [something] into law, or whatever they are doing. I would observe those people, and most of the time they won't bother to ask Asians. Because, I think, we have a poor voting rate.

Even in West Coast areas with many Asian Americans, some Asian American political organizations, and a few Asian American elected officials, Alex has noticed the lack of interest that activists have in soliciting Asian Americans to be involved in political petitions. Asian Americans do have a relatively low voter turnout rate, but that rate is steadily growing.[30] His statement also assigns responsibility to Asian Americans for not asserting their political interests and issues and for a low voting rate, but does not assess critically the possible reasons for this. In contrast, Asian American analyst Vijay Prashad explains this lack of political involvement as linked in part to historical exclusion and discrimination and thus to "being socially detached from U.S. life," which "justifies withdrawing even further from the social and political life of the United States."[31]

Taking Asian-on-Asian stereotyping and discrimination a step further, Frank, who lives in a city with large Asian American communities, reports often acting out of a perspective shaped by the white framing of Asian Americans:

I have my own company. I use an American white female and I send her out to sell, and then I send the Oriental girl out there. I found that the white American females consistently have higher sales. So as a business owner, ... of course I'm going to lean toward the white American girl. She's bringing more money for me. It's a simple fact of life. And you know, I don't think you can force that issue. At the end of the day, who's writing a check to your company, right, and if I send the white girl out there, and she gets more money for me, I'll be using her. Not because of race, just as a fact of life. I wouldn't say that it's fair or not fair. Nothing in life is fair. I look at it this way: life is not fair from the beginning to end. If you try to make everything fair, it won't work. If I was born as Brad Pitt, it would be great, but I'm not. Brad Pitt may be making a couple movies, making a hundred million dollars, but since I'm not, I make less than $150,000. Am I unhappy? Of course I'm happy. I'm happy. It's a fact of life.

Note how Frank uses the negative word "Oriental," one that whites invented and have long used to categorize and denigrate Asians and Asian Americans. His unreflective use of the term suggests acceptance of a stereotyped white framing of Asians, one that he openly acknowledges in various parts of his detailed interview. In addition, although many of his customers are Asian American, he prefers whites as salespeople. Complicating an assessment of his perspective, we observe too that Frank is adamant that life in the United States is "not fair," so he must just accept that racially biased reality.

Attacking Asian Americans Who "Rock the Boat"

Most of our respondents have refrained from openly protesting racist incidents that they have seen or been involved in, even if they live in areas with many Asian Americans. One reason is fear of white retaliation. As we have shown, acquiescing has long been an individual and group survival technique. Parents pass down these strategic techniques to children, often conjoined with admonitions to individual conformity. This conventional adaptation to racial hostility poses serious problems for those who choose to challenge that racial reality. Asian American activists thus have often found themselves alone when standing up against discriminatory incidents. They have been accused of "rocking the boat" and have been targeted with negative criticism from the very communities that they are attempting to serve and protect.

Take the example of Jessica, a Vietnamese American whose family situation we described earlier. At a major university with a substantial Asian and Asian American student population (approaching one-fifth), Jessica's student group published a well-documented report about problems of Asian and Asian American students there, with the hope of securing significant institutional change. The group made modest demands, including more Asian American representation in student government and one Asian American mental health counselor. After the report was released, the university administration claimed to be responsive to its findings and planned meetings to discuss the issues. The most intense criticism of this rather moderate report came from an unexpected sector—from other Asians and Asian American students in the university community. When word got to those students, as Jessica puts it, "the shit really hit the fan." She continues with her account:

But the students, that was the most hurtful because a lot of the criticism came from our own community. And I can see it. And it's like watching a video about the model minority being perpetuated. You know, it's like here it is. This is how the model minority is perpetuated, and then just look at it. I mean, people were saying, "Why do you have to rock the boat?" People saying, "Why are you looking for trouble? Why are you seeing things that aren't there? I've never experienced racism. It must not exist." It was ridiculous, and people were personally attacking the women of [the organization] ... and it was so hurtful for [the president], and it was really hard for me to see it. In Asian American Studies classes, people would say, "That's ridiculous," where I would think the most progressive Asian Americans would see. People saying that "this is crap" and like, "this doesn't exist."

Much criticism of the important report came from Asian American students, yet the intent was to provide better representation and support for that population. For these students fear of white backlash trumped even modest actions to bring campus change. Like the Japanese Issei and Nisei before and after World War II, Asian Americans today can work hard and become high-achieving citizens, yet still *greatly fear* losing everything at the whim of discriminatory whites. At Jessica's university, the Asian student population is the largest among the students of color, yet being critical of the university's often anti-Asian climate is still too difficult for many.

Fareena, a Bangladeshi American, was head of this bold student organization at the time. In her interview she discusses the backlash she received after the report was released:

There was a lot of hate mail from Asian American males. A lot of them were Asian Studies majors saying, "Why are you causing a ruckus? You're making us look bad." I remember taking an Asian American Studies class at that time. The women in that class hated me. I would get nasty little notes on my desk, "You're just doing this for your résumé." I thought, "If I was doing this for my résumé, I would get better grades. I wouldn't be messing up my classes," because that's what I was doing. One of them had said that I just "needed to take a Midol and cool down. These issues aren't that big of a deal." I thought the Midol reference was very interesting. I talked to her about it, and she just said, "It's a pain killer." These are all Asian American females, saying, "Why are you making Asian Americans look bad? Why are you saying that?" ... No group likes it when someone's rocking the boat. People think differently in terms of belonging to an imagined community or not. Some people are very defensive of it, and some are not.

Fareena bore the brunt of the criticism from the student community she was trying to serve. She was labeled an agitator, and many Asian Americans on campus worked to distance themselves from being associated with the "trouble seekers" in the Asian organization. She continues by describing some positive responses, as well as her personal costs:

> I've had a lot of nice e-mails and messages from people, but they were primarily people of color that were not Asian American. Or Asian Americans would send it in, but they would remain anonymous. I thought that was weird. I remember that it was a really bad semester for me. For me in the beginning I was like, "I'm ready to take it! I'm ready to take it! I don't care. If I believe in these issues and I made this report, I have to be responsible for whatever consequences come. I will learn from it. It will be an opportunity." But I had to seek counseling. I really did.

Interestingly, Fareena received much support from other racial groups, especially African Americans and Latinos, that many whites label as "troublemakers" when they openly resist the serious manifestations of white discrimination. She explains more about the character of the backlash and the major impact of the events on her:

> A lot of our members weren't expecting this big of a backlash from Asian Americans. One member quit because he felt like he was going to lose his friends and he felt like he shouldn't have to defend our organization to them.... Some of the members were questioning, "Did we go about this the right way? Should we have made this report? Should we have kept it quiet?" Which is what the person who quit had advocated for. Now that I think about it, I think we did do the right thing. But back then I felt silenced and I think I took it a little harder and I didn't tell people, and people didn't realize because I was quoted so much. I was also in Asian American Studies classes at the time, the other people were not.... I failed it. I never explained it to the professor, who was the adviser for Asian American Studies.... It was just hard and if it was hard to tell her, because the class would have discussions about it every day in the beginning. They would say things out loud very passive-aggressively to me or by even saying my name. Me being the person I am, I would want to say, "Actually, you have that wrong, because this is what happened." The professor would shut me down. I don't think she realized she was shutting *me* down, but she saw that it was becoming a back-and-forth argument.

Shortly after Fareena began being harshly criticized by other Asian students, she stepped down from the leadership of the organization.

Even with the Yellow Power movement near the end of the 1960s, successful pressures for reparations for imprisoned Japanese Americans, and the recent increase in Asian American Studies courses (some even being taken by her critics), the collective memory of racial oppression and resistance to it that is passed along to Asian Americans is relatively weak, indeed sometimes nonexistent. This greatly complicates the protest efforts of Asian American activists. Even later, fellow Asian students in Fareena's Asian American Studies courses still make similar remarks to her when there is news of a new racist incident in the campus area.

In her interview Jessica reasons in a sharp and probing way with regard to why many Asian American students reacted negatively to discussions of anti-Asian racism:

> It happens because we internalize that racism and that oppression. You know, it goes back to, you know, when you are little, and all you want to do is fit in. And if you feel like you fit in and someone else is making a racket.... I mean, like, *shut up,* you know, stop being such a [sore] thumb! You know, *stop!* I think that's part of what it is. And part of it is because the Asian American community is very diverse, and I mean some people may have not experienced that kind of discrimination. That doesn't mean it doesn't exist. I mean, it does, and maybe you just weren't aware of the discrimination that you experienced because it's everywhere. It's pervasive. It's the little things, and you can't deny the numbers when you talk about the professional world, and how many people you have—just look at the university—how many Asian Americans there are and how many of them are high ranking. So, I mean, it's undeniable it exists, but when we don't learn about our history, and we don't learn about our role here in this country and we're not even seen as Americans, I mean, we internalize all of that and we don't see it. A lot of times Asian Americans don't consider themselves people of color, and other people don't consider them people of color either. So they don't understand it, they don't get it. Or they say, well yeah, I guess you're right, but it's not as bad as, you know, the black community or the Latino community, so we should shut up.

When Jessica asserts that "we don't learn about our history," she is highlighting the lack of collective memory of historical oppression and resistance to it among most Asian Americans, an issue to which we will return later. Because many Asian Americans lack a substantial knowledge of the history of oppression, they sometimes do not even see themselves as people of color—or at least as people who need to organize and resist the racism they regularly face. This is highly problematical for those who not only understand that oppression but seek to organize and to change it.

At least one other study has found Asian Americans in similar situations. Thus, pioneering researcher Mia Tuan has concluded from her interviews with Asian Americans that

> some Asian Americans have embraced the model minority label, and see it as their ultimate ticket into gaining social acceptance.... Youth were convinced that with hard work, patience, and a little help from the model minority stereotype, they would someday gain the full approval of white Americans. They wrote off repeated incidents involving racism or discrimination as the acts of ignorant individuals, isolated experiences that they did not take seriously.[32]

Similarly, Fareena and Jessica's classmates are hoping that Fareena's brave actions do not "ruin it for the rest of them," as they too believe discriminators are just ignorant and they remain naively hopeful that whites will honor their hard work with success and real acceptance.

Stereotyping Other Americans of Color: Targets and Discriminators

In his pioneering analysis of Asian Americans, Frank Wu has argued that their in-between role in the U.S. racial hierarchy makes for a complexity of situations, which often shift and mutate significantly from one to the next: "When considering Asian Americans it is easier to realize that people can be both perpetrators and victims of racial discrimination. We can simultaneously play both roles, inferior to one, superior to the other. Asian Americans can feel ostracized by whites and terrorized by blacks. Asian Americans can even simultaneously play both roles in relation to the same group, regarding either blacks or whites with contempt only to have the favor returned."[33]

One point that Wu fails to address in his otherwise insightful analysis is that it is the centuries-old white racial frame that provides most major stereotypes that Asian Americans and other people of color adopt in regard to U.S. racial groups, including their own group. Like almost all critical analysts, Wu skirts around directly naming white discriminators as such even as he discusses the serious discrimination Americans of Asian descent face "in society" and assesses well how they often add to their somewhat favored position "by disparaging other people of color." Wu attributes this process to personal choices made by individual Asian Americans. However, these Asian Americans are making such choices within a societal context that is deeply and structurally racist, one where they are forced to collude to some degree with the existing racist system and where they often accept much of the white racial framing of society and the racial hierarchy that age-old frame buttresses.

The impact of U.S. racism is not confined to the borders of the United States. Indeed, U.S. economic, political, military, and mass media power makes the country very important, indeed often dominant, in many global settings. The United States not only exports commercial goods but also propagates important ideals and ideas as well. The U.S. media are very influential and perpetuate important aspects of the white racial frame to many countries around the world. Certain U.S.-oriented products and their advertising also spread a U.S. racial framing. One conspicuous example of the global perpetuation of this white racist framing can be seen even in brands of toothpaste used in some countries overseas. For example, in Taiwan the "Darkie" toothpaste brand still shows a man in "black face" with bright white teeth. Another toothpaste brand is not so subtly called "Whiteman"! The Darkie brand depicts a blatantly racist image of a white man mocking "blackness" in the fashion of the old white minstrels once commonplace in the United States, while the Whiteman brand overtly shows "whiteness" as the standard for beautiful and ideal oral hygiene. Other products, such as some candy packages in Europe, Asia, and Mexico, also carry extraordinarily racist representations. Moreover, U.S. movies and television shows, some from the 1930s–1950s era, are regularly shown around the globe, and they too often carry racist messages not only about white superiority and black inferiority but also about the inferiority of other Americans of color.

Thus, many new immigrants from overseas countries enter the United States with their heads already full of racist stereotypes and images—especially those targeting African, Latino, and Asian Americans—which they have picked up from their contacts with the U.S. mass media and other sources. Asians thus frequently receive racialized messages about Americans of color long before they step on U.S. soil. After immigrating, they and their children live under the aegis of the white frame and quickly learn many folkways of this still racialized society. Because of this, many learn and accept old racist stereotypes of themselves and other Americans of color long promoted by whites.

Sociologist Claire Jean Kim has studied conflict between Korean Americans and African Americans in New York City. She concludes from her research that "by celebrating Asian American 'success,' White opinion makers implicitly assert that nothing is standing in the way of other nonwhite groups except their own bad habits or cultural deficiencies."[34] This aspect of the white framing of the latter

Americans of color is often adopted by Korean and other Asian Americans. For example, Alex, a Korean American professional from the West Coast, discusses such views held by his grandparents:

> It's interesting because my grandparents ... just wouldn't like African Americans. For no particular reason.... They don't change their minds.... My grandpa, all the time he would like always, for whatever reason, he wouldn't like African Americans. And then they never really gave me any clear reason when I [said], "What did they do to you?" "Nothing." So that's pretty disappointing. But that's the way things are, I guess.... I think that in L.A., those riots going on, and there's a big conflict between Koreans and blacks. And I think that has something to do with it. Their interaction with African Americans is almost nothing. They go to church; they're in the Korean community, because understandably they don't speak the language, so they just stay in the Korean community. And what they know is what they see in the newspaper.... They read the Korean newspaper, and I don't know what the content areas [are], but I would guess the only time [African Americans] get a mention is when some kind of crime happens.

Alex is able to pinpoint the likely source of his grandparents' views—a Korean American newspaper and its reporting on 1990s conflicts between Korean American merchants and African Americans in cities like Los Angeles. However, his grandparents' antiblack sentiments likely preceded these conflicts. As we suggested previously, Korean and other Asian immigrants to the United States frequently have preconceived stereotypes about African Americans even before they immigrate, to a substantial degree because of contact with U.S. media operating overseas.[35] In addition, Korean-black conflicts in the United States, and the way they are reported in mainstream and Korean news media, seem to have worsened the stereotyping that Korean Americans hold in regard to African Americans (and, likely, vice versa).

Such conflict between Asian Americans and African Americans is not new. Since the importation of Chinese workers onto the West Coast in the 1850s, and into the state of Mississippi during the 1870s Reconstruction era after the Civil War, Asian immigrants have periodically been used by whites to undercut other workers of color. In Mississippi, these Chinese immigrants were brought in as cheap workers to harvest crops on former slave plantations, thereby undercutting newly freed black laborers. However, this effort did not work out well for the Asian immigrants, and some then opened small stores catering to the black southerners. Chinese immigrants were then mostly shut out of doing business with white customers, and whites' racist beliefs often kept whites from catering to black customers, thereby leaving this modest business opportunity open for these Chinese Americans.[36]

Many Asian Americans, like these Chinese merchants long ago, have continued to find ways to prosper by providing economic services for African Americans. Thus, recent Korean immigrants, some of whom cannot find jobs in line with their educational credentials because of various types of discrimination by white employers, sometimes use their economic resources to start small businesses catering to low-income communities, especially those of African and Latino Americans in central cities. The U.S. racial hierarchy thereby creates the possibility of serious conflict, as Korean American scholar Kim argues:

> Korean immigrants find themselves in a disadvantaged position relative to Whites but in an advantaged position relative to Blacks. It is in this way that the very economic opportunities that are closed to Blacks become the ticket to upward mobility for Korean immigrants. To the degree that Korean immigrants also buy into the racial constructions that underwrite the racial order—that is, to the degree that they accept that Blacks deserve their lowly status because they are lazy, unintelligent, undisciplined, etc.—they become further implicated in American racial dynamics.[37]

A number of our respondents articulated or discussed negative stereotypes of African Americans and other Americans of color. Frank, a Korean American, offers these comments about some people in his own ethnic group:

> I noticed that Koreans tend to discriminate a lot more than any other race. Yeah, they tend to make nasty comments about Mexican Americans and black Americans.... I think that the main damage of the movie media— every Mexican you see in the media is usually a drug dealer or crazed killer, or a sexual predator, or some very, very nasty role. Every movie you go and see, a drug dealer is usually a South American driving a Rolls Royce with a three-foot-long cigar in his mouth. But that's going [to] keep every Korean in their head that every Mexican must be like that. Then on the news, every news you hear, some Mexican group is killing people, you know, for no reason. But a lot of people think they *must* be like that. Every one of them. I told them, they are not. Believe me, they are not. You know. The African Americans too.

Like Alex above, Frank identifies the mainstream media as a major source for negative typecasting of Mexican and African Americans. He presents himself as someone who understands this mass media distortion, yet also articulates in his interview some strong stereotyped notions about Mexican Americans: "The main problem seems to be education. They do not have a concept of education, and one thing I noticed—I don't know whether this is true or not—they are truly much better at this element than Asians—but you know, I count the fifteen- or sixteen- or seventeen-[year-olds], they are fully grown, mature physically, but mentally they're not."

Here Frank seems to be accepting a negative image of Mexican American teenagers as too mature physically and perhaps as threatening, but not as mentally mature. We might note here the common framing of Latinos (and African Americans) as not being interested in education for themselves or their children. This too is a central stereotype in the old white racial framing of these groups, in part because it deflects attention from many years of white discrimination against these groups, including continuing discrimination in the provision of first-rate educational facilities and opportunities. Yet, numerous research studies show that most Latino parents, like most African American parents, are *committed* to securing good educations for their children and others in their communities.[38]

Frank continues with a mixture of insight and stereotyping about Mexican Americans:

> So also another thing I noticed about Mexican Americans is that, when I didn't have a contact with them, I could have a bad news, bad things about them, you know what they do and all that stuff. But once I got to know them I found most of them are very hardworking, most of them are very honest. There's a very few—one in a hundred—which make every Mexican American look bad. They do some crazy things, you know, crazy, crazy things that I just cannot comprehend.

After discussing the fact that the media reality is contradicted in his own positive everyday experiences with most Mexican Americans, Frank returns to his strong notions about self-help:

> I saw them for about two years. I talked to them, and I did find out that [what] Mexican Americans need are good role models, and then someone to really get on the podium and tell them to get an education.... You know, if I was an African American and I was a leader, I would tell all African Americans ... two things: one, it doesn't matter how much political pull you have if your group does not have economic power. And I'd tell the Mexican Americans too. The Mexican Americans are going to vote for, you know, people into the city hall and all that stuff, and I told them, "So what? So what?" Let's say, for instance, I go to Salinas, California. In that

town 85 percent of the east side is Mexican American.... They all work for somebody. You know what I found out? One hundred percent of the land is owned by white Americans. And then they think they have political power. I told them, you got nothing. Political power means ... you have to have a dollar sign behind there. You guys don't have it. And African Americans too.

Frank stereotypes Mexican Americans as not being interested in working for themselves and as not having good role models. He offers unsolicited advice to both Mexican Americans and African Americans that they need to aggressively get into business in order to have significant economic power. Here, of course, he overlooks the fact that these groups lack access to economic and political capital because of past and present racial discrimination, such as in the U.S. lending industry.

Then Frank provides yet more advice:

And one thing I like to tell African Americans is they got to stop saying about the racism from now on. Because they've been here long time, almost 200 years. See, the Chinese and Koreans and Indians can come over here, and then they can become a multi-multi-millionaire within one generation, why couldn't they do it? And then one thing that I'd like to tell them is they've got to have all those black kids into the school.... African Americans, I don't think they have a right now even to say racism is holding them back. I don't think so.... As a matter of fact, if you take a look at the government program, like ... all of those companies set aside over 15 percent of the proposition to the minority, specifically for African Americans, and they cannot fill it because there is not enough candidates. I just tell, would like to tell those African Americans, U.S. government is giving you every opportunity to get ahead, but you are not taking it. And if you go over to that [successful] school, everybody is busy, every student is busy because they are trying to catch up with homework, or whatever.... Most [black] kids are not doing anything inside the classroom. They're joking around, they're playing around. They're not reading. That's why they are not getting ahead. Also, it's a chance to improve. I don't think, from here on, I don't think anybody would say it's racism that is holding them back. That it's absolutely not true. Maybe 5 percent true, and 95 percent not.

Frank recites numerous stereotypes and related notions and thereby perpetuates the white framing long used to rationalize the subordination of both African Americans and Mexican Americans. Although he has personal experience with white discriminators in his own life, he embraces the white-generated "boot-straps" ideology, arguing that African Americans and Mexican Americans just need to get educations, work harder, and start businesses. His analysis does not recognize the role of institutional racism, and indeed he chides African Americans for asserting there is white racism, the longevity of which (approaching 400 years now) he seriously underestimates. Although he discusses in his interview the glass ceiling that prevents upward mobility for Asian Americans, he does not relate such institutional racial barriers to the job and educational problems faced by a great many workers of color.

In contrast to Frank's views, some Asian American scholars have critically analyzed white attempts to play off Asian Americans against African Americans. In his probing analysis, Wu puts it thus: "Telling African Americans they ought to be like Asian Americans ... only aggravates racial tensions among African Americans and Asian Americans. It is a paternalistic suggestion, as if whites were the elders telling the older siblings, African Americans, that they should be more like the younger ones, Asian Americans."[39] Similarly, Prashad underscores his role as an Asian American in the racial hierarchy: "I am to be the perpetual solution to what is seen as the crisis of black America.... Meanwhile, white America can take its seat, comfortable in its liberal principles, surrounded by state selected Asians, certain that the culpability for black poverty and oppression must be laid at the door of black America."[40]

Because Asian Americans are often used by the white-controlled media, politicians, and other analysts as exemplars and weapons against black Americans, it is unsurprising that respondents such as Mylene, a Filipina American, parrot stereotyped views of African Americans:

The thing in the news is there's racial profiling by the police, but I'm not really familiar with that. I don't see any correlation because if you are committing the crime, you are committing the crime. It doesn't matter what race you are. It's excuses, you know what I mean? If you are that race and you commit a crime, don't say you're targeted because they caught you.... You know what I mean? I don't know where that racial profiling, where they get that; [it] doesn't make sense.... Yeah, that they always study hard and what not. But also, African Americans, a lot of them [are] into sports, and they make millions of dollars, and they are more richer than lots of Asians. Sports figures, like Shaq and Kobe, all these sports figures, and family and friends. And there are some rap singers, they make millions more, lots of millions more than a lot of Asians.... So it can be equalized in that way, money-wise.

Mylene seems to misunderstand the serious problem of racial profiling, information on which she apparently has gotten from the news media. Many Americans
of color, including Asian Americans, have faced frequent discriminatory racial
profiling by police officers and other government officials, most of whom are
white. Indeed, several state and local police departments have recently had to
change their racial profiling policies because of community protests against this
type of institutionalized discrimination.[41]

Mylene believes that the reality of a very small proportion of African Americans
being well-off athletes and entertainers somehow equalizes the general economic
situations of African Americans and Asian Americans as groups. However, government income statistics indicate that the median income of African American
families lags well behind the median incomes of most major Asian American
groups as well as the median income of white Americans.[42] As with other respondents, and a majority of whites, Mylene relies heavily on the mainstream media,
yet these sources frequently offer much misinformation and a white framing of
society's racial issues for many millions of viewers of all backgrounds.

Katherine, who is Chinese American, is retired but now does substitute teaching. In her efforts to improve the relationships among the racially diverse students
at her school, she reports that she imparts to them some distinctive messages:

> I substitute teach here, and I also take care of kids with broken families,
> and they are in middle-school age now, twelve, thirteen. And this little girl
> that I've been caring for ever since she was eight, she started telling me, she
> said, you know in the cafeteria they sit in groups now. [She's] Hispanic, she
> would play with just any kids, and now she said they kind of sit together
> now, the black kids together. I said ... you and I both know that, especially
> the black kids, a lot of them are not black. They're half-black, half-white. It's
> just that the white kids don't want to claim them because their skin color
> is darker. And they think they are black. They're not black, you know. And
> there are some Hispanic kids that are not Hispanic, and there are some
> Asian kids that are not Asian. I mean, they are half-Asian and half-white,
> so I told my students that in class.

This respondent is concerned about what she views as self-segregation of black
children in the cafeteria, a phenomenon commonly misinterpreted as involving
just the unfortunate personal choices of black children—and not the recurring
impacts of a racist society on them. Katherine also relates how she has tried to
distance the biracial children from their non-European heritages. She is arguing
that they are not truly children of color because they are partly white. She appears
to be saying that if these biracial children accent their whiteness, they can be

relieved of their lowly status as children of color and be in effect "white" children. Although she does note the biased preference of the white children, she seems to be under the impression that African, Latino, and Asian American children with some white ancestry can personally choose how they will be identified in society, neglecting the reality that their racial identities are usually imposed on them by those discriminatory white children and other whites.

One cautious respondent, Ginzi, argues in his responses to our questions that Asian Americans get mistreated by other groups of color: "Are we treated on the same level as everybody in this country? More or less. Like, I think—I think—let me not say anything stupid. Hmm, by the white population we're treated pretty fairly. From other minority groups we get more shit than from white people." Ginzi carefully chooses his words so that he does not say anything too offensive against others of color. This suggests that he may have deeper feelings about these racial issues that he does not wish to share. Significantly, in his interview at no point does he suggest a substantial role for white discriminators in creating problems for Americans of color.

One older Chinese American respondent from an urban area with a substantial Asian American population, Henry, has been ridiculed and even physically harmed by racist whites over nearly five decades. Recall his comments about whites in Chapter 3: "Why do they want to make fun of you? Because that's the way the culture is, because they want to make fun of Chinese culture because of the movies they see. Take the N-word, they banned that word, but they are still calling the Chinese 'Chinamen.'" In spite of this white discrimination, he still articulates images of African Americans from the dominant racial frame. For example, he discusses differences between Chinese Americans and African Americans in how they respond to white discrimination: "The Chinese don't complain about it. The Chinese culture is not like black. If [you] do something they don't like, they either attack you, or frighten you, or even kill you. How many Asians got the guts to do that? We should try to get them to ban the word 'Chinaman.' I think we need Chinese people to get together, just like the blacks do. I think a lot of things should change."

Over the course of his interview, however, Henry offers no evidence from his experiences for this strong stereotyping of African Americans as routinely violent, but rather seems to be drawing his images from distorted and stereotyped "news" presentations in the mainstream media. Wu has suggested that "many whites and Asian Americans do not have enough contact with African Americans to have formed a sense of any individual African American as a human being."[43] Indeed, many of our respondents articulate racist stereotypes of African or Latino Americans with little reservation or qualifying, and probably with limited or no personal experience with them. In the U.S. case, systemic racism masterfully and routinely creates racial tensions and conflicts among Americans of color by making all who live within this society accept, at least to some degree, its powerfully invasive and white-imposed racial framing of Americans of color.

Conclusion

In 2007 *AsianWeek* published a controversial article by an Asian American author, Kenneth Eng, on "Why I Hate Blacks." In this opinion piece he listed reasons for his hatred. Among his stereotyped statements was this: "Contrary to media depictions, I would argue that blacks are weak-willed. They are the only race that has been enslaved for 300 years. It's unbelievable that it took them that long to fight back." Eng cited personal experience and historical reasons for his strained relationship with the black community, but his cursory analysis points to a much larger problem: a widespread lack of knowledge in the Asian American community about the historical background and development of nearly four centuries of racial oppression in this country.[44] In contrast to his view, the reality is that African Americans were enslaved for about 240 years in North America and did indeed fight back in many ways from the first days of enslavement. The harsh criticisms directed against African Americans and other Americans of color in his analysis—and indeed in other articles that he wrote for *AsianWeek*—underscore the extent to which an extensive white racist framing of society has penetrated the minds even of well-educated Asian Americans.

The interview responses showcased in this chapter demonstrate the depth of the penetration of the white racial frame and the racial hierarchy it rationalizes in the lives of these Asian Americans. All must struggle against these oppressive realities every day of their lives in the United States. They may resist, or they may conform. They all do both. Both strategies are defensive and imposed on them by the surrounding society.

As we have seen, substantial efforts are put forth by numerous respondents to copy, mimic, and extend the white framing and folkways, including in regard to the racial hierarchy. Many clearly take measures to protect themselves from future white discrimination by conforming and trying to enter once exclusively white economic and social spaces. The impact of systemic racism, including white discrimination of many kinds and at several levels, has forced these interviewees to take significant defensive measures to protect themselves, as several of them sagely analyzed. They have changed names and social networks, adopted what they deem as white values and political stances, and even chosen white partners. At rather young ages, many respondents reported feeling and understanding great pressures to conform to the white framing and folkways, and all have worked hard to be accepted into white social worlds. Indeed, some respondents no longer think of themselves, or choose not to openly identify, as Asian American.

The dominant racial frame is so powerful that numerous interviewees have adopted some negative stereotypes about Asian Americans, about themselves and their group, as well as about other Americans of color. Many observe the racially subordinate position of African Americans in society and respond in a rather distancing and protective way. As Wu sagely notes, they "benefit just by not being black.... It may be that the ability of Asian Americans to pass into whiteness depends on their ability to distance themselves from blackness."[45] As our interviews make evident, many people distance themselves from blackness and go to great lengths to cozy up to whiteness. Their own identities often seem to be muddled in their minds as they grapple with how the white framing of Asian Americans dictates who they should, and should not, be. These respondents have learned the racial stereotypes and images of Asian Americans that are central in that dominant framing, racialized lessons they have often internalized.

Significantly, all our respondents noted or recognized in some way during their interviews that they or their families do face significant racial hostility and discrimination at the hands of white Americans in various places. However, most do not seem to view this continuing problem as structural and systemic but rather as a matter of incidents generated by white individuals acting out of ignorance or various other nonracial reasons.

CHAPTER 6
ACTS OF RESISTANCE

In December 2013, writer Suey Park started a Twitter hashtag (#NotYourAsian-Sidekick) that began trending on the social media site. In less than one day, there were over 45,000 tweets where Asian Americans and others were sharing ways in which Asians are marginalized in society.[1]

Park explained that she started the discussion because "nobody will GIVE us a space. We need to MAKE a space to use our voices, build community, and be heard" and that the provocative hashtag is "MAKING room for those of us silenced by the AAPI mainstream." The Twitter trend received a great deal of media attention and Park was interviewed by a number of mainstream media outlets including ABC, NPR, *Time*, Salon, and the *Washington Post*. Park was calling for a new movement, a development of a critical mass, and for Asian Americans to speak out about racial injustice. Park confronted the "AAPI [Asian Americans/Pacific Islanders] mainstream" as being complicit with racism and urged Asian Americans to break racial stereotypes. She informed Twitter followers, "This is not a trend, this is a movement. Everybody calm down and buckle down for the long haul, please."

Is a new day coming for Asian Americans? Will we begin to see a critical mass standing up and speaking out against white racism? It is too early to weigh the long-term effects of Suey Park's efforts on Twitter, but perhaps the social media are a key component to social movements today. The anonymity of cyberspace and lack of face-to-face interaction could help some Asian Americans speak out without fear of physical retribution. It remains to be seen if this helps Asian Americans resist in their daily lives, including in their personal interactions with whites.

Noteworthy is the fact that our respondents provided significantly fewer accounts of active and overt resistance to racial discrimination than they shared about that discrimination and its painful impacts. Less than a third offered significant insights into and accounts of overt resistance techniques used to contend with everyday racism. This is not unusual, for the few other recent studies of Asian Americans that have been conducted also rarely report such acts of open resistance. Today, racial hostility and discrimination remain daunting to combat because of the strength and systemic character of U.S. racism. White acts of discrimination are pervasive, and their strength and omnipresence help us to understand why relatively few respondents have decided to fight openly against them. Many choose to suffer quietly as they cope with discriminatory acts on their own. In order to protect themselves, many go to great lengths to conform to aspects of the white racial frame and its allied racial hierarchy.

Thus, everyday resistance to racism comes in many guises. Clearly, it involves more than direct physical or verbal confrontation. As Patricia Hill Collins suggests, resistance to racism can take a confrontational form, but it also comes in the form of internally rejecting some of the dominant racial framing, of producing tangible social and political changes for one's self and others, and of creating positive self-definitions and self-valuations.[2]

Direct confrontation can be dangerous and costly. Challenging white discriminators can result in the loss of a resistor's livelihood, security, dignity, and even life. The interviewees who actively resist demonstrate great bravery in fighting for respect and dignity, yet this overt resistance often gets ignored or played down in their own communities and usually goes unnoticed in the larger society. Moreover, much of the everyday resistance of Asian Americans involves individual reframing and psychological opposition to at least some of the white racial frame and hierarchy, although such a transformation of an individual's thinking and feeling does not necessarily generate more overt antidiscriminatory actions. And such resistance has not yet created a strong and collective counterframing to the white racial frame in most Asian American communities.

Overt Strategies: Direct Confrontation

Few respondents reported feeling confident enough to directly confront white discriminators. This is frequently because of fear that such action would worsen their situations. Not surprisingly, thus, such confrontational actions are rarely reported in our interviews or in other recent studies of Asian Americans. Certainly, however, there are important examples of very overt resistance in Asian American history, but they are seldom discussed in U.S. textbooks or classrooms. For example, relatively new Chinese immigrants, railroad workers, went on a large-scale strike for better working conditions in 1867. When white employers cut them off from supplies, however, those who did not die of cold or starvation were forced to resume their dangerous work. Moreover, during the 1960s civil rights movements, some Asian Americans on the West Coast took part in a "Yellow Power" movement, and others worked with or alongside the African American movement.[3] Recently, a growing number of Asian American organizations have worked, sometimes successfully, to combat anti-Asian imagery in the mainstream media and pop culture, yet these efforts often go unnoticed by Asian and non–Asian Americans alike. They rarely make the mainstream news media, in part because whites who control most of these outlets likely think Asian Americans do not really face significant hostility and discrimination—that is, that they are in fact the "model minority."

Resistance in the form of direct confrontation can be dangerous. Our respondents periodically reflected on possible confrontation but usually opted out of directly confronting perpetrators of discrimination because they were outnumbered or frightened about retaliation. In the relatively rare cases of confrontation that we now consider, respondents addressed issues of racial hostility or discrimination in public places. Overtly racist actions by whites in public settings have declined in the past two decades, mainly because such are seen by most as unacceptable social behavior.[4]

Yet they still occur in significant numbers. Lara, a Taiwanese American professional, discusses in some poignant detail a racial incident at a grocery store that involved some white children:

> Just a couple of years ago I went into a grocery store, and these kids, they must have been eight and ten. They were two brothers. They looked at me and pretended to speak Chinese and kind of mocked me. I just looked at them and said, "You need to stop or I am going to tell your mom and dad." And I just went about my shopping, and I'm thinking, "You know what, those little kids actually pissed me off." So when I got to the checkout register, I saw the kids with their mom and dad. And I told them, "I am sure your young boys are fine gentlemen, but you need to talk to them about the racial slur they just directed at me." They looked at me and said, "What happened?" I said, "You can ask them; they are old enough to tell you what they did." And I just left. I didn't follow up to see or anything like that, but I wanted them to know that their sons were doing that.

Americans of color must deal with emotions such as anger when dealing with everyday discrimination, and Lara was one of few respondents who detailed for us such a strong activist and emotional response. When she allowed herself to replay the incident in her mind, she was "pissed off." Lara's response, though direct, may seem rather modest. She may have too much faith in the parental disciplinary process, for she assumed the parents would be disappointed that their sons behaved that way, but she indicated that it was important to take action. For those who experience recurring racism, feeling anger is necessary and reasonable, for it helps sentient human beings to survive. If they are to survive, those targeted by discrimination somehow must find a way to control their anger at discrimination, yet not totally repress it. This involves a difficult balancing act in suppressing their feelings while keeping this suppression from harming them too much, both physically and psychologically.[5]

As noted previously, Charlotte reports learning at an early age to block painful emotions when faced by young tormentors. That emotional disconnect process may link to the fact that she has since taken a relatively confrontational approach when dealing with whites' racist comments:

> What I developed was this really killer look that I use, so that if anyone started saying anything, I would just turn around and look at them. And I remember specifically in high school one time, and I was at some party. Some person started making a Viet Cong–type joke. And I turned around and looked. He stopped dead in the middle of the joke and apologized to me for having said anything. So I think that's just what I developed ... a sort of demeanor that would actually stop people dead in their tracks, and they would just not go there.

Charlotte has developed an effective method to protect herself from racist performances, yet she may be seen by whites as "far too serious," a common stereotype that whites hold about Asian Americans. Indeed, when Asian Americans or others protest such racist joking, the white commentators will often label the protestors as odd or humorless because they "can't take a joke." They are likely to be pressured to accept the offensive joking, and opposition may put them at risk of being socially ostracized.[6]

In his probing interview, Guang reports continual harassment from white classmates, as well as from some other students of color because he is Asian American. Eventually, he learned to defend himself, as this account reveals:

> When I was a little kid I got picked on more, but then, I don't know, I started being more of a punk, and people stopped picking on me. It doesn't matter if you are Asian; it doesn't matter if you are smaller. If you aren't

going to stand up for yourself, people are going to pick on you. And people are saying that it's because they are Asian that they get picked on. Well, it might well be, but you've got to do something about it yourself. You can't just blame it on your race or your size.... What can you do about it but say something? If you can't, you can't. Just get yourself out of the situation.... If we don't take crap from people, and we don't take shit when they see things happening—that's what you should do. But a lot of people are raised so conservative from their Asian parents that they don't mouth it, they don't think it's worth the *risk*. ... People give me shit, but I fight back now.

Guang has learned the value of standing up for himself, and, luckily, he has not been in a situation where his open resistance has caused him to be seriously injured. Very insightfully, he notes that other Asian Americans are often discouraged by parents to speak out against discrimination. The discriminatory status quo is maintained in part by this silence; the lack of overt resistance helps to keep whites in substantial control of Asian American lives and livelihoods. Although there have been important Asian American organizations and civil rights movements in the past and the present, most of these efforts do not seem to be widely known or discussed often among a majority of Asian American families, at least judging from our interviews.

Even as we completed interviews with a diverse group of Asian Americans who would be regarded by most Americans as successful by the usual educational and economic measures, we found it somewhat surprising how seldom these respondents report using their socioeconomic resources to openly confront the racial hostility and discrimination that they face. In our numerous interviews only a small handful recounted using their socioeconomic resources in this manner. This lack of confrontation and resistance seems to be linked to certain views of society articulated by the respondents, including the view that "there's no point" in combating discrimination and the view that such discrimination is just "a fact of life." Many also seem fearful of "rocking the boat" or feel that if "discrimination is just ignored, it will go away."

Some actions that at first appeared to be aggressively confrontational responses to discrimination by our respondents were in fact protests made "through proper channels," such as going to the supervisor of a biased worker or writing an e-mail to an executive about a case of discrimination at a company's workplace. While such actions are indeed an important type of resistance, a closer examination of our specific interview accounts suggests that these respondents were often avoiding a more direct confrontation with the white perpetrators of particular acts of discrimination.

Rejecting the White Racial Frame

Perhaps the most frequent form of resistance by our respondents involves a personal rejection of key elements of the white-imposed racial frame. Most indicate some conceptual grasp of the pervasive and injurious nature of white hostility and discrimination. Whether or not they have taken direct and overt action against white discriminators, all have made some efforts to reframe their understandings of their racialized worlds. For example, they often battle in their minds, and sometimes in their families' discussions, against accepting some of the anti-Asian and other racial stereotypes whites have developed for Asian Americans or other Americans of color.

Learning to Be Angry and Reject the Frame

Indira is one of the few in our sample who has become an activist in regard to anti-Asian racism. She has worked at a multicultural center, but she reports that she was not always critical of anti-Asian stereotyping and discrimination. She admits that she once believed in the myth of the model minority and the myth that people of color will do well if they just work harder and pull themselves up by their "bootstraps." That changed when she took a job as a summer orientation leader at her college, where she came to think deeply about the realities of systemic racism. In that position, she recalls, she earned a reputation for being a spokesperson for diversity, but she still lacked a critical view of racial matters. She discusses her further progression in understanding in this way:

> I started my master's program, and one of the very first classes you take in a higher ed program is called "the student." To understand the diverse types of college students that exist.... I had no background in Asian American issues and research. That's huge—talk about shifting your consciousness, and there was [not much Asian American research] in the mid-1990s, but enough and there were books, and so there were things that I could have found.... Our final paper for the class was to do a paper and a presentation on "subcultures." You know what? Years later ... they still do this. I hated that phrase then, and I hate it now because "sub" assumes that white is normal and that everything else is not. That's common sense to anybody, so why wouldn't you change that? We had a list of things to pick from, athletes, something on Title IX, so that would be women's athletics or just women's programs in general. You could do African Americans, Latinos. Asian Americans were not listed on that thing. I didn't notice because I didn't identify as an Asian American back then, I don't think.

I don't remember. But I did ask the question, "Can I do a project on me and my people?" I remember that much. I think I identified as Asian then or [had a] lack of the words. My instructor was like, "Oh yeah, I mean definitely that fits under international." So I did an entire paper on the needs of international students—somehow [I was] confused as to, "But that doesn't really apply to me ... but I guess it does, because maybe that's what I am." ... And I was just really very, very confused, and it wasn't until later on that I was like, "Whoa, there is a whole world of ... like Asian, and this is *not* it."

Indira's instructor was discounting her identity when he recommended that she do a report on what he apparently assumed, from a conventionally stereotyped perspective, was her particular group—that is, "international students." Yet she is actually a *third-generation* Asian American. Without protest at that time, she continued on with the inappropriate assignment. At the time she was unclear about her own identity, like numerous other respondents. As we have observed previously, some Asian Americans seem to have been lucky enough to navigate through this society without an incident or event that forced them to confront deeply just how they are regularly stereotyped by whites.

Numerous respondents seem to accept negative framing and discriminatory behavior by whites as the price for white acceptance in their lives. Others, however, at some point have come to see serious problems with passive acquiescence. Indira reflects further on the aforementioned event:

It made me very angry because I feel like in the higher ed program they should know better. In a higher ed program, they should be current, that shouldn't have happened to me. It makes me very angry that that happened to me and that I didn't know what to research or where to find it. And the fact that my own instructor, who is the one who heads the master's program, is not even current on this literature himself. So that's when I became angry. That's where my commitment became more than ... "diversity is important."

The way the white instructor went about stereotyping who she was, accentuating her as foreign even though she is a multigenerational Asian American, made Indira feel invisible and out of place. When her professor did not perceive her American identity, this was a major turning point for her.

Indira's shift in consciousness is evident in her sharply insightful interview. Over time she began to challenge the commonplace racial framing and became committed to furthering her racial and social awareness. Her change in attitude and the fact that she was vocal about the reality of racism also brought some changes in her social environment, as she underscores:

> I was really appreciated when I did, "Oh diversity, I am diverse, you're diverse, how can we be diverse together?!" But it really shifted when I started saying, "No, you are not *seeing me* and this is *your* problem, and this is a white people's problem." When my consciousness started to change, my demeanor started to change. When my demeanor started to change, all of the sudden people were like, "What's wrong with Indira? She used to be so cool before and now, you know." I think a lot of that is so interesting. This is not fair, but I feel like I need to bring this up as a point of comparison.... But let's speculate. I can't say this is always true, but if I were African American, or Latina, like, it would be expected that an African American person might be angry about race issues, right? I don't think that's a good thing, but the reaction to me being angry, I feel, was much more extreme than one who'd be African American and angry. Because all the sudden I didn't fit my stereotype anymore, I wasn't shy and quiet and happy-go-lucky and my good basic female, meek woman anymore. I was angry, and all of a sudden I went from the model minority to the problem minority. It's like I jumped ship almost. Like, "Wait, you were one of the good ones and what happened to you?" I feel like I was ... reacted to in a much more unforgiving way because I didn't act like [the model stereotype]. And I still get that, I feel like I get that now. I feel like I can't say things or do things in ways; it's very unfair.

Multiculturalism "lite" promotes an approach to diversity that, like a social broom, often sweeps serious racism issues under the rug. As long as Indira was a "well-behaved minority" she was valued and praised. However, when she started to directly address racism, she violated the dominant racial frame's stereotype of Asian Americans as docile. Note too that her move away from conventional acceptance of the dominant racial frame and hierarchy involved significant change in her demeanor and interpersonal style, as well as in her emotions, including overt anger at subtle and overt racism.

In his analysis of U.S. society, Prashad argues that whites have deemed, paternalistically, Asian Americans to be the "solution minority." Yet "to be the solution has its problems too. When one is typecast as a success, one's abilities cease to be the measure of one's capacity. A young Asian child now, like a pet animal, performs his or her brilliance."[7] Asian Americans are expected to perform like white "pets" and follow white commands and folkways. Indira, with her change in consciousness, now regularly rejects this pet status.

Indira continues on her journey of awareness and each day strengthens her commitment to social justice, as she next reports in her interview:

> I am on this social justice listserv, and I was disgusted when someone sent me this link, because the *Newsweek* edition.... I was so angry. I remember everything because I know I am going to be able to quote it when I'm older.... The edition was called "India Rising." What happens when you put people on a pedestal, right? You would think, OK, well it's India, and basically the question posed in this entire series of articles of *Newsweek* was "How exciting, the world's messiest democracy is partnering with the world's richest democracy." In this edition it has stuff on [the movie] *Harold and Kumar Go to White Castle*[8]; I'm like, "What does this have to do with India?" *Nothing!* Nothing, right? What does that have to do with us? *Nothing,* yet it was all lumped together. What does that do? It perpetuates the "perpetual foreigner." Two things: it perpetuates both the relationship of the perpetual foreigner and the model minority stereotypes together, and that's what these articles have always done. It couples those two.

Challenging a white-run magazine's framing of India and Indian Americans, Indira views this media report and its examples as coupling major stereotypes about Asians, both "model people of color" and "perpetual foreigner" stereotypes. The *Newsweek* cover suggests that India is a rising force, but the inside article is watered down with odd information about an irrelevant movie about Asian Americans. By challenging the article's approach, Indira is challenging an ultimately white-controlled (top *Newsweek* editors') framing of both Indians and Indian Americans.

She adds this comment about her e-mail response to the article:

> My theory and my point of rage in my angry e-mail—I said to my peers, consider, I was like, "What happens, once a giant rises? It has to fall. How long before now India becomes a threat because we have already been exoticized as this rising giant, so once the giant rises it has to fall." You know? India and China are compared in those articles as well. We set ourselves up. Many of the authors were South Asians from what you could gather from their names, so we participate in our own oppression in that way.... It's not that I don't want to hear wonderful things. I read those articles with a feeling of a bittersweet emotion. On the one hand, I want to be proud of what my people do, but not at the expense of my citizenship, in terms of my perceived citizenship. I guess that's a better way of saying it.

Indira's words recall Frank Wu's assertion that the model minority myth is used "both to deny that Asian Americans experience racial discrimination and to turn Asian Americans into a racial threat."[9] She recognizes the U.S.-centric and exoticized framing, and the underlying messages of national and racial threat, in this series of articles. She also perceives the internalized oppression evident in some South Asian American journalists' active participation in this rather slanted framing. Their participation exemplifies the complicated positioning of Asian Americans in a white-dominated society. To achieve mainstream representation in the media, Asian American writers and movie actors usually must adhere to guidelines suggested by common stereotypes of the "model" people of color. Significantly, in her interview Indira further suggests that her critical questioning of the white framing has allowed her a new freedom, as compared to when she blindly accepted those racially framed media portrayals of Asians and Asian Americans.

Constructing a Counterframe

Numerous respondents actively resist racism, albeit to varying degrees, by questioning and resisting various racist ideologies. The construction of a strong counterframe to the preexisting white racist frame is a daunting task and has, judging from our interviews, yet to be fully accomplished by the majority of Asian Americans. Indeed, it appears that among all groups of color, only African Americans have managed to create a very strong counterframe and to regularly teach it to successive generations—though even African American families vary in how well they pass this counterframe along.[10] Our Asian American respondents do often attempt to gain more control of their lives by reevaluating and re-creating certain definitions of their social worlds. Specifically, they have frequently worked to construct views of Asian Americans that contrast with prevailing racist stereotypes. Yet, there is a cost to constructing such a counterframing, at least in more public ways. Those who start to be critical of white racism often face criticism and rejection not only from white teachers, coworkers, and supervisors but also from some Asian family members and acquaintances.

Jessica, a Vietnamese American, actively works to dispel the model minority myth in Asian American student groups but is quite honest in discussing the difficulty in staying committed:

> I can see in the African American community, somebody that wouldn't [fight racism] would be called an Uncle Tom, but in our community they would just be called practical. Don't you see? Like our parents would just call

them smart. Not rocking the boat, not causing trouble. And I think that it's just minority myths that we perpetuate within ourselves. And I mean, even me, it's hard to think sometimes, "Why do I have to stop everything and [why can't I] just concentrate on school and not worry about this [racism] because it doesn't have to do with me, it just has to do with other people who come after me? Why does it even matter?" And I could totally get by and not fight. Totally get by, and be *mildly content.*

Jessica thus views conformity as a choice. Like many Asian Americans, she is aware of the myth that resigned practicality and conformity to white folkways will likely award success and satisfaction. That is probably one reason why the dominant racial frame is rarely attacked openly. Asian Americans like Jessica believe they can be "mildly content" if they accept subordinate positions quietly. Even though Jessica is active against the surrounding racist system, she notes that even she is sometimes exhausted by these efforts and isolated from an Asian American community that mostly does not recognize the importance of her efforts. We observed the power and pervasiveness of the dominant racial frame and hierarchy in most of the interviews we conducted. People who publicly challenge white racism usually suffer significant social isolation and retaliation, frequently including attempts to make them believe they are impractical or irrational.

Whereas whites do not have to expend energy on everyday battles with U.S. racism, Asian Americans have to weigh what is more important, social acceptance or social justice. Although the task is daunting, Jessica explains why she does not want to stop fighting against racism:

I mean, we fight because the [majority of] the population does not. And it's hard because you see it. We do it for them, but they don't appreciate it. And I think that some do. They see what we do and they commend us for it and the change that we enact.... The ones that are vocal, I think, are the most scared. Like, that divides. The ones that say that we are doing the wrong thing, that we're ignorant, that we are the racists, they are just scared and they just don't know the facts. And that's where the biggest problem lies, I think, that if we were educated about our history, they wouldn't feel that way.

In her discerning comments, Jessica underscores the fears of retaliation and the lack of a strong collective memory in typical Asian American communities in regard to the long U.S. history of racial hostility and discrimination. Most Asian Americans do not have easy access to the missing pieces of their racial history and often seem to make decisions based on little understanding of the important dimensions of that history. Jessica articulates the importance of studying Asian

American history, a strategy that we will examine further in the next section. Like others in this chapter, she also defends the importance of speaking out.

Correcting Miseducation

Somewhat surprisingly, the majority of our respondents had never heard of the brutal killing of Vincent Chin in 1982 (see Chapter 2). Furthermore, those who had heard of Chin noted that they usually became aware of this hate crime long after it happened. This lack of knowledge reveals not only an absence of a collective memory of white racism within Asian communities but also the severe neglect of past and recent Asian American history in U.S. elementary, middle, and high school courses. Without such historical knowledge, Asian Americans may not realize why it is important to combat racial hostility both individually and collectively.

In their interviews numerous respondents were uncomfortable even in calling their mistreatment by whites "discriminatory" or "racist." As a survival tactic, these Americans may choose, consciously or unconsciously, to ignore the racial discrimination directly affecting them. Those who consciously work against anti-Asian framing often do so by constructing at least a partial counterframe—and usually in response to discriminatory incidents or because they have been exposed to a critical history of Asians in the United States. Joel, a Hmong American, has worked to reject the dominant frame. He discusses some reasons for raising community and societal awareness:

> I think that one of the main priorities is getting people, Asian American and non–Asian American individuals, aware that a lot of injustice is going on. And how we refer to the model minority myth. Oftentimes, that idea creates an illusion that the Asian American community is doing exceptionally well, and we don't need any assistance. But at the same time, within the Asian American category, there are so many groups within that classification that we still need to assist the Southeast Asians and the Hmong population ... not only that, but recent Chinese immigrants, recent Filipinos, etc. So, it's kind of like we need more awareness that this is going on and just because there's that notion that Asians are the model minority, we still need assistance, government funding, a lot of resources. There's this—Asian Americans are not the model minority because we are still fighting for social justice.

Joel may have had an easier time seeing social injustice because he grew up among whites who openly stereotyped Hmong Americans as inferior and because he experienced numerous racist incidents in his West Coast city, one that has a large Asian American and Pacific Islander population. When he went to college, he took courses addressing Asian American history, which has reportedly helped him to identify and assess the discrimination he has witnessed.

Reflecting on possible solutions for racial problems, Jessica too recognizes the importance of studying Asian American history. She notes that this is

> where the biggest problem lies. I think that if we were educated about our history, [Asian Americans] wouldn't feel that way. If we knew [how] oppression started and how it affects us every day, and how Asian Americans even came to be in this country, then I think that they would feel differently about what we say. A lot of them, they only see their own personal history. They only see that their parents came here, ... maybe not even when their parents came here, depending on the circumstances from which their parents came here.... My mom and dad never talk about, like, their journey here. So, you only see what happens in your life, and it's a short period of time in the history of Asian people in this country.
>
> I mean, if you are East Asian, and you have no concept of the South Asian community, then you [do not] understand the oppressions they face every day. Every day! Especially post 9/11.... The hate crimes for Asian Americans have increased a ridiculous amount, like 500 percent since 9/11, and I completely believe that. So I think that divide definitely comes from ignorance. That can be remedied, but it's still present, educating people about what that means.

U.S. history curricula are often white-centered and ethnocentric, especially below college levels, with many historical errors of commission and omission when it comes to Americans of color.[11] Again, the suggestion of recovering history, of critically educating Asian Americans, is an important way to build a substantial collective memory. Those respondents who were most cognizant of discrimination and inequality frequently stressed the importance of understanding the history of Asian Americans and of anti-Asian discrimination. Gaining accurate knowledge of this history has frequently served as an important turning point in their lives.

Learning more about this history may have a significant effect on people's orientations and interpersonal relationships. Adam, a multiracial Asian American, discusses the change in his friendship groups:

> I did take an Asian American course in college, mostly historical. It's like learning the history of Asians, which I found was not largely in my textbook

literature when I was growing up, other than maybe the Chinese, like on
the railroads or whatever in Hawaii. But I learned a lot. I only know that
after that I identified even more, but I think as time went on . . . I felt more
at home among Asian Americans or Asians. I just feel like, more comfortable being around them, which is strange because I spent most of my life
growing up with non-Asian friends. Then I felt, you know, I didn't feel any
different, but now suddenly I do feel a little different. . . . When I go and
visit Asia, whether or not it's Chinese or Japanese country, I still feel like
. . . I'm home there, even though I've never lived there. I feel at *home*. . . .
Maybe it's some of the cultural values and the mannerisms, or maybe it's
something as simple as, everyone looks kind of similar to me, although
not all the same. But, I mean, I wouldn't say it's like any one particular
thing. Maybe it's just where I identify myself now. And even though those
people—like over in Asia they're not Asian American, so obviously I would
have a more difficult time communicating with them—I still feel like . . . I
would be more *accepted* there than I would here, at least just at face value.

Just as Jessica was aided by historical education to reach a new level of racial
awareness, learning about Asian American history has brought Adam to a new
consciousness. Like most U.S. students, Adam was not exposed to much Asian
or Asian American history in high school, even though he grew up in a northern
city with a large Asian population. The historical information from his college
course has helped him piece together the subordinate and racialized role that
Asian Americans have played in U.S. history. Adam explains that he is now more
comfortable with Asians, including those overseas, than with white Americans
with whom he grew up. One key to understanding his statement is that he would
be treated better and feel more accepted by these Asians, by those who know
what being different from whites means. Although in his interview Adam had
a difficult time recalling specific incidents of discrimination he has faced, such
discriminatory incidents may lie behind the fact that, as he has gotten older, he
has significantly reduced contact with whites.

Judging from our interviews, seriously lacking for many Asian Americans is
a strong tradition of passing along important family and community histories.
This lack of knowledge appears to add to the identity struggles and related stress
involved in having an Asian heritage in a racist country. An accurate history of
Asian Americans puts contemporary experience with racist framing and discrimination into a helpful and appropriate context. Without understanding that long
history, as our interviews frequently show, many Asian Americans have difficulty
comprehending why they, their families, and friends are regularly mistreated and
marginalized by white Americans.

Like other activists in our sample, Brian became committed to activism on behalf of Asian Americans in part because he became better educated about this history. He reports that he does not remember much overt discrimination during his formative years. However, when he moved into a college setting, a few courses enlightened him as to this country's racial hierarchy and power structure. He comments on his development thus:

> The model minority myth wasn't something I understood until I got to college. Stereotypes about being good at math, and all that, it challenged me to break through some of those stereotypes. Because there was a time I was really strong at math, but I didn't focus in that area at all. I took, like, the minimum amount of math in college and said, "Forget it, I'm done with that." And just resisted the stereotype, and I think I was being intentional by it—to the point that as an adult, I see Black Lava[12] that has that T-shirt out that says, "I suck at math!" And heck yeah, I'm going to buy that shirt, wear that shirt proudly, and today it causes great conversation in regards to continuing to break the stereotypes—and why not do it on a shirt that starts conversation? So I think it started back in college when I took these courses. It [racial stereotyping] continues on in grad school....
> [I remember speaking with an] African American classmate, who didn't understand how the model minority myth was detrimental. That was one of the toughest conversations I had, because here was a person of color who didn't understand how "positive" could be detrimental to Asian Americans. That was one of the toughest conversations about race.

Brian's interview again illustrates how the allegedly "positive" model minority stereotyping puts Asian Americans in a difficult bind. Given the numerous overtly negative stereotypes about Asian Americans, being received as a model student can serve as a point of pride for a young Asian American. As we have seen continually in our interviews, however, this model stereotyping is at best a backhanded compliment, one that signals that whites are in control and get to assign the grades on the "minority report card" that Asian Americans and other Americans of color receive in their daily lives.

Exemplifying the important transition that numerous activists have made, Brian began to reject imposed Asian stereotypes after he became better educated about stereotyping and the white racist frame. Significant too is his comment about a conversation with an African American who had accepted the dominant framing of Asian Americans. Similar to the situation in a previous chapter where Ethan assumed that other Asian Americans would help him when he was a victim of a hate crime, Brian incorrectly assumed that his black colleague would easily understand the danger in white-generated model minority stereotyping.

Reexamining Various Stereotypes

To some degree, numerous respondents have challenged common stereotypes about Asian Americans, at least in their own minds and in informal friendship groups. Some have also begun to analyze critically the negative stereotypes and images of other people of color. John, a Chinese American, indicates that he is currently able to relate to the situations of other people of color: "There's a huge amount of effort to blame blacks that they are lazy, or Hispanics are lazy. Once you actually look at the poor, it's just amazing how much they are working and what *table scraps* they are getting, and it's not fair. And the reason why I feel sympathy for that is because ... I don't think it is a shame to wait tables, I don't think it's a shame to go across the border because you do what you have to do to survive." John identifies prominent racial and class stereotypes that are often part of the common white framing of African and Latino Americans, and he has reframed the latter groups. In his extended interview John seems to extrapolate from his experience as an Asian American and uses an empathetic eye when evaluating other people of color. He understands their hard work to survive and also has a critical understanding of the economy, which requires hard work yet often underpays and keeps many workers economically subordinated.

Similarly, Lin, also Chinese American, comments insightfully about structural barriers in U.S. society: "Well, like I said before, you know the system is set up not to encourage our group and to our detriment. When people give you enough *scraps* they accept it as essentially [adequate]. As a scientist, you get comfortable with that livelihood. You must struggle, as far as the basic needs, and to have a higher aspiration to really bring the community along." Both John and Lin use the word "scraps" for what people of color often receive from whites. John is referring to a more literal meaning, but the scraps to which Lin is referring appear in the form of certain middle-class rewards for high-achieving Asian Americans. Yet, for Lin these rewards are still socioeconomic morsels whose provision is largely controlled by whites, and it alarms her that most Asian Americans are content with the scraps stemming from white paternalism.

Surrounded by Familiarity: Shifts in Peer Groups

As we described previously, one respondent, Guang, was teased and beaten regularly by young whites when growing up. He is still grappling with, and in conflict with, the racialized identity that has been imposed on him. In describing his search for his place in society, he asks an important question: "I guess at that time I looked for more Asian friends because … in middle school, towards the end of middle school, I started meeting other Asian people. But I didn't know what to think of it. I thought it sucked that people picked on me…. So I had a really restricted social life for a long time and I didn't like, I mean, I didn't not like being Asian. It's just *damn,* what am I going to do about it?"

In his extended interview Guang indicates that he initially sought out white friends in elementary school. He did not intentionally refrain from seeking Asian friends, but his acceptance of the dominant racial frame inclined him to put a higher value on white friends. After being mistreated by whites, however, he sought out Asian American friends with shared experiences. Living in an Asian-populated area in the North, he still found that he did not relate well to certain Asian American male groups in his neighborhood because of class differences and their aggressive conformity to white ways. Guang then sought friends among other Asian Americans and other people of color. He has attempted to find personal answers in interactions with these friends, but has yet to feel like he fits well into society.

Others too have found solace from racism in friends of color. Jessica's Asian friends and other friends of color are better able to empathize with her experiences. In contrast, the white students at her school made her feel like a racialized outsider. She explains in some detail:

[Whites] don't have to deal with your mother rubbing you with this oil … when you are sick and coming to school smelling funny. Or, your mom packing French bread sandwiches for you when you really want a Lunchable, and that's all you really want. It's like, "Can you please buy me a Lunchable?" And she gives you soy milk and you don't know what to do. It's like, "Please, please let me fit in, Mom," and not being able to do it because she didn't understand what that meant to fit in…. When I found those Asian American students, we were just attracted to one another. It's just like, even though, like, we were all Southeast Asian—Vietnamese, Laotian, Thai, very different—but it didn't matter because *you got it*! You are Asian, you *get it* that ramen is not Asian food, and that thank goodness there is someone who is like me, that understands why my parents are the way they are. Because those are the things that you think of when you're little. Those are the things that bother you. Like, "Why are your parents like this?" Not like, "Who am I?" and "What am I going to do with my life." And "How does this affect me?" but "Why? Why can't I fit in?"

In this probing social psychological analysis Jessica describes her struggle in adolescence with family background, identity, and self-esteem. She felt very different and an outsider, but finally found support in friends who could understand well her Asian American family, style, and experiences. These friends helped her to feel comfortable in her identity. Assisting further in her identity development, she notes in her interview, was an Asian American student group in college. She is now proud of her heritage and who she is.

Still, Jessica has a serious concern about her younger siblings, as they do not have the same advantage of making Asian American friends:

> But it's weird because my younger siblings have a completely different experience than me. They don't really understand who we are. They don't understand that we are Vietnamese American. They don't understand that.... I mean, for a while my little brother thought that he was Mexican American because everybody in his class that was a person of color was Mexican American, and he knew that he was not white.... He knew that his house didn't speak English, but he didn't know what it was. He just thought we were speaking Spanish and that we were Mexican American, which is really hilarious. Because my mom said something to him like, "Throw away the trash," and he's like, "Mom, I don't speak Spanish." And she was like, "What?!" So, yeah, but they get it now, kind of. They don't understand what it means exactly, but they know that it is different.

Jessica was fortunate to have numerous Asian American classmates during her school years, but the demographics of her hometown have changed significantly as much of the Asian American population has moved to other parts of town. Her younger siblings are much more isolated from other Asian Americans than she was. In her interview Jessica reveals that her parents have rarely talked about life in Vietnam or coming as refugees to the United States. Her siblings have little understanding about where they come from, their cultural background, or what sacrifices their parents have made. Even though they are sometimes confused about their ancestry, they know they are not like other people, especially those in the dominant white group. They know they are treated as a subordinate social group, yet lack of access to a strong collective memory of oppression prevents them from more substantial understandings of racism.

Guang and Jessica were not the only respondents to discuss changing their peer groups to encompass mostly Asian Americans or other people of color as they began to critically analyze their social situations and group identities. In fact, the majority of our second-generation respondents reported adjusting their peer groups away from whites after their adolescent years, if young people of color were readily available in their areas. They have recognized that Asian Americans and other friends of color usually provide them a greater sense of belonging and much less threat to self-esteem than friendship groups that are predominantly white.

Producing Tangible and Political Change for Self and Others

Some respondents who have challenged U.S. society's dominant racial framing and its array of negative racial stereotypes and images have decided to do so because of their personal experiences with this framing and its discriminatory impact. Their experiences have led them to channel their energies into producing tangible social and political changes for themselves and others. Other respondents have produced such community changes without directly challenging the dominant racial framing. For example, one female respondent felt inclined to suggest to a white restaurant owner that he put up better lighting in a parking lot because a Chinese American had been assaulted outside his establishment. While in her interview she indicated a lack of awareness of the dominant racial frame and hierarchy—and suggested that the attack was an isolated incident by ignorant white individuals—she still took it upon herself to attempt to make a significant change for the better in her community environment.

In contrast, other respondents have chosen organizational methods to create change—through group educational efforts, by joining organizations, and by providing important services to the community. In her interview, for example, Alice describes what the Nisei generation and her Sansei generation are doing in this regard:

> I see them [the Nisei] a lot at the Japanese American Museum, and some of the things that Japanese Americans have done is to really make sure, there's so many people committed to making sure that the story's not lost. I think they turned their anger into a more productive, educational mode. Everybody's written a lot of films and books, and so we are sort of over the psychological hump. Because the Nisei are, like, retiring or dying to a certain degree, it's really the time now where the … mantle is going to the Sansei. And many Sansei, they are making sure with the museums and supporting all these activities. Especially the recordings of the World War II veterans, and things like that. The story's not lost, and I don't think Nisei are angry anymore because there have been so many overtures by the government to offer the camps as historical sites and grants and reparations. You know, the whole educational thing.

Once again we see the liberating effects of education about the history of white racism. Alice interprets many of the efforts of the Nisei to educate and share the pains of World War II internment as getting over the "psychological hump." They have used these techniques to heal from the pain of past racial discrimination. In addition, they are trying to build a substantial collective memory and to impress on future generations that they should be wary of white authorities and prepared to combat future racial oppression. Their efforts in creating such things as museums have, in fact, generated relatively rare institutional contexts—usually in cities with large Asian American populations—where accurate accounts of past discrimination are passed along. Many Nisei, and many Sansei like Alice, are heavily invested in educating future generations of Asian Americans.

Aggressive Community Action

Several respondents reported being involved in more aggressive actions aimed at reducing discrimination and increasing support facilities in particular communities. Recall from previous chapters the substantial efforts that several Asian American college students put into a well-researched report about Asian American affairs on their major university campus. This organizational effort involved efforts to redress the overt, subtle, and covert discrimination many Asian and Asian American students reported facing. As individuals, these students took risks and paid a significant price for standing up against individual and institutional racism at this major historically white institution of higher learning.

Other respondents reported taking aggressive actions to improve conditions for Asians and Asian Americans in their communities. Lin, who has years of experience in social services, is head of an Asian American community center. When she observed in previous workplaces that non-Asian social workers often requested her help with Asian clients, she decided to open a center designed to help Asians and Asian Americans with their particular problems. She wrote a support proposal and presented it to her city council but encountered serious problems:

> I went to the city council; I made a proposal. I wanted to set up an office for Asian Americans in town, and I asked just for 500 square feet of space.... The words came back to me from the city council; one of the council members is a friend, and she actually told me when they looked at my proposal. A Hispanic city council member actually looked at the proposal and looked at where I live, ... in an affluent part of town. And it is known to people as "Eagle Mountain." He actually told the other council members, "Look at where she lives, she lives on 'Eagle Mountain' and they don't need our help." I have never forgotten that. I have not resolved that because for another minority to do this to another minority group, so I don't think ... they're saying just words [in that] "at where she lives." Don't you think that's some racial undertone? That I'm not supposed to live there? "If she lives there then she doesn't need our help." I think there are some racial undertones there, and that the person who said that may not know that. That is so ingrained, so ingrained, so insidious.

A committed community director here takes action to counter discrimination and other problems faced by Asian Americans. As she illustrates, not all significant discrimination faced by Asian Americans comes directly from whites. In some cases, other Americans of color accept the dominant racial framing and impose its standard stereotyping on Asian Americans as "model minority" or "honorary white" in various discussions and settings. Once defined thus, Americans from all backgrounds, like the Hispanic American here, may accept this framing of Asian Americans and take discriminatory action based on that. Looking to reach out to Asians and Asian Americans in need with a rare community organization serving them, Lin is assumed unworthy because she lives in a predominantly white and affluent neighborhood. There may also be an assumption, common among non-Asians who accept the white framing, that Asian Americans do not face serious social or economic problems. Building coalitions across groups of color becomes more difficult when Americans of color conform too much to white folkways, adopt the white frame, and thereby isolate themselves from each other.

Even though Lin was denied public funding, she remained motivated to open up the important center and accomplish her goals:

> I used to work at [a] . . . crisis center, . . . and I got a lot of phone calls from different nonprofits or public agencies, like the health department, once they found out that there's actually an Asian working in the social services. I got a lot of phone calls about being an interpreter; that made me realize that these are the people that come forward to ask for help—and usually [agencies do] not even meet . . . their needs. There are so many that may not even know the system, to come forward to ask for help. Why don't they know about it? I feel like we need a place that we can call home that people will feel comfortable to come home and talk about it. So at that time I only have a very humble request for 500 square feet, and I will volunteer my service for people to come and ask, because I feel like I understand the system. I can direct people to different places to ask for help, but people have to know where to find me—I cannot have it in my home, right? So that's why I asked for [the office space]. . . . Since I didn't get it, so I feel like "Well, then I have to create." They don't want to help me, then, I have to help myself, because this needs to be done. So, if I don't get it this way, then I will get it some other way. So, I got it through private . . . contributions.

Lin demonstrates great resilience and eventually accomplishes her goals. Contrary to some common assumptions, the reality in the United States is that people of color, including Asian Americans, frequently meet with financial and real estate obstacles when they try to open their businesses and build organizations.[13]

Putting her experiences in a critical historical perspective, Lin explains why she works so hard for fellow Asian Americans:

> I really think if we truly believe that we have our rightful place here because … our ancestors have put down their lives here for us. They helped to build the railroad. They helped to really develop the economy and the future of this country. They have already [given us] our rightful space here in this country. It is up to us to take it. In the past they cannot do it, because they were not protected by the law. You know, like the Chinese Exclusion Act and all of that, is utterly racist, especially against us. But we have to thank the brothers, the black brothers and sisters and all the people that were in the civil rights movement that [by] … claiming their space by working on fairness and justice of this nation, they also claimed the space for us. So, it's really up to us to move into our rightful place.

Lin accents an important point about how being knowledgeable in regard to past oppression against Americans of color can serve as a motivator to combat racism today. Her knowledge of Asian American history and of the civil rights movement, as well as other historical realities, gives her important data to reference and draw upon in assessing the racially hostile world around her. She is appreciative of the African American struggle, and that seems to help her be hopeful that her community efforts will pay off.

Katherine, a retired Chinese American professional, immigrated several decades ago. She was the only Asian undergraduate at her U.S. university but describes feeling welcomed there. Katherine realized that her presence there was novel and took the opportunity to teach classmates and teachers about her homeland. She had her parents ship her slides from home so that she could make a presentation about China. As time progressed, however, she came to this conclusion: "They treated me very well, very, very well. You know why? I came to the conclusion that if you are just one of very, very few, you are not a threat." Her mind-set has changed as she has seen that the population growth nationally in Asian immigrants and their children has become more of a "problem" in the minds of many whites.

Katherine now volunteers with a national political organization that seeks to mobilize Chinese Americans to vote, in part so that current politicians will take notice of them and their political interests. The organization also works as a watchdog organization for hate crimes and negative Asian representations in the mass media. She reports being glad to share in a successful campaign against Asian American defamation: "Abercrombie and Fitch that one time with that

T-shirt. They came out with this T-shirt that was racially derogatory.... And so, our president called them right away and said that if you don't take that [off the racks] and issue an apology, we'll mass e-mail out to our one-million-plus e-mail list, and then we will boycott your product, and they pulled it."

Katherine was referring to the incident involving T-shirts sold by Abercrombie and Fitch clothing stores that mocked Asian Americans with racially offensive cartoons and captions such as "Wong Brothers Laundry Service" and "Two Wongs Can Make It White," as well as others making light of rickshaws and the Buddha.[14] Katherine is proud to be part of a group that exists to promote Asian American interests. That this organization has over one million members calls into question the image of Asian Americans as uniformly politically apathetic. When necessary, many will join in and support antidiscrimination groups like this one in taking some group action against certain types of racism. Katherine further notes the increase in the Asian American population in recent decades as a cause of increased anti-Asian sentiment in the non-Asian population, because "we are a threat" and non-Asians are "jealous." She is working now to maintain a better representation of Asian Americans in U.S. political bodies.

Recall too the case of Indira, who gained her "angry" voice of concern about racism and then moved into organizational action. She is unapologetic about her fight for visibility and redress for Asian Americans in a variety of settings:

I became the adviser of the Indian [student group], Indian [cultural organization]. Those were groups that naturally gravitated towards me. The [Asian] Greek scene had emerged. And Greek life had also realized that we need somebody, and I had relationships with people. I was able to do pretty obnoxious things like, "No, I'm not meeting with the Asian American students up there, they don't feel comfortable in the dean of students' office, they are meeting with me down here because they are students of color. And they need to know!" It was so funny because I think at that point I'd also developed a reputation that ... no one could say "no" to me, and I knew that, and I wanted that. It doesn't matter, you have to use the power that you have. So, I take it very seriously and I do use the power that I have. I wanted Asian Americans to circulate. Any time I had training with any kind of Asian American group, I would make them do it here in the middle of the room because we are in a fishbowl. And what happened was this space, it's almost been perceived as a space for just certain populations, just African American or Latino populations, but that was never true. If people don't know that they could frequent the space then they don't, right? So I had changed that.

Indira developed a relatively intimidating persona, seen by many whites as atypical for an Asian woman, in order to effect change. She would not have been able to be influential in changing the racial climate at her university without breaking free from stereotyped images of docile Asian women. She worked hard to promote the visibility of Asian American students, building up important organizations and alliances. Her aggressive approach awarded her some access to opportunities formerly unavailable. In the struggle for fair treatment, Americans of color have frequently found it difficult to be awarded that treatment by just being polite or quiet. For example, during the civil rights movement of the 1960s, the Student Nonviolent Coordinating Committee (SNCC) found that more aggressive action was necessary to bring changes in legal segregation. Sociologist Rod Bush has explained that the SNCC members "drew the lesson that patient suffering was not sufficient to bring about federal intervention.... Activists learned that the sporadic acts of nonviolent resistance were not enough. More was needed to dismantle the enduring structures of racism in the Deep South."[15]

For Indira, quietly suffering was not a viable option. Still, many Asian Americans adopt a less aggressive approach to the hostility they face. As we saw in Chapter 2, Ethan remained relatively silent even after he was a victim of a violent hate crime. His actions after the incident do not match his strong words in his interview, wherein he articulates his views about political apathy among Asian Americans:

> I am not OK with that [apathy]. This event has made me willing to be involved now. That's why I wanted to make sure I talked to you about how important it is. You know, some of my Asian American friends think this was just an isolated experience. I don't. I am optimistic to see the change in terms of Asian American activists. I will be one of them. Growing up here and being educated here, I want to get rid of the "don't rock the boat" mentality. I have no problem doing it. I am OK letting people know.... You know if an incident like this happened in the African American community, they would be enraged, but because it was an Asian American, "Oh, it's not that bad." If the same incident happened to an African American, they would have Jesse Jackson there. The NAACP would be boycotting. There would be a huge response from the community in support. With the Asian American community, there was no response, and none that I could see in the media anyways.

Earlier in the interview, Ethan admitted to staying out of the spotlight after the racist attack on him. He did seek help from police officials and community leaders, but he assumed that they would be responsible for redressing his assault, just as he now hopes that we may assist in telling his story through such channels as our research. In a contrasting comment, however, he says that he now wants to take "boat rocking" actions for the betterment of Asian Americans and criticizes their lack of overt political action. Ethan is an example of how powerful and nuanced the racist system is in controlling lives. He discusses being unaware of his subordinated status as a man of color until the racist assault, then discovering the reality of racism, and now desiring to be politically active. Yet he apparently refrains from actually taking such overt action even as he is still haunted by the vicious hate crime that he suffered.

Other Strategies for Survival

In Indira's quest for justice, she has sought to recruit a new generation of activists. In order to do that, she has utilized tactics that accommodate the omnipresent Asian American focus on socioeconomic achievement. The pressures for achievement are complicated. They result in part from strategizing against the constant threat of discrimination by whites, which often leads Asian American parents to apply great pressure on their children. Indira has had to find a way to get in the door to appeal to other Asian Americans to take action:

> Two years ago, we were having struggles with recruiting Asian American students to be student directors for [the Asian organization], mainly because again [of] Asian American consciousness, and the diversity of our groups. African American student population, and the same case for the Latino population, they come to the table, so what was different? I think it was, what did it for me is, "What's in it for me? What do we get out of this?" I didn't approach it from the issue of race, I approached from the issue of, "This is your space and you deserve to be here just like all of our students deserve to be here." I also tapped into … "How do we benefit, how does our community benefit?"

Indira describes a certain "Asian American consciousness" as being an obstacle to finding leaders. Making recruitment difficult, she suggests in her interview, is the choice of Asian Americans to conform and seek a white-modeled identity. To recruit future Asian American campus leaders, Indira has chosen to be more subtle in her approach and to purposely avoid raising racial issues, with the hope that the solicited students will eventually get to a place where she can be more forthright. Indira has had to cite personal and community benefits for them. She continues by discussing some strategies:

So, I developed an Asian American [leadership program] because I know our community will come to things that are leadership driven, or you get something out of it. So the [program] was a multi-week institute where you met once a week and you did things on public speaking, fund-raising, programming, you are really here to get something out of it, professional development, and your role is to plan an Asian American conference for Asian American students. At the end of this institute, you get a letter of recommendation that documents everything that you did. It will always be on file, and you can always use it for whatever you need. We'll change it, for whatever you need it [for]. But of course you get to know these students over the [the program] so it's not very hard to, right? Through that, that became almost an underhanded recruitment process because it also got Asian American students comfortable in this space. Because they were planning programs that they had to frequent, using the resources here, and when you're here you start hearing these conversations, you start joining them, you start hanging out, that then becomes that perpetuating, "Oh, OK, I belong here."

Indira has had to invoke some aspects of the model minority imagery in order to educate the students, with an ultimate goal of rejecting that stereotype. She is very proud of her Asian American identity and is astute about anti-Asian racism, but chooses to conceal much of that understanding in her recruitment of students. She is creating safe campus space for them to do things of benefit to Asian American students, including sharing their accounts of racial prejudice and discrimination. By being able to share experiences jointly, they are also gradually building a collective memory of oppression.

Peter, an Asian Indian who works in the entertainment business, likewise uses subtle methods in combating the barriers of a racist society. Although the comedy material he shares with his audience appears to play up certain Asian stereotypes, this material is in fact used to force whites to think. Peter states that he could be more direct, but that is not the route he chooses in his comedy act:

I don't have to be political for forty-five minutes. I try to make it as subtle as possible when I'm talking about the national spelling bee and stuff like that. It's really subtle, like, I'm really making a dig, but it's really subtle. But it's really why I watch the national spelling bee. That's the real reason I watch it, you know? ... [What are you digging at when you're making those statements?] I honestly think that white people should win the national spelling bee every single year. They should win a competition featuring the language they invented, OK. Ninety percent of the time I do that, the audience is just silent. Like, it's a dig. It's basically saying you're not as educated as us. That's basically what I'm saying and then I just soften it by saying you don't see any white people winning the spelling bee in India. So I flip it back around, but it really is a dig. Then I do the joke about the valedictorian sitting in the fire drill.

The valedictorian joke concerns a school catching on fire. The teachers line up the students alphabetically to exit the building, but this results in a distinctive racial bias in the line. The white children in the front of the line to escape the fire have names such as Adams, Barnes, and Carter, while the students at the end are Asian in heritage, with names like Tuan, Vargas, Wong, and Zhou. Peter ends the joke by making the sound of something being engulfed by flames and stating, "There goes another valedictorian." In his interview he assesses the reason for this joke: "And that's a complete dig, because everybody knows it's just a complete dig on [whites]—but it's a dig. But it's not really a slam. It's just kind of a 'where we are' speaking for our generation, you know. I used to see so many comments [by] comedians because I just watch comedy all the time—and whenever they would talk about Indians and Asians it's just stereotype bullshit."

Peter has developed barbed jokes that play off of the substantial achievements of Asian Americans as compared to whites. His audiences are primarily comprised of whites, so he uses his position as the entertainer to make social commentary where a white audience cannot control his remarks. Peter is not aggressively challenging the model stereotype but addressing it indirectly. In his interview he differentiates his material from that of other entertainers who frequently perpetuate the old white racist stereotypes in their comedy routines.

Peter next discusses his hopes for some empowering consequences from his rather innovative joking approach:

I do this joke about the Asian people changing their names when they move to this country to fit in. It's the truth. It's not like I'm saying, "Oh, we have goofy long names, and here's a goofy long name." I could do that, I could do that and people would laugh, but I'm trying to look at, actually why people do that. It's basically the same thing [as when] I talk about how Americans don't go to India and try to fit in. It's the same thing; it's a dig again. It's not like a "it hurts my feelings," it's just what I always felt like Chris Rock would kind [of do] if he was Asian. We don't get uplifted or empowered enough on TV, and I'm trying to make us look like we are. To me we are.

In additional commentary he describes other Asian American entertainers who use Asian images and stereotypes from the old racist frame, including stereotypes about Asians using kung fu and karate as well as mock language. He cites Asian Indian entertainers who caricature an Asian Indian clerk at a convenience store and use mocking language or accents to make white audiences laugh. Peter refuses to present Americans of color in a negatively and racially stereotyped light. For example, he never uses the word "terrorist" in his act because he does not believe in perpetuating such crude stereotyping of Middle Eastern and South Asian men. According to his interview comments, he seeks to be appreciated as an entertainer because of talent, not for an ability to play into conventional and negative racial stereotyping.

Creating Self-Definition and Self-Valuation

Research on African Americans has long shown that creating a strong black self-valuation can be a method of successful resistance to racism. This method of resistance involves African Americans personally and collectively reframing the negative definitions and valuations placed on them by a racist society. They resist by giving themselves new positive valuations (for example, "black is beautiful") that contrast with how they are stereotyped in traditional white racist framing.[16] Some Asian Americans adopt a similar positive approach. Typically, this method of resistance first develops privately but then may evolve into a more public form of resistance.

Some Asian Americans have chosen to resist discrimination and stereotypes applied to them in very individual and personal ways. Creating a positive self-definition and self-valuation does not necessarily require a critical understanding of the racial frame and hierarchy, but it does require a strong desire for self-preservation. For example, Charlotte explains her innovative path in this regard:

> I guess this all stems back to what I went through in fifth grade, when I turned off my emotions. That it was good and it was bad. The good part was that I stopped crying every day. The bad part was that I lost track of my emotions. But the other good part was I really had a good way of being able to divorce myself with what was going on. And saying, "You know, it's your loss. You don't want to get know me? Weird, because I don't fit your model? It's tough, but I have a lot of talents that I can add to you. And if you've got issues that you've got to overcome, that's your problem, not mine." So in that respect, I think it gave me a lot of confidence.

By divorcing herself from the desire for social approval from whites, Charlotte gained greater self-esteem and self-confidence. She is now a strong, independent person and credits her character building to this brave and innovative coping mechanism, which she has since used to deal with recurring discrimination by whites of all ages. After developing this form of covert resistance, Charlotte took further action that helped her deal with ridicule and harassment. Recall from our previous discussion of her interview that she early on developed a "killer look," which she directs at whites who harass her.

Other innovative strategies are reported by several respondents. In a poignant part of her interview, Indira recounts the use of a subtle, yet public, form of resistance that she engages in to honor her mother and national identity:

> The reason I started to wear Indian clothes is because of my mother. My mother used to wear Indian clothes when I was a little girl, and I used to always be like, "Wow, I wish I could be like her." … After I was in college, my mother stopped wearing Indian clothing in public. To Indian things, [her] social circles, that's fine, but she wouldn't elsewhere. I asked her, "You know, I don't see you wearing [Indian] stuff to work anymore." She was like, "Yeah, I feel like a cartoon." [long pause] "I feel primitive." That just made me so angry. That I was like, "That will not happen." That is a legacy that I will carry with myself. She feels like a cartoon. Definitely in any space, whenever I am ever present in public, where I speak in public, I will always honor this identity because of what she felt.

As we have observed in previous commentaries, and as a few other scholars have demonstrated, attempts at promoting diversity in the United States have sometimes reinforced various forms of "Oriental" stereotyping.[17] Asian American children, who are usually under significant pressure to conform to white folkways, frequently know little about their ancestors and national backgrounds, indeed often only what they have gleaned from an Anglocentric textbook, or perhaps from an encyclopedia entry read for a show-and-tell session at school. Indira's mother was tired of being viewed by whites as a primitive museum exhibit or cartoon, for whites do frequently use exoticized images of Asians to accent whites' supposed superiority.[18] When Indira was retelling the story, her emotions seemed heightened, and long pauses provided an opportunity for her to keep from getting more upset. Her eyes became wider and her breath heavier as she was deliberate in relating this moment that changed how she presents herself and her national-origin identity in public.

Conclusion

Clearly, Americans of color put a lot on the line when they openly or directly resist whites' racist framing and discriminatory actions in everyday life, and that is a major reason that a great many acquiesce in their racialized environments and suffer mostly in silence. Much research shows how whites for several centuries have used overt, subtle, and covert methods to keep people of color under control and compliant. Even though the threat of retaliation and backlash persists, a brave contingent of Asian Americans has chosen to fight back with their fists, minds, and hearts. While relatively few report feeling protected or confident enough to be openly confrontational and aggressive against white discriminators, many have grappled in one way or another with the white racist framing of Asian Americans and have attempted to reframe the anti-Asian and other racist stereotypes, images, and understandings that have been embedded in their own minds by society's mainstream media and other influential sources of socialization in the white racist framing of society.

Among our diverse group of respondents, those who have chosen to take more direct and overt countering action have tried to produce important social and political changes in the system of oppression that they and other Americans of color routinely face. They have joined important political groups, worked hard in an array of societal institutions to educate others, created their own community and campus organizations, and labored actively to increase Asian American visibility, status, and power. Yet they face many social constraints, some internal to the Asian American community and some external barriers imposed from the larger society. Thus, one activist has used creative techniques to educate other Asian Americans about issues of campus racism, but she must conceal her critical views in order to appeal to them in a less threatening manner. Still, the most common countering of everyday racism among our respondents involves their choosing to reframe their own understandings, identities, and sense of self-worth away from the racist stereotyping and valuations that they have imbibed from living in this still-racist society.

CHAPTER 7
REPRISE AND CONCLUSIONS

Like other Americans, Asian Americans are diverse in terms of their interests, experiences, and backgrounds. The omnipresent model minority image is usually an attempt by whites and others to do rather simpleminded categorizing. Being labeled "model minority" does not mean, as we have shown throughout this book, that Asian Americans are free of strong negative stereotyping and discrimination and are fully accepted by whites. Some European groups that immigrated to the United States, such as the Irish and Italians in the nineteenth and early twentieth centuries, were once labeled as not white, and they soon became white in the eyes of almost all Americans.[1] In spite of media and scholarly commentaries about the attainment of "model status" or "honorary whiteness" by Asian American groups, however, this has not happened for any Asian American group. The only survey of whites that we know on this subject, which we cited in previous chapters, suggests that the overwhelming majority of whites now reject the idea that any Asian American group can be viewed today as clearly "white."[2] In everyday life, Asian Americans are still seen by a majority of whites as inferior in certain significant ways to whites, and thus frequently as appropriate targets for racial hostility and discrimination.

We begin this chapter by examining the orientations and views of two Asian Americans in regard to their experiences with racial hostility and discrimination and to their ways of coping with the difficulties created by that racism. As we will see, they have decided to deal with the challenges of U.S. racism in dramatically different ways. In this comparison the often confusing and complex choices and pressures with which Asian Americans struggle every day become clear. They are always set within a racist world that whites have created and still maintain. Some of our respondents have lost faith in ever being fully and fairly accepted by whites, while others still have faith that they eventually will be. Even within the latter group there are divergent views on how to obtain that acceptance. Aggressive conformity to white folkways, to the dominant racial frame and associated racial hierarchy, is one important method to gain acceptance, but there are some who have chosen to put up a strong fight against the common straightjacket that is contemporary racism.

A Tale of Two Asian Americans

Two of our most accomplished and interesting respondents, Lin and Frank, have each lived in the United States for more than four decades. Both have spent much of their lives in large cities. Both have been fortunate enough to avoid being targets of violent attacks and other extreme forms of racial hostility and discrimination, and both see clearly the lack of power that Asian Americans have in the economic and political worlds of the United States. But in numerous other respects there are major differences in their lives and life choices. Frank has chosen to adapt, often aggressively, to the white frame and hierarchy and to "whiten" himself as much as possible on the inside so that whites will accept him regardless of his physical appearance. In contrast, Lin has chosen to reject the intense pressures to conform passively to the white racial framing and hierarchy, and instead to fight back as much as she can, for herself and her community.

The cultural analyst Raymond Williams has suggested that there are both "indicative" and "subjunctive" commentaries on society. Indicative comments assess what is actually taking place in the surrounding society, while subjunctive commentaries are "attempting to lift certain pressures, to push back certain limits," to press toward significant change even where that is very difficult.[3] We see both Frank and Lin making numerous indicative statements about their social worlds, but it is Lin who embeds in her insights more of a strong subjunctive concern with possibilities for significant societal *change*.

Seeking "Whiteness" as Personal Creed

Many Asian Americans have immigrated to the United States since the 1960s civil rights movement. Frank's family settled on the outskirts of a western city with a large Asian American population. Living outside the central city area, Frank's family was the only Asian American family in the area at the time.

Upon his arrival in the United States, Frank recalled, "The first thing I noticed immediately is that, one, I couldn't speak English, and two, you couldn't find the rice." He soon began to change what he could control:

> At that time it was very, very difficult to assimilate, but I learned English very, very quickly. At that time it was very difficult to make friends with Mexican Americans or white Americans or African Americans. As a matter of fact, when I got here, there were almost no African Americans and Spanish Americans and Mexican Americans too. Mostly white.... But I had to start making friends, mostly white friends. And, I didn't have any Oriental friends.

In his interview Frank offers a relatively problem-free picture of his years in school. He looked up to whites, aspired to imitate them, and sought them as friends. His view of this period, during which he was the only Asian American student in his junior high, reminds us of a comment by another respondent, who pointed out that if you are just one of very few, "you are not a threat."

When Frank moved into a professional career after his years in predominantly white schools, his rose-colored-glasses view of whites began to be challenged. In reply to a question asking if he felt "accepted in the white world," he at first answers strongly, "Yes, I do. Yes, I am." But when he elaborates on this answer, his demeanor and tone change significantly:

> Number one is that when I . . . could you repeat the question again? I didn't get the context. [If you've been accepted by whites, you know, as an equal?] One thing. Once when I was at the lower management area, and I kept on climbing to upper management, at the time I reached the vice president position, and I was competing with a white person, I felt something, but I kind of discounted it. And also I accept my Asian heritage as one of the handicaps. I accepted it as a fact of life. I didn't look at it as any other issue.... It's changing a little bit, but large American corporations, it's still the same thing. The glass ceiling is still there. That's why a lot of smart, really well-educated, and really well-connected Asians are starting their own companies, because they can't go through that glass barrier.

Frank initially answers without hesitation that he is certainly accepted in the white world. Asked to explain his answer, he finds it difficult to find words and asks us to repeat the question. His answer then changes; he discusses feelings and experiences that indicate that Asian Americans are definitely at a disadvantage to whites in corporate America. As we have noted, most respondents insisted initially that they had faced no significant discrimination but then admitted to incidents of white-generated hostility or discrimination as the interviews continued.

Frank is a vocal proponent of more education for Americans of color, including Asian Americans. Indeed, in his interview Frank indicates that he holds some stereotypes of African and Latino Americans as not doing well economically because of lack of educational effort, and of Asian Americans as doing well because of their significant educational efforts. Yet, he professes in the preceding excerpt that, in fact, his Asian heritage is a "handicap." Like some other respondents, Frank thus adheres to two somewhat contradictory views: (1) education is the great equalizer in U.S. society and will bring success for Asian Americans; and (2) no matter how educated they become, Asian Americans will be disadvantaged because of their "heritage," while whites get disproportionate advantages. Evidently, Frank exerts substantial mental energy to reconcile these rather antithetical beliefs, a dilemma faced by a great many other Americans of color.

Frank believes that with more effort, and by conforming more aggressively to white values and folkways, Asian Americans will still have a good shot at gaining socioeconomic success. He comments, "So you just have to know the rules, and then just follow the rules, you know. I think that's the best way of you becoming successful here. Just follow the rules. Knowing the rule is needing education. Because whites are not going to teach you; teaching you that kind of rule is expensive."

Frank's language is somewhat coded. The "rules" that he has followed to become successful have involved conforming to white ways and embracing much of the dominant framing and ideology. White society benefits from Frank's and others' conforming because that helps to keep the traditional racial framing and hierarchy intact. Failing to teach certain "rules" to people of color could in fact be expensive for whites, not just in an economic sense but in terms of the power and privilege they would have to relinquish if people of color more actively challenged them. Indeed, at one point Frank describes himself with the harsh term "banana"—that is, "Asian in the face, but inside is pure white." Frank seems to be convinced that holding white views and orientations keeps him in good standing with whites as a member of the heralded "model minority."

At the same time, Frank knows well that the white world to which he aspires is a straightjacket with significant restrictions for people like him:

> Let's say I have a white friend, and I go out [to a restaurant]. We try to be fair. Most customers are white Americans. [Your white friend] did not want to be there with you because you're Asian. It's like this. Koreans have this saying: "If you make a fist with your hand, it goes one way." It doesn't go the other way. I learned that from my parents. You try to make a fist right

here, right? Your hand only goes towards the way you make a fist, which means let's say I raise my hand, try to make a fist, all my fingers will go toward left. It's just like that. It's just a thing, you just cannot change it.

The Korean saying that Frank references here accentuates the physical reality that fingers curl naturally inward toward the palm when making a fist. Fingers do not curl backward toward the backs of hands. Similarly, the white racist context is just such a fact of life and forces one to adapt to that reality. As he views it, Asian Americans cannot change that reality. Thus, for him substantial conformity is the sensible thing to do to gain the "most acceptance" from whites in the face of white racism. Frank seems to be resigned to being racially subordinate.

Crumbs Do Not Satisfy: Present Action and Future Hopes

Like Frank, Lin reports that she has lived a life free of violent racism. She too remembers being treated reasonably well in school. Unlike Frank, her education in the United States began at the college level. As a result, she had no experiences with the racist taunts and other racial hostility that plagued the early lives of many of our respondents. Even without negative childhood experiences, Lin has come to understand how Asian Americans of all ages are viewed and treated negatively as foreigners and outsiders by a great many whites and other non-Asians. She indicates in her extensive interview that she did not set out to become a community activist but has done so because at specific points in her life certain troubling incidents raised her awareness. They served as turning points in life that steered her to a life of community service. The rise of the feminist movement, the death of Vincent Chin, and working with rape victims all have opened her eyes to the realities of social inequalities in U.S. society.

In a revealing and searching interview, Lin offers many insights into being Asian American in this racist society. For example, she offers this view of where she and other Asian Americans stand in the eyes of many whites:

So we are good enough to be "gangs, goons, geeks," and all of them. But we are not good enough to be president, senators, Supreme Court justices, all of them, because we are just not good enough. They [whites] don't see us as good enough because of our look. Now, if you are Jewish, you know the anti-Semitism in the old days, but you don't *look* different. If you don't tell people you are a Jew, people cannot tell you are a Jew. You can *pass*. You can get by, and then when you get by, you get to the place where you can make policy. You will change it, and we cannot even do that! With this face? With these eyes? This nose? This cheekbone? You know? We cannot even pass that. You know some of the blacks, sadly, some of the blacks they are so fair they can pass as white. It is sad in a different sense, but at least when they get there, they get a chance to get there. For us, that is not even possible. Now, there is strength in that too. Because I can't change this, I might as well be who I am.

In her opening sentence, Lin references the stereotyped images that whites hold of Asian Americans, a categorizing influenced by the list of such negative image terms ("gangsters, gooks, geeks, and geishas") that journalist Helen Zia has assessed in her writings on Asian Americans.[4] Similar to Frank, Lin recognizes that there is a "glass ceiling" for Asian Americans and accents the difficulties they have in breaking through such barriers. Yet, unlike Frank, she uses this recognition of white hostility and discrimination as a source of directed anger, strength, and resistance. Facing this reality, Lin has decided to be a strong Asian woman, the identity she asserts for herself, and to ignore the omnipresent pressures to conform to white stereotypes of Asian women. Her major goals are not wed to mimicking or pleasing whites.

Lin believes that her efforts can make a difference in the fight for social justice for Americans of color. She is not afraid to take action. In Chapter 2 we cited her story of assisting one of her employees who had faced discrimination at a car dealership. In dealing with the manager of that auto firm about this discriminatory act, she rejected the advice of others in her community who pressured her to ask for a new car or money as compensation. Instead, the direction she took was to deal with the white manager in a "relational" way. She wrote a strong report of this incident to an Asian American political association of which she is a member, making her action clear to the manager but not demanding compensation. She stood firm in her decision, with the hope of publicizing the incident and thereby achieving a broad impact that could benefit the entire Asian American community: "I want us to stand on high moral ground. The reason why I bring it to his attention is, first, he [the dealership manager] is a policymaker. He can make changes. Secondly, the reason why we sent out this report [is] because we expect people to be better; that's the high moral ground." Lin took assertive action and addressed the racial incident that happened at a particular business, but she did not want to "cheapen" her response to the discrimination by demanding a new car or money. Instead, she has sought to build a continuing relationship with a white businessperson who holds the power to make situations better for Asian American customers in the future.

Accenting a "subjunctive" orientation, Lin hopes that this manager will make changes at his dealership because it is the "right thing to do" or because he feels the pressure of losing future business. In her interview Lin further explains why she fights in this manner:

I am not prepared to ease his conscience. But you see how many people do that? Do you see the practical thinking of some people? I think if people throw you some crumbs, or some goal, or give you a car then that makes it okay? Then we have lost our cause. So this is again, I have this driving … integrity. And this comes from the women's movement, coming from watching all these great women in the past fighting for voting rights, fighting for all of these; I am standing on their shoulders.

Lin spoke with great conviction when recounting her experiences. Over her decades in the United States she has seen significant societal changes come about because of the civil rights and feminist movements. She remains confident that her efforts will also help to bring about significant changes for Asian Americans in her local community.

Still, Lin admits to us that she has not always been so confident. In addition to becoming better educated about racial issues, she has needed some encouragement to move from this awareness of inequalities to becoming a strong community activist. A college professor once helped her out of her shell by assuring her that whatever she had to say in class was worthy of others listening to:

One of my turning points, I have to tell you, in college, is really from my Jewish professor. Coming from Hong Kong, you are not even encouraged to speak up. I was not like this. We were trained to look at the notebook, take whatever teachers are telling you, and don't question. I didn't even know how to formulate a question. Then in college I had to take a seminar course. Fifty percent of your grade was depending on your participation on your speaking out, on presentation. So, halfway through the class, I could not. I didn't know how to speak up. So my professor, a Jewish woman, talked to me in her office and said, "Lin, I have been observing you; you haven't really spoken." I said, "Yes, I know I am in trouble." She said, "You know, Lin, I just want you to know that your experience is just as important as everyone in this class. Without your participation, this class will not be the same." First of all, she held a space for me to step in, that I am just as important. Then she gave me my responsibility that this class will not be the same if I don't speak up. This was very powerful. It was motivation and empowerment. The rest is history, and I haven't stopped talking [she laughs].

In her life Lin has continued speaking up against other social injustice. Dealing with discriminatory events like the car incident has been central to her development as an outspoken activist. She now views silence as a hindrance to change. This racist society is set up to discourage dissent on most racial matters, but at a key point Lin had a professor who helped her to speak out, and thus to start on the road to fighting injustice. Indeed, she and other respondents who have chosen to actively combat racial hostility and discrimination have usually gotten to that point by first being educated about the pervasiveness and reality of that racism, and then by being encouraged by significant others to act to bring about community change.

Significant collective memory is created and reshaped when Asian Americans begin to be educated in depth about their extensive history and are given a chance to share their personal stories and listen to others who have shared similar experiences. The five respondents in our sample who are currently activists working against racism in their daily lives all mentioned that educating Asian Americans about discriminatory events of the past is one key to creating awareness and understanding for change. Respondents like Frank seem to have little in the way of historical understandings to put their own racialized mistreatment into a historical context, and they tend to view their experiences with discrimination mainly in a present-day context. Understanding racial discrimination in its present context can of course be important, but without the collective memory of many decades of discrimination and of the strategies that Asian Americans have developed to resist that discrimination, a particular Asian American may well feel isolated, confused, or overwhelmed. Thus, many Asian Americans have great difficulty in making sense out of why they are treated as both "perpetual foreigners" and "model minorities." Without that deeper historical understanding it is difficult for them to counter racial hostility and discrimination effectively.

Judging from our revealing interviews, Asian Americans generally have a painfully complex relationship with the white-dominated United States. Many have resigned themselves to accept the racist status quo. However, Lin views her situation in a way that enables her to be hopeful that she can make changes:

> In Hong Kong it was a British colony. We don't have that many nonprofit grassroots organizations. I was not even given a chance to vote in Hong Kong. I never voted in Hong Kong. Not until I came here is when I got to vote. So, how can this not be my home? It has given me all the privileges, but it is still not fair, but I have more privileges when I am over here than as a British second-class citizen, right? So I chose this to be my home. And I want to make this a better home.

Like numerous other respondents, Lin feels a debt to the United States for providing her with opportunities that were not as available in her home area (now China). Like Frank, she realizes that life is not egalitarian and fair in the United States, but unlike Frank she uses her accomplishments and socioeconomic status to actively counter the imposed white pressures and "rules," so that hopefully she can make life better for herself and other Asian Americans.

Like all Asian Americans, the particular situations of Frank and Lin are both unique and complex, and we do not presume to capture all aspects of their very productive lives in this rather brief comparison. Still, their stories do suggest two divergent paths that Americans of color, including Asian Americans, often take in their lives when they are dealing with the everyday realities of systemic racism. Both want to live happily and without facing racial hostility and discrimination in this country. Frank has chosen to take what he can get and to try to ignore the injustice that he does perceive. By working very hard and playing by the white rules, he seeks to be happy in life, yet he realizes that he is "handicapped" by white views of his Asian heritage. Lin, in comparison, believes that actively and directly addressing white racism and its impact on Asian Americans will lead to a better future for all Americans. These accounts demonstrate that the Asian American experience is not easily captured or explained by statistical studies on their socioeconomic achievements or by "model minority" stereotyping. Behind the figures, tables, and model labels one finds distinctive, unique, and complex individuals trying to do the best they can in a difficult and trying societal world that is frequently racist and inhospitable to people like them.

This brief comparison of Frank and Lin also demonstrates that Asian Americans are *not* just targets or victims of racism but possess much personal agency, either to bring about change or to accept the racial status quo. Lin is an example of how Asian Americans can in fact be knowledgeable about the white racial frame and the racial hierarchy and take action as an individual to bring some changes in this disturbing reality to benefit a local Asian American community. She is impassioned and desires to make her life in the United States better even though she is aware that she is viewed by many whites as an outsider. She has been actively involved in local, state, and national politics, even to the point of once running for a local government position. Indeed, numerous people in the Asian American community have sought her out and look to her as a reliable resource when they must deal with racial mistreatment. Hers is an example for other Asian Americans seeking to resist the always burdensome realities of systemic racism.

Conclusion and Reflections: Continuing Efforts for Social Change

We conclude by considering a few additional implications that arise from our in-depth interviews. The responses of these Asian Americans reveal that being viewed individually or collectively as a "model minority" does not save them from racial hostility and discrimination. As we have documented in these interviews, white Americans often cite and use Asian Americans as an example of a "solution minority" for other people of color to follow. However, the reality is that Asian Americans face hostility and discrimination regularly at the hands of whites of various ages, both genders, and all classes. Even with advanced degrees and respectable jobs, they still find themselves excluded and othered just because of the way they look and because of their cultural backgrounds. There are no historically white places in the United States where Asian Americans are free from the threat of stereotyping, harassment, and other discrimination. Within neighborhoods, schools, workplaces, and most places in between, racial hostility and discrimination remain omnipresent threats. At times, acts of hostility and discrimination are overt and obvious, yet in other cases this white racism puts on a subtle or covert face, leaving its targets to wonder if an incident was indeed generated by discriminatory intent.

Wasting energy evaluating white actions is a chronic burden for people of color in this still-racist society. Broadly considered, long-term exposure to whites' discriminatory actions over the life course is very costly in physical and psychological terms. In dealing with everyday hostility and discrimination, these men and women engage in substantial mental gymnastics just to cope and survive. They use various methods to protect themselves from this hostility and discrimination, such as emotional disconnecting, suppression of memories, and compliant conformity. The weight of everyday racism can and does significantly affect their self-esteem and self-image. Asian Americans, like other Americans of color, have the burden of a "double consciousness," as they learn how they are negatively viewed by whites, yet still seek to assert their own self-crafted identities.

Certainly, this research raises new questions in need of much further research. Few researchers have examined the lives of Asian Americans as they face everyday white racism. The commonplace reports on educational and economic successes often mislead and paper over the painful racial stereotyping and discrimination they regularly face. For example, only a little research has examined areas like housing discrimination. Yet, one recent study by the U.S. Department of Housing and Urban Development found that discrimination against Asian American homebuyers by housing providers is substantial, as the latter are significantly less likely than similar white homebuyers to be given information on, and shown, available houses. Those who are renters also face rates of discrimination by housing providers that are similar to or greater than those of African Americans and Latinos.[5] In addition, very little attention has been paid to contemporary Asian American health problems, especially as they link to the stresses of everyday racism. Human suffering and loss because of such racism is an old story, yet social science and medical researchers have done very few studies that document in detail the impact of recurring racism on the health of Asian Americans.

Among the urgent questions are these: How much are Asian Americans suffering physically and mentally from the stereotyping and discrimination that we have documented? And what should private agencies and governments at all levels be doing about that reality?

Relatively compliant conformity is a common coping mechanism described in our interviews. These Asian Americans are often hopeful that their conformity, hard work, and achievements will, or should, eventually gain them full acceptance from the dominant group. Numerous respondents are candid about their efforts to conform to white mores and folkways and about what they hope to obtain by this conformity and whitening. Both first-generation and later-generation respondents have assumed that such adaptation and compliance would gain them full and fair acceptance in white worlds, yet they have all discovered that this is not the case, for they still face major racial barriers. Parents who have faced substantial discrimination frequently place great pressures on their children to conform in hopes that such adaptation will protect them from similar mistreatment at the hands of whites. Yet, by compliantly conforming to white folkways, and especially to the dominant racial frame and hierarchy, our respondents and other Asian Americans accept a negative framing of their own groups, as well as of other people of color. Such one-way conformity is but one sign of the great power that the white framing and the conventional racial hierarchy still have in U.S. society.

Unmistakably, anti-Asian views and framing remain quite commonplace and deadly in their effects across the United States. We should note too how much anti-Asian sentiment is now being extended by powerful whites well beyond U.S. borders. Take the cases of large-scale recalls of Chinese-made toys and food products imported into the United States. Beyond the issue of the quality of the recalled Chinese products is that of how the U.S. media—and much of the U.S.-influenced world media—have portrayed recalls of Chinese-made products. The U.S. and world media have generally ignored the preexisting international economic structure within which such recalls have taken place. The mostly white corporate executives, in office complexes in the United States and Europe, are the ones who have often made important decisions to utilize Chinese manufacturers and pressure the latter to cut costs to maximize corporate profits. These corporate elites have replaced many U.S. manufacturing workers of various racial-ethnic backgrounds with highly exploited, low-wage workers in Asia, thereby securing lower production costs. U.S. and European corporate executives are ultimately responsible for unsafe products being recalled, yet Western policymakers and the media have rarely highlighted this critical point about global capitalism.

Consider too the treatment of certain food products from China, a small percentage of which have been found to be contaminated. With sensational headlines such as, "Is China Trying to Poison Americans *and* Their Pets?" and "The Chinese Poison Train Is Still Out There, Lurking on a Container Ship Headed Our Way,"[6] yet more images of the old "yellow peril" are being invoked in the U.S. media. Headlines such as these support our assertion that the old white racial framing of Asian people is now a global reality. Moreover, some strong actions have been taken on the basis of these negative Asian images. In February 2008, for example, the U.S. Olympic Committee announced that, because they were concerned with the safety of Chinese meat, they would import 25,000 pounds of U.S. meat for the 2008 Summer Olympic Games.[7] Contrast this reaction to Chinese food products with the more restrained U.S. reactions to recent major recalls of U.S. food products, such as meat products and spinach packages produced by U.S. farmers. In February 2008, within a few days of the U.S. Olympic Committee decision, the U.S. Department of Agriculture announced the *largest recall of U.S. beef in history,* some 143.4 million pounds produced by one major company.[8] Note the double standard. In the latter cases only a particular U.S. farming operation that produced tainted meat or spinach products became the focus of blame from politicians or the media, not U.S. farming or the U.S. economy as a whole. Yet bias in the Western media's reporting has frequently caused the Chinese product recalls to become racialized as a distinctive "Oriental" or "Chinese" problem. In this manner, the media have called into question the "trustworthiness" or "ethics" of an entire nation of people. As one journalist put it, the Western media's treatment of the Chinese product recalls "reinforces the notion that befouled food is the consequence of a foul culture."[9]

Judging from our detailed interviews, only a handful of Asian Americans have chosen to aggressively and openly resist the omnipresent racial framing of Asians and Asian Americans or the associated racial hierarchy. Few Asian American individuals are willing to risk directly confronting white discriminators or institutions. Our interviews suggest that such confrontational resistance to racial hostility and discrimination is infrequent, but that some significant internal resistance to such racism by individuals is much more common. Many respondents reported their substantial fear that confronting racist actors will only worsen difficult situations with these discriminators. Indeed, they have often adapted their own behavior so as to accept racial harassment and other acts of racial entitlement from whites, small and large, including racial stares, racist epithets, workplace discrimination, and even hate crimes on the street. The few respondents who have become activists, who have directly challenged the racist frame and discriminators, reported not only negative responses from whites but often significant negative responses from some other Asian Americans. Other Asian Americans have made it clear to them that they are uncomfortable even with moderate activists because they "rock the boat" and may "ruin" existing opportunities for Asian Americans by generating a significant white backlash.

A large majority of Asian Americans have immigrated to the United States since the 1960s or are the children of immigrants. In most cases their understanding of the history of systemic racism in the United States is as yet modest or incomplete. Numerous respondents spoke of being taught by their parents that they should assimilate and conform as much as possible to the dominant white framing and folkways, but not about the resistance strategies that Asian Americans have used historically to fight the omnipresent anti-Asian discrimination. Without a shared and strong memory of Asian American history, these respondents have more easily accepted negative stereotypes and images of Asian Americans and other Americans of color.

Some respondents made it clear that increasing and sharpening the collective memory of anti-Asian discrimination among Asian Americans can be an important starting point for individual and group efforts to bring change in discriminatory patterns. These respondents generally indicated that learning more about their history in the United States has reshaped their views about resisting everyday racism. They better understand the racial discrimination and inequalities lying beneath their everyday intergroup interactions, especially in historically white institutions. The more they have learned about the history of racial oppression and about their own position in the contemporary hierarchy, the more they are likely to resist actively the hostility and discrimination they encounter. In addition, those who have developed some counterframing to the prevailing racist framing are much more likely to have developed empathy for, and significant relationships with, other Americans of color. Becoming better educated in their history and developing at least a partial counterframe have also given these respondents a new consciousness about who they are and what needs to be accomplished to make the United States a better society. Although burdensome at times, understanding better the hows and whys of systemic racism has empowered these men and women. For the most part, they no longer view themselves as just the victims of racism but rather as active agents who can bring egalitarian change to this society.

Creating a network of allies is also imperative. Since the publication of the first edition of this book, we have been humbled by the number of non–Asian Americans who have responded so passionately to understanding anti-Asian racism. The first response is most often, "I had no idea that Asian Americans faced these obstacles." Undergraduates of color, in particular, see the connection that all groups of racial minorities have with each other and to white supremacy. By debunking the "model minority" myth, we can move beyond the "oppression Olympics" and build multiracial coalitions. These coalitions already exist, but are few and far between. Beyond racial justice coalitions, we also need to understand the ways that systems of oppression intersect. The Occupy Wall Street movement of the 2000s was successful for a time in mobilizing a critical mass of activists. However, the largely class-based movement did not fully integrate people of color into its protests, and it also suffered from significant issues of sexism. If it could be fully realized that racism, classism, sexism, homophobia, ableism, and nationalism are all interconnected and reinforcing, groups fighting for social change could truly develop a critical mass.

As we see in the case of Lin and other activists in our sample, some courageous Asian Americans have long worked to build collective efforts and organizations against racial discrimination. These Americans have dedicated their lives to bringing organizational and institutional changes now, as well as to educating and inspiring future generations to do the same. Such activists have been critical to the development of new civic and civil rights organizations. Among the first influential Asian American organizations to develop were those of Japanese Americans, organizations created in West Coast cities in the 1920s and 1930s. These include the Japanese American Citizens League (JACL), now the oldest national civil rights organization among Asian Americans. The JACL initially advocated assimilation and self-help strategies for Japanese Americans but did press moderately and increasingly for increased voter registration and for changes in discriminatory laws targeting Asian Americans.[10] After World War II, the JACL pressed federal and state governments to eliminate all anti-Asian laws, including those preventing land ownership and citizenship for the Issei, and struggled to secure repayment for huge economic losses resulting from the removal to U.S. concentration camps during World War II. Only in 1987, after long years of fighting white opposition, did they and allied organizations succeed in getting congressional leaders and the White House to agree to legislation providing modest reparations and an official apology to Japanese Americans.[11]

During the late 1960s and early 1970s a significant but small "Yellow Power" movement developed alongside the Black Power movement, mainly in college communities like that of Berkeley, California. This movement was more influenced by Malcolm X and the Black Power movement than by the earlier black civil rights movement. As one legal scholar, Chris Iijima, has noted, the "focus of a generation of Asian American activists was not on asserting racial pride but reclaiming a tradition of militant struggle by earlier generations," and this movement focused not on racial identity but on "questions of oppression and power." The students and other individuals involved in this movement were politically oriented and sought not just representation in society but liberation from white oppression. They created the term "Asian Americans" as a counter to "Orientals" and proceeded to organize "other Asians for a larger political end rather than an end in itself."[12] They were the first in the 1960s to be aggressive and protest-oriented in insisting on much more education about Asian American history in schools, colleges, and communities, and on a complete end to racial discrimination against Asian Americans. Substantial numbers of Asian Americans from different nationality backgrounds organized together and shared their experiences with white racism. By the 1970s, pan-Asian organizations and media were helping to create an Asian American umbrella consciousness among students, professionals, and other Asian Americans with common experiences in fighting discrimination. However, then as now, Asian Americans had varied reactions to these pan-Asian civil rights efforts, with support from some Asian Americans but much opposition from others fearful of white retaliation.[13]

Indeed, only in the 1980s, with the substantial growth in the number of Asian immigrants to the United States, did national pan-Asian organizations begin to address broad Asian American civil rights concerns. One umbrella political effort was the founding of the Asian American Voters Coalition, which included Japanese, Chinese, Asian Indian, Filipino, Korean, Vietnamese, and Thai American organizations. Groups like this have worked to bring Asian Americans together in a powerful voting bloc seeking to influence elections in states such as California, as well as to fight anti-Asian media images, hate crimes, and other discrimination. Similarly, since the 1980s, the Asian Pacific American Legal Center of Southern California, the country's largest legal organization serving Asian-Pacific Americans, has often taken legal action to protect Asian immigrants' rights and addressed numerous other civil rights issues.[14]

Since the 1990s the number of Asian Americans dedicated to moving Asian American communities in a more conservative direction seems to have increased. In response, the older progressive Asian American organizations, including the JACL and the Organization of Chinese Americans, joined together in a major coordinated effort to form the National Council of Asian Pacific Americans (NCAPA). This relatively young civil rights organization now articulates strong civil rights positions and coordinates efforts to get better legislation on and prosecution of anti-Asian hate crimes and other racial discrimination and to improve immigrants' rights.[15] In addition, the Media Action Network (MANAA) has worked to combat anti-Asian stereotyping in the media. Such an organization seems quite necessary; since the 1990s dozens of overtly racist media incidents have been countered by MANAA and allied organizations.[16] There has also been growth in organizations seeking goals of particular interest to specific Asian American communities. Beginning in the 1990s, for example, Filipino Americans organized to generate political efforts to win offices in cities where they have substantial populations and to press for the passage of the Filipino Veterans Equity Act, congressional legislation that would provide Filipino veterans of

World War II the government benefits long promised to them. Similarly, in the 1980s the Korean American Coalition was formed as an advocacy organization seeking to increase Korean American participation in political affairs with voter registration and citizenship drives. In addition, the Southeast Asia Resource Action Center (SEARAC) in Washington, D.C., has engaged in political action and educational efforts for Cambodian, Laotian, and Vietnamese Americans and has worked on expanding domestic social programs, on immigrant rights, and on leadership training assistance for community organizations.[17]

As we have seen in this brief historical overview, and throughout our interviews, there are several levels at which Asian Americans can and do counter the racial hostility and discrimination that they face. Some work at the individual level, and others do so at an organizational level. While some groups mobilize to attack anti-Asian discrimination aggressively and directly, other groups, often at the local level, mobilize to assert traditional cultural understandings, values, and language as a more subtle or symbolic way of countering stereotyping and discrimination. While such efforts are not always successful, they do provide a type of resistance to stereotyping and Anglo-conformity assimilation pressures. For example, in the Houston area some local Vietnamese and Chinese American groups successfully positioned street signs in their home languages next to the old English signs. However, in another area of Houston, Korean Americans have tried to do the same, but white resistance has so far blocked these efforts. Local individuals and groups in several cities have quietly resisted in yet other ways, such as in regard to urban architecture. Thus, in an inner suburb of Houston where the Chinese and other Asian American communities are growing, one finds numerous new buildings reflecting traditional Chinese architectural design. This is an important type of symbolic resistance. In addition, in Houston, Los Angeles, and numerous other cities local organizations concerned with advancing Asian American political interests have been created to raise money and to support Asian American candidates for local political office.[18]

Clearly, one current and future challenge, at both the local and national levels, is to encourage many more Asian Americans to be willing to openly challenge the hostility and discrimination that they face and to engage in more aggressive antidiscrimination efforts through existing and future civil rights and other antidiscrimination organizations. Coalitions with other Americans of color who have come to a similar viewpoint also seem essential. The 1960s civil rights movements made it clear that social organization and interracial coalitions of Americans can bring about alterations in the structure of U.S. racism. In the previous decade or two we have seen a growing number of coalitions between Asian and non-Asian groups of color. For example, Latino, African, Vietnamese, Korean, Chinese, and other Asian American leaders in Los Angeles created the

Multicultural Association for Voter Registration to help citizens of color register and become active politically there. In another example, in the labor sphere, Korean American community organizations in Los Angeles helped Latino hotel workers' unions in a dispute with a major hotel owner. These mostly West Coast coalitions among citizens of color suggest a growing awareness that intergroup cooperation can mean greater political and economic power.[19]

Moreover, in 2012 a record number of Asian Americans ran for national political offices—thirty Asian American candidates, up from ten in 2010. In 2013, seven Asian Americans were in the U.S. House of Representatives, two were in the U.S. Senate, and three were serving in President Obama's cabinet. Asian Americans are getting more attention from established political parties as voter turnout continues to steadily increase. Nonetheless, Asian Americans are still underrepresented in political offices so mobilization of a critical mass in this arena is imperative in order to improve persisting inequalities in political power.

Finally, we should add that dealing with white Americans will be necessary to any ultimate solution to anti-Asian and other white racism, for whites' centuries-old racial framing and imposed racial hierarchy are indeed the *major* problem of "race" in U.S. society. As long as a majority of whites, especially of policymakers and others with power, deny that Asian Americans face everyday racism, little government and other policymaking effort will likely be directed at problems of anti-Asian discrimination, or at dealing with discrimination's impact seen in the suicide, substance abuse, and depression rates of Asian Americans. For most whites, Asian Americans continue to be rather invisible people in regard to their actual, as opposed to imagined, lives. Indeed, until a majority of white Americans can be made to see that U.S. society has a deep and pathological foundation of white racism that still has malign influences in most contemporary institutions, until they recognize that they and others must take aggressive action to end personal and societal racism—not only for moral reasons but also for the very survival of a truly democratic society—the racist foundation and its surface structures will likely persist. Educating significant numbers of white Americans to think critically about white racism is not easy, but it is possible and, as we and some of our respondents see it, a good place to start. Once this problem of the white mind and white racial framing is critically analyzed and admitted, especially in public ways by large numbers of white (and indeed many other) Americans, then the public and private solutions for replacing systemic racism can be better envisioned and, we hope, democratically implemented.[20]

Bringing significant changes in the white racial frame and in the society's racial hierarchy will, of course, be *very* difficult. However, the white racial frame and associated racial hierarchy have been challenged and partially altered twice in U.S. history—once during the slavery era, when organized white and black abolitionists helped to end slavery, and again during the 1950s and 1960s civil rights movement era, when African Americans and their allies in numerous other racial and ethnic groups helped to end the extreme forms of legal apartheid in the United States. In both cases Americans who were committed to racial change generated major societal crises, and many whites, especially leaders, eventually came to see the need for some reduction in racial oppression and inequality. Today, most whites are too constrained by their racial privileges and white racial frame, by their own racial biographies, to see the need for radical societal change.

Nonetheless, change will likely come, for human history has a way of creating what complexity theory calls "cascading bifurcations," surprising shifts that generate great societal instability and possibly a new social order.[21] In such situations the racial framing and hierarchy can be restructured again, perhaps even replaced, if substantial numbers of Americans of diverse backgrounds can be brought to a full consciousness of how racial oppression operates in society—and if they *organize* collectively and effectively to bring about that significant societal restructuring.

Notes

Notes for Chapter 1

1. This information is taken from a local newspaper, which is unnamed to protect the family's identity.

2. Ian Shapira and Michael E. Ruane, "Student Wrote about Death and Spoke in Whispers, but No One Imagined What Cho Seung Hui Would Do," *Washington Post*, April 18, 2007, www.washingtonpost.com/wp-dyn/content/-article/2007/04/18/AR2007041800162_pf.html (retrieved October 15, 2007).

3. Vickie Nam, "Introduction," in *YELL-Oh Girls!*, ed. Vickie Nam (New York: Quill, 2001), pp. 111–116; Michael Kim, "Out and About: Coming of Age in a Straight White World," in *Asian American X: An Intersection of Twenty-First Century Asian American Voices*, ed. Arar Han and John Hsu (Ann Arbor: University of Michigan Press, 2004), p. 141.

4. See Vijay Prashad, *The Karma of Brown Folk* (Minneapolis: University of Minnesota Press, 2003).

5. Paul Spickard, *Mixed Blood* (Madison: University of Wisconsin Press, 1988), p. 347. On assimilation perspectives, see Talcott Parsons, "Full Citizenship for the Negro American? A Sociological Problem," in *The Negro American*, ed. Talcott Parsons and Kenneth B. Clark (Boston: Houghton Mifflin, 1966), p. 740; for a critique, see Rubén G. Rumbaut, "Paradoxes (and Orthodoxies) of Assimilation," *Sociological Perspectives* 40 (1997): 483.

6. In this and later sections we draw on Joe R. Feagin, *Systemic Racism: A Theory of Oppression* (New York: Routledge, 2006), pp. 1–45 and 290–299; and on Joe R. Feagin and Clairece B. Feagin, *Racial and Ethnic Relations*, 8th ed. (Upper Saddle River, NJ: Prentice Hall, 2008), chaps. 10–11.

7. See Feagin and Feagin, *Racial and Ethnic Relations*, chaps. 10–11.

8. Robert G. Lee, *Orientals: Asian Americans in Popular Culture* (Philadelphia: Temple University Press, 1999), p. 8.

9. See Joe Feagin, *Racist America: Roots, Current Realities, and Future Reparations*, 3rd ed. (New York: Routledge, 2014), chap. 3; and Feagin, *Systemic Racism*, pp. 1–99.

10. *Plessy v. Ferguson* 163 U.S. 537, 561 (1896).

11. *Takao Ozawa v. United States*, 260 U.S. 178 (1922). See E. Manchester-Boddy, *Japanese in America* (San Francisco: R and E Research Associates, 1970), pp. 25–30.

12. Jacobus tenBroek, Edward N. Barnhart, and Floyd W. Matson, *Prejudice, War, and the Constitution* (Berkeley: University of California Press, 1968).

13. Frank Furedi, *The Silent War: Imperialism and the Changing Perception of Race* (New Brunswick, NJ: Rutgers University Press, 1998); Roger Daniels, *The Politics of Prejudice* (New York: Atheneum, 1969); tenBroek, Barnhart, and Matson, *Prejudice, War, and the Constitution*.

14. DeWitt is quoted in Daniels, *The Politics of Prejudice*, pp. 3–6. Italics added.

15. Quoted in Ronald Takaki, *Strangers from a Different Shore: A History of Asian Americans* (New York: Little, Brown, 1989), p. 370.

16. See Robert G. Lee, "The Cold War Construction of the Model Minority Myth," in *Contemporary Asian America: A Multidisciplinary Reader*, 2nd ed., ed. Min Zhou and J. V. Gatewood (New York: New York University Press, 2007), pp. 475–480.

17. Janice Tanaka, *When You're Smiling* (Janice Tanaka Films, 1999).

18. Long Le, "The Dark Side of the Asian American 'Model Student,'" August 2, 2006, http://news.newamericamedia.org/news (retrieved January 5, 2007).

19. Rosalind Chou, *Asian American Sexual Politics: The Construction of Race, Gender, and Sexuality* (Lanham, MD: Rowman and Littlefield).

20. For more, see Rosalind S. Chou's video "Linsanity: A Sociological Look," http://vimeo.com/37290995.

21. Alexandra Wallace, "Asians in the Library," last modified March 2011, www .youtube.com.

22. Associated Press, "Alexandra Wallace, Student in Anti-Asian Rant, Says She'll Leave UCLA," *Huffington Post*, March 19, 2011.

23. "Daphne Kwok, Organization of Chinese Americans, and John O'Sullivan, *National Review*, Discuss Recent Cover Story for That Magazine That Asian Americans Are Saying Is Offensive and Racist," NBC News Transcripts, March 21, 1997; Mae M. Cheng, "Magazine Cover Ripped; Coalition Calls *National Review* Illustration Racist," *Newsday*, April 11, 1997, p. A4.

24. Doris Lin, "The Death of (Icebox.com's) Mr. Wong," USAsians.net, http:// us_asians.tripod.com/articles-mrwong.html (retrieved December 14, 2006).

25. Jennifer Fang, "Team America: Racism, Idiocy, and Two Men's Pursuit to Piss Off as Many People as Possible," Asian Media Watch, October 28, 2004, www .asianmediawatch.net/teamamerica/review.html (retrieved December 17, 2006). We draw here in part on Feagin and Feagin, *Racial and Ethnic Relations*, chap. 11.

26. Helen Zia, *Asian American Dreams: The Emergence of an American People* (New York: Farrar, Straus, and Giroux, 2000), pp. 134ff.

27. Steven A. Chin, "KFRC Deejay Draws Suspension for On-Air Derogatory Remarks," *San Francisco Examiner*, December 6, 1994, p. A2; "Current Affairs," *JACL News*, www.jacl.org/index.php (retrieved December 19, 2006); Media Action Network for Asian Americans, "Latest Headline News," www.manaa.org (retrieved December 18, 2006); Jennifer Fang, "Racism Abounds following Rosie," www.racialicious.com /2006/12/15/racism-abounds-following-rosie (retrieved September 25, 2007).

28. Fang, "Racism Abounds."

29. Jane H. Hill, "Mock Spanish: A Site for the Indexical Reproduction of Racism in American English," unpublished research paper, University of Arizona, 1995.

30. Rosina Lippi-Green, *English with an Accent* (New York: Routledge, 1997), pp. 238–239.

31. Feagin and Feagin, *Racial and Ethnic Relations*, pp. 292–293.

32. Tim Wise, *Affirmative Action: Racial Preference in Black and White* (New York: Routledge, 2005), pp. 136–137.

33. Feagin and Feagin, *Racial and Ethnic Relations*, pp. 292–293.

34. The National Coalition for Asian Pacific American Community Development, "Spotlight on Asian American and Pacific Islander Poverty: A Demographic Profile," June 17, 2013, http://nationalcapacd.org/spotlight-asian-american-and -pacific-islander-poverty-demographic-profile.

35. Ibid.

36. Marlene Kim, "Unfairly Disadvantaged? Asian Americans and Unemployment during and after the Great Recession (2007–10)," Economic Policy Institute, April 5, 2012, www.epi.org/publication/ib323-asian-american-unemployment/.

37. See Ronald Takaki, "Is Race Surmountable? Thomas Sowell's Celebration of Japanese-American 'Success,'" in *Ethnicity and the Work Force*, ed. Winston A. Van Horne (Madison: University of Wisconsin Press, 1985), pp. 218–220.

38. Paul Taylor et al., "The Rise of Asian Americans" (Washington, DC: Pew Research Center, 2012–2013).

39. William Petersen, "Success Story, Japanese-American Style," *New York Times*, January 9, 1966, p. 21.

40. "Success Story of One Minority Group in the U.S.," *U.S. News & World Report*, December 26, 1966, pp. 73–76.

41. See J. N. Tinker, "Intermarriage and Assimilation in a Plural Society: Japanese Americans in the United States," *Marriage and Family Review* 5 (1982): 61–74; V. Nee and J. Sanders, "The Road to Parity: Determinants of the Socioeconomic Achievements of Asian-Americans," *Ethnic and Racial Studies* 8 (1985): 75–93; and D. A. Bell, "The Triumph of Asian-Americans," *New Republic*, July 15, 1982, pp. 24–31.

42. See, for example, James T. Madore, "Long-Quiet Asian Group Starts to Mobilize," *Christian Science Monitor*, May 20, 1988, p. 7.

43. Senate Judiciary Committee, "Capitol Hill Hearings," September 20, 1991.

44. Kathleen Wyer, "Beyond Myths: The Growth and Diversity of Asian American College Freshmen, 1971–2005," Research Report, Higher Education Research Institute, UCLA, 2007.

45. Sharon S. Lee, "Satire as Racial Backlash against Asian Americans," *Inside Higher Ed*, February 28, 2008, http://insidehighered.com/views/2008/02/28/lee (retrieved March 1, 2008).

46. See, for example, Susan Lee, *Unraveling the "Model Minority" Stereotype: Listening to Asian-American Youth* (New York: Teachers College Press, 1996); S. M. Nishi, "Perceptions and Deceptions: Contemporary Views of Asian-Americans," in *A Look Beyond the Model Minority Image: Critical Issues in Asian America*, ed. Grace Yun (New York: Minority Rights Group, 1989), pp. 3–10; Mia Tuan, *Forever Foreigners or Honorary Whites? The Asian Ethnic Experience* (New Brunswick, NJ: Rutgers University Press, 2003); Frank Wu, *Yellow: Race in America Beyond Black and White* (New Haven, CT: Yale University Press, 2003); and Ronald Takaki, *Iron Cages: Race and Culture in the 19th-Century U.S.* (New York: Oxford University Press, 1994).

47. Pyong Gap Min and Rose Kim, "Formation of Ethnic and Racial Identities: Narratives by Asian American Professionals," in *Second Generation: Ethnic Identity among Asian Americans*, ed. Pyong Gap Min (Walnut Creek, CA: Altamira, 2002), pp. 167–175; Won Moo Hurh and Kwang Chung Kim, "Adhesive Sociocultural Adaptation of Korean Immigrants in the U.S.: An Alternative Strategy of Minority Adaptation," *International Migration Review* 18 (1984): 188–216; and Kwang Chung Kim and Won Moo Hurh, "Beyond Assimilation and Pluralism: Syncretic Sociocultural Adaptation of Korean Immigrants in the U.S.," *Ethnic and Racial Studies* 16 (1993): 696–713.

48. Nazli Kibria, *Becoming Asian American: Second Generation Chinese and Korean American Identities* (Baltimore: Johns Hopkins University Press, 2002), pp. 3–41.

49. See, for example, Tuan, *Forever Foreigners*. A recent search on Google for the phrase "honorary white" coupled with the word "Asian" found only 1,900 web pages. Most use of the phrase "honorary white" seems to be by scholars and some web commentators, not by ordinary whites. In contrast, a search for the phrase "model minority" and "Asian" found 153,000 web pages.

50. Mari J. Matsuda, "We Will Not Be Used," in *Where Is Your Body and Other Essays on Race, Gender, and the Law* (Boston: Beacon Press, 1996), pp. 148–151.

51. Prashad, *The Karma of Brown Folk*, p. 6.

52. Wu, *Yellow*, p. 91.

53. For example, Wu, *Yellow*; and Prashad, *The Karma of Brown Folk*.

54. Claire Jean Kim, "The Racial Triangulation of Asian Americans," *Politics and Society* 27 (March 1999): 105–138; and Claire Jean Kim, *Bitter Fruit: The Politics of Black-Korean Conflict in New York City* (New Haven, CT: Yale University Press, 2003), p. 16.

55. Kim, *Bitter Fruit*, p. 45.

56. Gary Y. Okihiro, "Is Yellow Black or White?" in *Asian Americans: Experiences and Perspectives*, ed. Timothy P. Fong and Larry H. Shinagawa (Upper Saddle River, NJ: Prentice Hall, 2000), p. 75.

57. Joe R. Feagin and Danielle Dirks, "Who Is White? College Students' Assessments of Key U.S. Racial and Ethnic Groups," unpublished manuscript, Texas A & M University, 2004.

58. Christine Yeh, "Age, Acculturation, Cultural Adjustment, and Mental Health Symptoms of Chinese, Korean, and Japanese Immigrant Youths," *Cultural Diversity and Ethnic Minority Psychology* 9 (2003): 34–48.

59. Won Moo Hurh, "Adaptation Stages and Mental Health of Korean Male-Immigrants in the United States," *International Migration Review* 24 (1990): 456–477; Center for Medicaid Services, *Medicaid Managed Care Enrollment Report: Depression Diagnoses for Adolescent Youth* (New York: Medicaid Statistics Publications, 2002). Other studies report similarly high rates for Native American teenagers.

60. Jei Africa and Majose Carrasco, "Asian American and Pacific Islander Mental Health," a report for the National Alliance on Mental Illness, February 2011.

61. See, for example, C. Browne and A. Broderick, "Asian and Pacific Island Elders: Issues for Social Work Practice and Education," *Social Work* 39 (1994): 252–259; Laura Harder, "Asian Americans Commit Half of Suicides at Cornell," *Cornell Daily Sun*, March 29, 2005, p. 1; and Tanaka, *When You're Smiling*.

62. The data and quotes are from Elizabeth Cohen, "Push to Achieve Tied to Suicide in Asian-American Women," www.cnn.com/2007/HEALTH/05/16/asian .suicides/index.html (retrieved May 16, 2007).

63. Abraham Kardiner and Lionel Ovesey, *The Mark of Oppression: Explorations in the Personality of the American Negro* (Cleveland: World Publishing, 1962); William H. Grier and Price M. Cobbs, *Black Rage* (New York: Bantam Books, 1968); and Joe R. Feagin and Karyn D. McKinney, *The Many Costs of Racism* (Lanham, MD: Rowman and Littlefield, 2003).

64. Tanaka, *When You're Smiling*.

65. See Feagin and Feagin, *Racial and Ethnic Relations*, chap. 10.

66. Feagin and McKinney, *The Many Costs of Racism*.

67. See Debra Van Ausdale and Joe R. Feagin, *The First R: How Children Learn Race and Racism* (Lanham, MD: Rowman and Littlefield, 2001); and Joe R. Feagin and Melvin P. Sikes, *Living with Racism* (Boston: Beacon Press, 1994).

68. Maurice Halbwachs, *On Collective Memory*, ed. and trans. Lewis Coser (Chicago: University of Chicago Press, 1992), pp. 38, 52.

69. We draw here on Feagin, *Systemic Racism*; and on Yanick St. Jean and Joe R. Feagin, *Double Burden: Black Women and Everyday Racism* (New York: M. E. Sharpe, 1998).

70. A few respondents are from the Pacific Islands, but in this book we will usually use "Asian American" as the collective term. Readers should keep in mind that the term "Asian Americans" includes people from East and South Asia, as well as from Pacific Islands near the Asian mainland, such as the Philippines. All but two of our respondents claim heritage from mainland Asia. The first six interview participants were located by word of mouth and through websites for Asian community organizations and student groups. These respondents suggested other interviewees. To diversify, we made numerous

contacts by word of mouth, especially using Asian American group websites. We posted on a public website in three metropolitan cities with large Asian American populations. Candidates were informed by phone, e-mail, or in person that we were studying Asian Americans and were interested in hearing them talk about experiences. We have lightly edited the interview quotes for grammar, stutter words ("you know"), and clarity. Pseudonyms are given to all respondents to conceal their identity, and some details have been omitted or disguised in the quotes from interviews to increase the anonymity of participants.

71. One multiracial respondent is half Chinese and half Mexican American; one is half Chinese, one-quarter white, and one-quarter Mexican American; one is half Chinese and half white. One listed as Japanese is also part Okinawan.

72. The only hesitancy encountered involved English skills. Twenty interviews were in person, and the remaining twenty-three were conducted and recorded over the phone. In-person interviews were conducted in several states at a specific location, date, and time of the respondents' choice. The majority were conducted in public areas such as coffee shops, libraries, or restaurants. Five took place at the respondent's workplace. One interview involved tagging along with a director of a community center; we began at her place of work, went to a copy center, returned to the community center, went to the post office, and ended at a local eatery for lunch. Each interview lasted between forty-five minutes and three and a half hours. Before each interview, informed consent and demographic information were collected. All but one interview was audiotaped. The tapes were later transcribed and analyzed for recurring themes.

Notes for Chapter 2

1. Jennifer Gonnerman, "Pvt. Danny Chen, 1992–2011," *New York Magazine*, January 6, 1012; Kirk Semple, "Army Charges 8 in Wake of Death of a Fellow G.I.," *New York Times*, December 21, 2012.

2. Semple, "Army Charges 8."

3. John Mataxas, "Pvt. Danny Chen's Family Speaks Out against Military Hazing as Final Soldier Faces Punishment," CBS News New York, December 18, 2012, http://newyork.cbslocal.com/2012/12/18/pvt-danny-chens-family-speaks-out-against-military-hazing-as-final-soldier-faces-punishment/.

4. See U.S. Commission on Civil Rights, *Civil Rights Issues Facing Asian Americans in the 1990s* (Washington, DC: U.S. Government Printing Office, 1992), pp. 26–29; "The Trail of the Suspected Drive-By Killer," CNN.com, July 5, 1999, www.cnn.com/US/9907/05/illinois.shooting.timeline/index.html (retrieved September 1, 2007); and "Hate Crime in Queens," *AsianWeek*, August 25, 2006, http://news.asianweek.com (retrieved December 18, 2006).

5. See Mia Tuan, *Forever Foreigners or Honorary Whites? The Asian Ethnic Experience* (New Brunswick, NJ: Rutgers University Press, 2003).

6. NAPALC, *Backlash Final Report: 2001 Audit of Violence against Asian Pacific Americans* (Washington, DC: NAPALC, 2002); U.S. Commission on Civil Rights, *Civil Rights Issues*, pp. 5–6; Jocelyn Y. Stewart, "Lest Hate Victim Be Forgotten," *Los Angeles Times*, January 25, 2001, p. A1; Orange County Human Relations Commission, "Hate Crimes and Incidents in Orange County," http://64.233.161.104 /search?q=cache:2B69Ym6YOgAJ:www.ochumanrelations.org/pdf/Hate_Crime _report.pdf+%22orange+county%22+reported+%22hate+crimes% 22+2005&hl=en &gl=us&ct=clnk&cd=3 (retrieved January 1, 2007); FBI, *Hate-Crime Statistics, 2011* (Washington, DC: U.S. Department of Justice, 2012). In this section we draw in part on Joe R. Feagin and Clairece B. Feagin, *Racial and Ethnic Relations*, 8th ed. (Upper Saddle River, NJ: Prentice Hall, 2008), chaps. 10–11.

7. Mimi Ko, "Forum to Examine Police Harassment," *Los Angeles Times*, June 11, 1994, p. B2; see also Mara Rose Williams, "Asian Americans Say Police Are Biased," *Atlanta Journal and Constitution*, September 9, 1994, p. C5; Maryland Advisory Committee, U.S. Commission on Civil Rights, "City Services and the Justice System: Do Korean American Storeowners in Baltimore, Maryland, Get Equal Treatment?" July 2004, http://64.233.161.104/search?q=cache:3QEAKAn-g9wJ:www.usccr.gov/pubs /sac/md0704.pdf+%22adequate+police+protection%22+%22asian+americans%22&hl =en&gl=us&ct=clnk&cd=1 (retrieved January 1, 2007); and Utah Task Force on Racial and Ethnic Fairness in the Legal System, "Perceptions of Racial and Ethnic Fairness in the Criminal Justice System: Listening to Utahns," Client Committee Report on Public Hearings, 1999, http://64.233.161.104/search?q=cache:2i_I1Gbt5K0J:www.utcourts .gov/specproj/retaskforce/clrpt24.pdf+photographing+youths+%22gang%22 +%22racial+profiling%22+%22asian+american%22&hl=en&gl=us&ct=clnk&cd=4 (retrieved January 1, 2007).

8. For reviews of numerous studies, see chapters on specific groups in Feagin and Feagin, *Racial and Ethnic Relations*.

9. Joe R. Feagin and Karyn D. McKinney, *The Many Costs of Racism* (Lanham, MD: Rowman and Littlefield, 2003), p. 11.

10. See Joe Feagin, *Racist America: Roots, Current Realities, and Future Reparations*, 3rd ed. (New York: Routledge, 2014).

11. Ibid.

12. See Feagin and McKinney, *The Many Costs of Racism*.

13. Mark Potok, "Anti-Sikh Crimes Hard to Quantify but Very Real," Southern Poverty Law Center, *Intelligence Report* 48 (Winter 2012), www.splcenter.org /get-informed/intelligence-report/browse-all-issues/2012/winter/anti-sikh-hate -crimes.

14. Joe R. Feagin and Danielle Dirks, "Who Is White? College Students' Assessments of Key U.S. Racial and Ethnic Groups," unpublished manuscript, Texas A & M University, 2004.

15. W. E. B. DuBois, *The Souls of Black Folk* (New York: Bantam Classic Books, 1989 [1903]).

16. Brynn Gingras and Shimon Prokupecz, "Sikh Professor Who Wrote about Hate Crimes Gets Attacked by Teens." New York 4 NBC News, September 23, 2013, www.nbcnewyork.com/news/local/Sikh-Columbia-Professor-Attacked-Beaten-Possible-Hate-Crime-Harlem-224809352.html (retrieved December 17, 2013).

17. We draw here on Jackie Jebens, "Where Is the Love? Criminalization in Valentine's Day News," unpublished research paper, Texas A & M University, Spring 2008.

18. Jean Kim, "Asian American Identity Development Theory," in *New Perspectives on Racial Identity Development: A Theoretical and Practical Anthology*, ed. Charmaine L. Wijeyesinghe and Bailey W. Jackson (New York: New York University Press, 2001), pp. 67–90.

19. Tuan, *Forever Foreigners*, p. 71.

20. Otto Santa Ana, *Brown Tide Rising: Metaphors of Latinos in Contemporary American Public Discourse* (Austin: University of Texas Press, 2002).

21. See Joe R. Feagin and Melvin P. Sikes, *Living with Racism* (Boston: Beacon, 1994); and Feagin and McKinney, *The Many Costs of Racism*.

22. Feagin and McKinney, *The Many Costs of Racism*.

23. Nazli Kibria, *Becoming Asian American: Second Generation Chinese and Korean American Identities* (Baltimore: Johns Hopkins University Press, 2002), pp. 41–54; Tuan, *Forever Foreigners*, p. 68.

24. See Feagin and Sikes, *Living with Racism*; and Feagin, *Systemic Racism: A Theory of Oppression* (New York: Routledge, 2006).

25. See Debra Van Ausdale and Joe R. Feagin, *The First R: How Children Learn Race and Racism* (Lanham, MD: Rowman and Littlefield, 2001).

26. See, for example, José A. Cobas and Joe R. Feagin, "Language Oppression and Resistance: The Case of Latinos in the United States," *Ethnic and Racial Studies*, 31 (February, 2008): 390–410.

27. Frank Wu, *Yellow: Race in America Beyond Black and White* (New Haven, CT: Yale University Press, 2003), p. 70.

28. Rosina Lippi-Green, *English with an Accent* (New York: Routledge, 1997), pp. 238–239.

29. Suein Hwang, "The New White Flight," *New York Times*, November 19, 2005, p. 1B.

30. Brad Knickerbocker, "U.S. Japanese Retain Cultural Ties," *Christian Science Monitor*, July 27, 1993, p. 11; see also Tuan, *Forever Foreigners*, p. 15.

31. For example, Kibria, *Becoming Asian American*, p. 64.

Notes for Chapter 3

1. "Bullying against Asian Students Roils Philadelphia High School," *USA Today*, January 22, 2010, http://usatoday30.usatoday.com/news/education/2010-01-22-asian-bullying-philadelphia_n.htm.

2. Ibid.

3. Paul Wong, Chienping Faith Lai, Richard Nagasawa, and Tieming Lin, "Asian Americans as a Model Minority: Self-Perceptions and Perceptions by Other Racial Groups," *Sociological Perspectives* 4, no. 1 (1998): 95–118.

4. See Wendy Moore, *Reproducing Racism* (Lanham, MD: Rowman and Littlefield, 2007).

5. Debra Van Ausdale and Joe R. Feagin, *The First R: How Children Learn Race and Racism* (Lanham, MD: Rowman and Littlefield, 2001), p. 191.

6. Nazli Kibria, *Becoming Asian American: Second Generation Chinese and Korean American Identities* (Baltimore: Johns Hopkins University Press, 2002), pp. 29–32.

7. Frank Wu, *Yellow: Race in America Beyond Black and White* (New Haven, CT: Yale University Press, 2003), p. 59.

8. See Debra Van Ausdale and Joe R. Feagin, "Using Racial and Ethnic Concepts: The Critical Case of Very Young Children," *American Sociological Review* 61 (October 1996): 779–793. See also the magazine *Teaching Tolerance*, published by the Southern Poverty Law Center.

9. See Ralph Ellison, *Shadow and Act* (New York: Random House, 1964).

10. William H. Grier and Price M. Cobbs, *Black Rage* (New York: Bantam, 1968).

11. Hernan Vera and Andrew Gordon, *Screen Saviors: Hollywood Fictions of Whiteness* (Lanham, MD: Rowman and Littlefield, 2003).

12. Sarah Lubman, "Good Grades Are Just Part of the Story for Asians at UC," *San Jose Mercury News*, February 21, 1998, http://modelminority.com/modules.php ?name=News&file=article&sid=89.

13. See Leslie Houts Picca and Joe R. Feagin, *Two-Faced Racism: Whites in the Backstage and Frontstage* (New York: Routledge, 2007).

14. Eduardo Bonilla-Silva, *Racism without Racists: Color-Blind Racism and the Persistence of Racial Inequality in the United States* (Lanham, MD: Rowman and Littlefield, 2003).

15. W. E. B. DuBois, *The Souls of Black Folk* (New York: Bantam Classic Books, 1989 [1903]).

16. See Joe Feagin, *Systemic Racism: A Theory of Oppression* (New York: Routledge, 2006).

17. See Wu, *Yellow*, pp. 218–227.

18. See Ronald Takaki, *Strangers from a Different Shore: A History of Asian Americans* (New York: Little, Brown, 1989).

19. See Joe R. Feagin and Clairece B. Feagin, *Racial and Ethnic Relations*, 8th ed. (Upper Saddle River, NJ: Prentice Hall, 2008), pp. 327–328; and Asian American Justice Center, *Backlash Final Report: 2001 Audit of Violence Against Asian Pacific Americans*, Annual Report (Washington, DC, 2002), at www.napalc.org/en/cms/?116 (retrieved March 7, 2008).

20. The first study here is Pyong Gap Min and Rose Kim, "Formation of Ethnic and Racial Identities: Narratives by Asian American Professionals," in *Second Generation: Ethnic Identity among Asian Americans*, ed. Pyong Gap Min (Walnut Creek, CA:

Altamira, 2002), p. 175. The second study is Paul Taylor et al., *The Rise of Asian Americans* (Washington, DC: Pew Research Center, 2012–2013), p. 97. The professional study is Ryan A. Smith, *Changing the Face of Public Service Leadership: A Research Report and Call to Action* (New York: National Urban Fellows, 2010), pp. 19–21, 43.

21. Holly Coughlin, *My Breakup with Miss Saigon* (St. Paul: Minnesota Women's Press, 1999); Susan Lee, *Unraveling the "Model Minority" Stereotype: Listening to Asian-American Youth* (New York: Teachers College Press, 1996).

22. Indira preferred the use of "Asian Pacific Islander Desi American" to describe the umbrella group of what we have defined as Asian Americans in our text.

23. Joe R. Feagin and Melvin P. Sikes, *Living with Racism* (Boston: Beacon, 1994).

24. Kibria, *Becoming Asian American*, pp. 72–73.

25. Deborah Woo, *The Glass Ceiling and Asian Americans: The New Face of Workplace Barriers* (Walnut Creek, CA: Altamira, 2000); Gloria Luz R. Martinez and Wayne J. Villemez, "Assimilation in the United States: Occupational Attainment of Asian Americans, 1980," paper presented at the American Sociological Association meetings, Chicago, 1987, pp. 31–32; and U.S. Commission on Civil Rights, *Civil Rights Issues Facing Asian Americans in the 1990s* (Washington, DC: U.S. Government Printing Office, 1992), pp. 103–136. On recent studies of glass ceilings and other discrimination, see Lei Lai, "The Model Minority Thesis and Workplace Discrimination of Asian Americans," *Industrial and Organizational Psychology* 6 (2013): 93–96.

26. "Federal Panel Reveals That Most Top Jobs Are Still Held by White Men," *Jet*, April 3, 1995, p. 24; Crosby Burns, Kimberly Barton, and Sophia Kerby, *The State of Diversity in Today's Workforce* (Washington, DC: Center for American Progress, 2012), p. 4.

27. Feagin and Sikes, *Living with Racism*; and Woo, *The Glass Ceiling and Asian Americans*.

28. See Coughlin, *My Breakup with Miss Saigon*.

29. Ibid.

30. Jonah Spangenthal-Lee, "Woman Arrested after Spraying Baby with Soy Sauce," *Seattle Police Department Blotter*, August 26, 2013, http://spdblotter.seattle.gov/2013/08/26/woman-arrested-after-spraying-baby-with-soy-sauce/.

31. See Feagin and Sikes, *Living with Racism*.

32. See Kibria, *Becoming Asian American*, pp. 72–147.

33. Chris K. Iijima, "The Era of We-Construction: Reclaiming the Politics of Asian Pacific American Identity and Reflections on the Critique of the Black/White Paradigm," *Columbia Human Rights Law Review* 29 (1997): 48.

34. Lei Lai and Linda C. Babcock, "Asian Americans and Workplace Discrimination: The Interplay between Sex of Evaluators and the Perception of Social Skills," *Journal of Organizational Behavior* 34 (2013): 310–326.

35. Leland Saito, *Race and Politics: Asian Americans, Latinos, and Whites in a Los Angeles Suburb* (Urbana: University of Illinois Press, 1998), pp. 39–54; Leland T. Saito,

"From 'Blighted' to 'Historic': Race, Economic Development, and Historic Preservation in San Diego, California," *Urban Affairs Review* 45 (2009): 166–187.

Notes for Chapter 4

1. Hunter Stuart, "'Why I'd Hate to Be Asian' Video Goes Viral, Prompts Apology from Sam Hendrickson," *Huffington Post*, March 8, 2013, www.huffingtonpost.com/2013/03/08/why-id-hate-to-be-asian-sam-hendrickson-apologize_n_2839926.html (retrieved January 17, 2014).

2. William H. Grier and Price M. Cobbs, *Black Rage* (New York: Bantam, 1968), p. 24.

3. Joe R. Feagin and Karyn D. McKinney, *The Many Costs of Racism* (Lanham, MD: Rowman and Littlefield, 2003).

4. Nazli Kibria, *Becoming Asian American: Second Generation Chinese and Korean American Identities* (Baltimore: Johns Hopkins University Press, 2002), p. 27.

5. Grier and Cobbs, *Black Rage*, p. 24.

6. Alvin N. Alvarez and Linda P. Juang, "Filipino Americans and Racism: A Multiple Mediation Model of Coping," *Journal of Counseling Psychology* 57, no. 2 (2010): 167–178.

7. William Petersen, "Success Story, Japanese-American Style," *New York Times*, January 9, 1966, p. 21.

8. Janice Tanaka, *When You're Smiling* (Janice Tanaka Films, 1999).

9. Peter J. Burke, "Identity Processes and Social Stress," *American Sociological Review* 56 (1991): 836–849.

10. Ronald Takaki, *Iron Cages: Race and Culture in the 19th-Century U.S.* (New York: Oxford University Press, 1994).

11. Joe R. Feagin and Melvin P. Sikes, *Living with Racism: The Black Middle Class Experience* (Boston: Beacon, 1994); Joe R. Feagin, Hernan Vera, and Nikitah Imani, *The Agony of Education: Black Students in White Colleges and Universities* (New York: Routledge, 1996).

12. Cynthia Feliciano, *Unequal Origins: Immigrant Selection and the Education of the Second Generation* (New York: LFB Scholarly Publishing, 2006); and Cynthia Feliciano, "Does Selective Migration Matter? Explaining Ethnic Disparities in Educational Attainment among Immigrants' Children," *International Migration Review* 39 (2005): 841–871.

13. Grier and Cobbs, *Black Rage*, p. 29.

14. Leela Gandhi, *Postcolonial Theory: A Critical Introduction* (New York: Columbia University Press, 1998), p. 9.

15. Leslie Houts and Joe R. Feagin, *Two-Faced Racism: Whites in the Frontstage and the Backstage* (New York: Routledge, 2007).

16. See Grier and Cobbs, *Black Rage*.

17. See Feagin and Sikes, *Living with Racism.*

18. Grier and Cobbs, *Black Rage*, p. 19.

19. Rosalind S. Chou, *Asian American Sexual Politics: The Construction of Race, Gender, and Sexuality* (Lanham, MD: Rowman and Littlefield, 2012).

20. Ibid.

21. Grier and Cobbs, *Black Rage*, p. 40.

22. W. E. B. DuBois, *The Souls of Black Folk* (New York: Bantam Classic Books, 1989 [1903]), p. 3.

23. See Mia Tuan, *Forever Foreigners or Honorary Whites? The Asian Ethnic Experience* (New Brunswick, NJ: Rutgers University Press, 2003).

24. Joe R. Feagin and Danielle Dirks, "Who Is White? College Students' Assessments of Key U.S. Racial and Ethnic Groups," unpublished manuscript, Texas A & M University, 2004.

25. Tuan, *Forever Foreigners.*

26. Min Zhou and Yang Sao Xiong, "The Multi-Faceted American Experiences of Children of Asian Immigrants: Lessons for Segmented Assimilation," *Ethnic and Racial Studies* 28, no. 6 (2005): 1119–1152.

27. Karen Pyke, "'The Normal American Family' as an Interpretive Structure of Family Life among Adult Children of Korean and Vietnamese Immigrants," unpublished paper, Gainesville, University of Florida, 1997.

28. Tuan, *Forever Foreigners*, p. 162.

29. Feagin and Sikes, *Living with Racism*, pp. 295–296.

Notes for Chapter 5

1. NewsOne staff, "Teens Brutally Beat Asian Boy While Calling Him N-Word," January 17, 2012, http://newsone.com/1801685/video-white-teens-brutally-beat-asian-boy-while-calling-him-n-word (retrieved January 19, 2014).

2. YouTube video: www.youtube.com/watch?v=Iseu8MpXhjQ.

3. Frank Wu, *Yellow: Race in America Beyond Black and White* (New Haven, CT: Yale University Press, 2003).

4. Joe R. Feagin, *Systemic Racism: A Theory of Oppression* (New York: Routledge, 2006), p. 47.

5. See Wu, *Yellow.*

6. Ibid.

7. Vijay Prashad, *The Karma of Brown Folk* (Minneapolis: University of Minnesota Press, 2003), p. 123.

8. Joe R. Feagin and Karyn D. McKinney, *The Many Costs of Racism* (Lanham, MD: Rowman and Littlefield, 2003), p. 32.

9. Hung Cam Thai, "Formation of Ethnic Identity among Second-Generation Vietnamese Americans," in *The Second Generation: Ethnic Identity among Asian Americans*, ed. Pyong Gap Min (Walnut Creek, CA: Altamira, 2002), p. 76.

10. Debra Van Ausdale and Joe R. Feagin, *The First R: How Children Learn Race and Racism* (Lanham, MD: Rowman and Littlefield, 2001), p. 127.

11. The research is cited in Stephen Steinberg, *Race Relations: A Critique* (Palo Alto, CA: Stanford University Press, 2007), p. 131.

12. Chiderah Monde, "Julie Chen Reveals Workplace Racism Led Her to Get Plastic Surgery for 'Asian Eyes,'" *New York Daily News*, September 12, 2013, www.nydailynews.com /entertainment/tv-movies/julie-chen-reveals-plastic-surgery-asian-eyes-article-1 .1453535.

13. Ibid.

14. "Japanese Model Spends over $100k on Plastic Surgery to Look Like French Doll," *Your Health Asia One*, May 8, 2013, http://yourhealth.asiaone.com/content /japanese-model-spends-over-100k-plastic-surgery-look-french-doll.

15. C. N. Le, "Cosmetic and Plastic Surgery," *Asian-Nation*, www.asian-nation .org/cosmetic-surgery.shtml (retrieved December 21, 2006); the quote is from Olivia Chung, "Finding My Eye-Identity," in *YELL-Oh Girls,* ed. Vickie Nam (New York: Quill, 2001), p. 139 (italics omitted).

16. Jeff Lindsay, "Why the Hmong Are in America," *Future Hmong Magazine*, June 14–15, 2002.

17. Feagin, *Systemic Racism*, pp. 252–258. See also Joe R. Feagin, *White Party, White Government* (New York: Routledge, 2012).

18. Tanaka, *When You're Smiling.*

19. See Kenneth B. Clark and M. P. Clark, "Segregation as a Factor in the Racial Identification of Negro Preschool Children," *Journal of Experimental Education* 8 (1939): 161–163; William H. Grier and Price M. Cobbs, *Black Rage* (New York: Bantam, 1968); and Kiri Davis, *A Girl Like Me* (New York: Media Matters, 2005).

20. U.S. Census Bureau, *Current Population Survey,* November 2004; Joe R. Feagin and Clairece B. Feagin, *Racial and Ethnic Relations*, 8th ed. (Upper Saddle River, NJ: Prentice Hall, 2008), pp. 297 and 336–337.

21. Kumiko Nemoto, "Intimacy, Desire, and the Construction of Self in Relationships between Asian American Women and White American Men," *Journal of Asian American Studies* 9 (2006): 51.

22. Feagin and Feagin, *Racial and Ethnic Relations*, pp. 336–337.

23. Greg Mayeda, "Japanese Americans Don't Lose Identity," *New York Times*, December 28, 1995, p. A20; Feagin and Feagin, *Racial and Ethnic Relations*, chap. 10.

24. Ronald Takaki, *Strangers from a Different Shore* (Boston: Back Bay, 1998).

25. Karen D. Pyke and Denise L. Johnson, "Asian American Women and Racialized Femininities," *Gender and Society* 17 (2003): 33–53; Alexandra Suh, "Military Prostitution in Asia and the United States," in *States of Confinement*, ed. Joy James (New York: St. Martin's, 2000), p .150.

26. Rosalind S. Chou, *Asian American Sexual Politics: The Construction of Race, Gender, and Sexuality* (Lanham, MD: Rowman and Littlefield, 2012).

27. Kat Chow and Elise Hu, "Odds Favor White Men, Asian Women on Dating App," NPR's Code Switch, November 30, 2013, www.npr.org/blogs

/codeswitch/2013/11/30/247530095/are-you-interested-dating-odds-favor-white
-men-asian-women.

28. Three were South Asian and two were East Asian.

29. Min Zhou, "Are Asian Americans Becoming White?" *Context* 3, no. 1 (2004):
29–37.

30. U.S. Census Bureau, *Current Population Survey*, November 2004.

31. Prashad, *The Karma of Brown Folk*.

32. Mia Tuan, *Forever Foreigners or Honorary Whites? The Asian Ethnic Experience*
(New Brunswick, NJ: Rutgers University Press, 2003), p. 8.

33. Wu, *Yellow*, p. 30.

34. Claire Jean Kim, *Bitter Fruit: The Politics of Black-Korean Conflict in New York
City* (New Haven, CT: Yale University Press, 2003), p. 45.

35. See also Feagin, *Systemic Racism*; and Feagin and Feagin, *Racial and Ethnic
Relations*.

36. James Loewen, *The Mississippi Chinese: Between Black and White* (Longrove,
IL: Waveland, 1988).

37. Kim, *Bitter Fruit*, p. 41.

38. See Feagin and Feagin, *Racial and Ethnic Relations*, chap. 8.

39. Wu, *Yellow*, p. 67.

40. Prashad, *The Karma of Brown Folk*, p. 6.

41. See Joe Feagin, *Racist America: Roots, Current Realities, and Future Reparations*, 3rd ed. (New York: Routledge, 2014), pp. 157-201.

42. See U.S. Census Bureau, *Current Population Survey*, November 2004; and
Feagin and Feagin, *Racial and Ethnic Relations*, chaps. 10–11.

43. Wu, *Yellow*, p. 318.

44. Kenneth Eng, "Why I Hate Blacks," *AsianWeek*, February 25, 2007, www
.asianweek.com (retrieved June 2007).

45. Wu, *Yellow*, p. 66.

Notes for Chapter 6

1. Casey Capachi, "Suey Park: Asian American Women Are #NotYourAsianSidekick,"
Washington Post, December 17, 2013, www.washingtonpost.com/blogs/she-the-people
/wp/2013/12/17/suey-park-asian-american-women-are-notyourasiansidekick/.

2. Patricia Hill Collins, *Black Feminist Thought: Knowledge, Consciousness, and the
Politics of Empowerment* (New York: Routledge, 2000), pp. 201–225. We are indebted
to Karen S. Glover for suggestions here.

3. See, for example, Ronald Takaki, *Strangers from a Different Shore* (Boston:
Back Bay Books, 1998); and Ronald Takaki, *Iron Cages: Race and Culture in the 19th-
Century U.S.* (New York: Oxford University Press, 1994).

4. Eduardo Bonilla-Silva, *Racism without Racists: Color-Blind Racism and the
Persistence of Racial Inequality in the United States* (Lanham, MD: Rowman and Littlefield, 2003).

5. Joe R. Feagin and Karyn D. McKinney, *The Many Costs of Racism* (Lanham, MD: Rowman and Littlefield, 2003).

6. See Joe R. Feagin and Melvin P. Sikes, *Living with Racism* (Boston: Beacon, 1994); and Leslie Houts and Joe R. Feagin, *Two-Faced Racism: Whites in the Frontstage and the Backstage* (New York: Routledge, 2007).

7. Vijay Prashad, *The Karma of Brown Folk* (Minneapolis: University of Minnesota Press, 2003), p. 6.

8. This is a film by New Line Cinema (2004) that perpetuates some Asian American stereotypes.

9. Frank Wu, *Yellow: Race in America Beyond Black and White* (New Haven, CT: Yale University Press, 2003), p. 49.

10. Joe R. Feagin, *The White Racial Frame*, 2nd ed. (New York: Routledge, 2013), p. 163ff; and Joe R. Feagin, *Systemic Racism: A Theory of Oppression* (New York: Routledge, 2006).

11. See James Loewen, *Lies My Teacher Told Me: Everything Your American Textbook Got Wrong* (New York: Touchstone, 1994).

12. Black Lava is a clothing company that makes apparel to appeal to Asian Americans, often with humorous commentary.

13. See Feagin and Sikes, *Living with Racism*.

14. Jenny Strasburg, "Abercrombie and Glitch: Asian Americans Rip Retailer for Stereotypes on T-shirts," *San Francisco Chronicle*, April 18, 2002, p. A1.

15. Rod Bush, *We Are Not What We Seem: Black Nationalism and Class Struggle in the American Century* (New York: New York University Press, 1999), p. 163.

16. See Collins, *Black Feminist Thought*; and Feagin and Sikes, *Living with Racism*.

17. See Prashad, *The Karma of Brown Folk*.

18. Ibid.

Notes for Chapter 7

1. See, for example, Joe R. Feagin and Clairece B. Feagin, *Racial and Ethnic Relations*, 8th ed. (Upper Saddle River, NJ: Prentice Hall, 2008), chaps. 3–5.

2. Joe R. Feagin and Danielle Dirks, "Who Is White? College Students' Assessments of Key U.S. Racial and Ethnic Groups," unpublished manuscript, Texas A & M University, 2004.

3. Raymond Williams, "Forms of Fiction in 1848," in *Literature, Politics, and Theory*, ed. Francis Barker et al. (London: Metheun, 1986), p. 16.

4. Helen Zia, *Asian American Dreams: The Emergence of an American People* (New York: Farrar, Straus, and Giroux, 2001).

5. Margery Austin Turner et al., *Discrimination against Racial and Ethnic Minorities* (Washington, DC: Department of Housing and Urban Development, 2012).

6. "Is China Trying to Poison Americans *and* Their Pets?" Homeland Insecurity Column, *World Net Daily*, May 27, 2007, www.worldnetdaily.com/news/article

.asp?ARTICLE_ID=55892 (retrieved March 12, 2008); and Jeff Yang, "A Taste of Racism in the Chinese Food Scare," *Washington Post*, July 15, 2007, p. B02.

7. Bud Poliquin, "U.S. Olympic Team Rejects Chinese Food," *Post-Standard*, February 22, 2008, www.syracuse.com/articles/sports/index.ssf?/base/sports -0/1203674380303860.xml&coll=1 (retrieved March 1, 2008).

8. James R. Healey and Julie Schmit, "USDA Orders Largest Beef Recall: 143.4 Million Pounds," *USA Today*, February 18, 2008, www.usatoday.com/money/ -industries/food/2008-02-17-slaughterhouse-recall_N.htm (retrieved March 1, 2008).

9. Yang, "A Taste of Racism," p. B02.

10. See Ivan H. Light, *Ethnic Enterprise in America* (Berkeley: University of California Press, 1972), pp. 174–179; and Bill Hosokawa, *The Nisei* (New York: Morrow, 1969), pp. 199–200.

11. Nathaniel C. Nash, "House Votes Payments to Japanese Americans," *New York Times,* September 18, 1987, p. A15. In this and the following few paragraphs we draw on Feagin and Feagin, *Racial and Ethnic Relations*, pp. 279–340.

12. Chris K. Iijima, "The Era of We-Construction: Reclaiming the Politics of Asian Pacific American Identity and Reflections on the Critique of the Black/White Paradigm," *Columbia Human Rights Law Review* 29 (1997): 57–58.

13. Roger Daniels, *Asian America: Chinese and Japanese in the United States since 1850* (Seattle: University of Washington Press, 1988), p. 113; Min Zhou and James V. Gatewood, "Introduction: Revisiting Contemporary Asian America," in *Contemporary Asian America: A Multidisciplinary Reader,* ed. Min Zhou and James V. Gatewood (New York: New York University Press, 2000), pp. 27–35.

14. Yen Le Espiritu, *Asian American Panethnicity* (Philadelphia: Temple University Press, 1992), pp. 19–51; Paul Sweeney, "Asian Americans Gain Clout," *American Demographics* 8 (February 1986): 18–19.

15. Frank Wu, "Asian Americans Finally Organize the NCAPA," New America News Service, November 27, 1997. On neoconservative efforts, see Glenn Omatsu, "The 'Four Prisons' and the Movements of Liberation," in *Contemporary Asian America: A Multidisciplinary Reader*, 2nd ed., ed. Min Zhou and J. V. Gatewood (New York: New York University Press, 2007), pp. 71–72.

16. Steven A. Chin, "KFRC Deejay Draws Suspension for On-Air Derogatory Remarks," *San Francisco Examiner*, December 6, 1994, p. A2; "Current Affairs," *JACL News,* www.jacl.org/index.php (retrieved December 19, 2006); Media Action Network for Asian Americans, "Latest Headline News," www.manaa.org (retrieved December 18, 2006); Zia, *Asian American Dreams*, p. 134.

17. Michelle Mizal, "Filipino Americans Hope to Build Unity: Group Also Hopes to Build Political Clout at D.C. Event," *Virginian-Pilot* (Norfolk, VA), August 21, 1997, p. B1; Bong-Youn Choy, *Koreans in America* (Chicago: Nelson-Hall, 1979), pp. 141–189; "Programs," Korean American Coalition, www.kacdc.org/programs/index.html (retrieved January 3, 2007); Carolyn Leung, "Redefining Advocacy for the Southeast Asian American Community," *Journal of Asian American Studies* 3 (2000): 237–241.

18. We are indebted here to suggestions and information provided by Nestor Rodriguez, October 28, 2007.

19. See Carla Rivera, "Orange County Focus," *Los Angeles Times*, April 28, 1992, p. B3; K. Connie Kang, "Korean Groups Back Union Fight for Jobs," *Los Angeles Times*, November 17, 1994, p. B1.

20. Joe R. Feagin, *Systemic Racism: A Theory of Oppression* (New York: Routledge, 2006), p. 321.

21. See John Briggs and F. David Peat, *Turbulent Mirror: An Illustrated Guide to Chaos Theory and the Science of Wholeness* (New York: Harper and Row, 1990), p. 177.

INDEX

✳

About the Authors

Rosalind S. Chou, Assistant Professor of Sociology at Georgia State University, is the author of *Asian American Sexual Politics*.

Joe R. Feagin is Professor of Sociology at Texas A&M University. He is author of 65 scholarly books, including *The White Racial Frame* (2nd ed., Routledge, 2013) and *Racist America* (3rd ed., Routledge, 2014).

CPSIA information can be obtained
at www.ICGtesting.com
Printed in the USA
FFHW011913081118
49329096-53600FF